Understanding Victimology

Understanding Victimology: An Active-Learning Approach explains what the field of victimology is—including its major theoretical perspectives and research methods—and provides insight into the dynamics of various offline and online crimes from the victims' vantage point. It is the only textbook to provide numerous innovative active-learning exercises to enhance and reinforce student learning, and it addresses important contemporary topics that have thus far not been covered by other victimology texts, including identity theft, hate crimes, and terrorism. This unique and relevant work is ideal for students, academics, and practitioners who are interested in a comprehensive introduction to victimology.

Dr. Shelly Clevenger is an Assistant Professor at Illinois State University in the Criminal Justice Sciences Department. She has authored peer-reviewed journal publications and books on the topics of sexual assault, intimate partner abuse, and cybervictimization. Dr. Clevenger presented her research at the *United Nations Women* in New York City in December 2016. She has also done speaking engagements throughout the state of Illinois on her work and activism. Dr. Clevenger is also the recipient of the 2016 Feminist Criminology Article of the Year Award. She has two other forthcoming books, *Teaching Theory* and *Gendering Criminology: Crime and Justice Today*. She has also been recognized for her teaching in these areas by Illinois State University with both college and university Faculty Teacher of the Year Awards; the 2016 Outstanding Teacher of the Year Award from the American Society of Criminology's Division of Victimology; and the 2017 Teacher of the Year Award from ASC's Division of Critical Criminology and Social Justice.

Dr. Jordana N. Navarro is an Assistant Professor of Criminal Justice at The Citadel. Dr. Navarro grew up in south Florida where she aspired to a career in law enforcement. After studying sociology at the University of Central Florida, Dr. Navarro developed a passion for understanding victimization perpetrated both offline and online.

Dr. Catherine D. Marcum is an Associate Professor of Criminal Justice at Appalachian State University. Dr. Marcum grew up in West Virginia and aspired to a career in higher education. Her research interests include cybercrime victimization and offending, sexual victimization, and correctional issues. As of the publication date of this text, she has authored or coauthored over 45 peer-reviewed journal articles and 10 books in her areas of expertise.

Dr. George E. Higgins is a Professor in the Department of Criminal Justice at the University of Louisville. Dr. Higgins received his Ph.D. in Criminology at Indiana University of Pennsylvania in 2001. His research focuses on testing criminological theories. Dr. Higgins publishes consistently with students and colleagues from around the world.

"This is the most dynamic victimology text on the market. It is truly intersectional and comprehensive in its treatment of victims, contains hands-on active learning exercises that increase understanding and empathy, and provides great information for future practitioners of every stripe. I've been looking for this text for 20 years."

—Elicka Peterson Sparks, *Department of Government and Justice Studies, Appalachian State University*

Understanding Victimology

An Active-Learning Approach

Shelly Clevenger, Jordana N. Navarro,
Catherine D. Marcum, and
George E. Higgins

Routledge
Taylor & Francis Group

NEW YORK AND LONDON

First published 2018
by Routledge
711 Third Avenue, New York, NY 10017

and by Routledge
2 Park Square, Milton Park, Abingdon, Oxon, OX14 4RN

Routledge is an imprint of the Taylor & Francis Group, an informa business

Library of Congress Cataloging-in-Publication Data
Names: Clevenger, Shelly, author.
Title: Understanding victimology : an active-learning approach / Shelly Clevenger [and three others].
Description: New York, NY : Routledge, 2018. | Includes index.
Identifiers: LCCN 2017048658 | ISBN 9780815399902 (hardback) | ISBN 9781498772846 (pbk.)
Subjects: LCSH: Victims of crimes.
Classification: LCC HV6250.25 .C625 2018 | DDC 362.88—dc23
LC record available at https://lccn.loc.gov/2017048658

ISBN: 978-0-8153-9990-2 (hbk)
ISBN: 978-1-4987-7284-6 (pbk)
ISBN: 978-1-315-15157-1 (ebk)

Typeset in Frutiger
by Apex CoVantage, LLC

Visit the eResource: www.routledge.com/9781498772846

I dedicate this book to all of the victimology students I have had over the years who have taught me so much! In addition, I dedicate it to two former students who have changed my life in so many wonderful ways: Kelsie Langheim and Mia Gilliam. If I ever needed them, they were "always" there in a "flash!" Shelly Clevenger

I would like to dedicate this textbook to my family, who remain steadfast sources of support in my career. Jordana Navarro

I dedicate this book to so many of my students, past and present, who demonstrated bravery in the face of so many struggles and challenges. Cathy Marcum

I dedicate this book to my family and my students (past, present, and future). George Higgins

Contents

Preface

The privilege of working in the criminal justice community is interaction with a variety of stakeholders, such as judges, probation officers, and, of course, offenders. However, there are others who play an integral part of the system, yet are often overlooked in the process of trying to punish and treat the offenders: the victims. Victims of crime include every combination of race, sex, religion, age, and sexual orientation. They range from the highly educated to someone with barely a third-grade education. They are white-collar or blue-collar workers, or the unemployed. Furthermore, victims of crime can also be offenders as well.

The purpose of this text is to explore the world of victimology through the lens of not only *who* is victimized but also *how* they are victimized. In addition, our text will discuss the history of victim advocacy and what we are doing now to help victims of crime, and what is still left to do. Most importantly, we want students to be able to critically apply this information through active learning exercises. We understand that instructors will choose to teach this class in very different ways, and there are online resources available to them to accomplish various goals. Some of the students who use this book will become victim advocates, and some may have other direct or indirect interactions with victims of various types of crime. Our goal is to help them emerge from this literature with better insight into this strong, yet fragile group of individuals who deserve a voice.

Chapter 1

Introduction to Victimology

Keywords

- Assistance-oriented Victimology
- Criminology
- Critical Victimology
- Feminists
- General Victimology
- Interactionist
- Victimology
- Penal Victimology
- Positivist Victimology
- Radical Victimology
- Victim Blaming
- Victim Facilitation
- Victim Precipitation
- Victim Provocation

Introduction

Benjamin Mendelsohn, often referred to as the father of victimology, describes the field as "the science of victims and victimity. By victimity, we mean the general concept, the specific common phenomenon which characterizes all categories of victims, whatever the cause of their situation" (1976, p. 9). In other words, Mendelsohn continues, "it [victimology] must take into account all phenomena which *causes* victims, to the extent that society takes an interest in them" (1976, p. 9; emphasis added). Taking into account these statements, victimology is the study of victimization that includes the analysis of the victim-offender relationship as well as the victim's experiences with the criminal justice system during the administration of justice (Mendelsohn, 1976; van Dijk, 1999; Viano, 1983). Ultimately, the field of victimology includes two overarching goals: (1) to prevent victimization from happening in the first place and (2) to minimize the harm post-victimization as well as prevent repeat victimizations (Mendelsohn, 1976).

Media Byte 1.1: Perfect Victims—Revictimizing Survivors of Crime

As the victimology field has developed, there has been greater recognition and understanding of crime victims as unique individuals. Specifically, journalists and scholars alike have continued to challenge the idea of a "perfect victim," because factors associated with that concept are largely not grounded in reality and are often based on inaccurate beliefs about crime. In this Media Byte, read the following news article:

Katie McDonough. "The 'Perfect Victim' Myth: How Attempts to Discredit Rape Survivors Stand in the Way of Real Change." Salon. February 3, 2015. (www.salon.com/2015/02/03/the_perfect_victim_myth_how_attempts_to_discredit_individual_survivors_stand_in_the_way_of_real_change/)

After reading the above news story, answer the following questions in a brief response:

In thinking about rape and sexual assault, what actions and characteristics immediately come to your mind when you think of "offender" and "victim"?
After writing down how you conceptualize those two terms, check out Project Unbreakable (http://projectunbreakable.tumblr.com/). Note the survivors' stories and whether they challenge the list created to address question 1.

Describe in a brief reaction paper the consequences associated with upholding the idea of a "perfect victim" on a societal level, in terms of how crime is understood and responded to, and on an individual level for both the offender and the survivor.

The following quote from Frederick Wertham's (1949) text entitled *The Show of Violence* underscores the importance of victimology in the overall understanding of crime: "One cannot understand the psychology of the murderer if one does not understand the sociology of the victim. What we need is a science of victimology" (as cited in Fattah, 1989). While this holistic understanding of crime has steadily progressed since the 1970s, most studies prior to the 20th century placed little emphasis on crime victims (Mendelsohn, 1976; Schneider, 2001; van Dijk, 1999; Viano, 1983, 1976). Interestingly, as Fattah (2000) notes, some of the earliest works examining crime victims were outside academia and are found in literature and poetry. To understand the state of victimology then, it is important to revisit this history, including the work of its pioneers, and learn how the field progressed.

Textbook Author Spotlight

Dr. Shelly Clevenger, Illinois State University

Biography: Dr. Clevenger grew up in Pennsylvania. She is an Assistant Professor at Illinois State University. Her research interests include sexual assault, intimate partner abuse, and cybervictimization. She has authored peer-reviewed publications on these topics appearing in such journals as *Feminist Criminology*, *Sexual Abuse*, *The Security Journal*, *The Journal of Criminal Justice Education*, and *The Journal of School Violence*. Clevenger also served as an editor, as well as contributor, for the edited volume *The Virtual Enemy: The Intersection Between Intimate Partner Abuse, Technology, and Cybercrime*. She has been recognized for her teaching in these areas by

Illinois State University and the American Society of Criminology Division of Victimology with Outstanding Teaching Awards.

Favorite Part of Teaching: Interacting with students in the classroom and outside the classroom through civic engagement projects

Research Interests and Areas: sex offenses, victimology, animal cruelty

Education:
Ph.D.   Criminology, Indiana University of Pennsylvania
M.A.   Criminology, Indiana University of Pennsylvania
B.A.   Criminology, Indiana University of Pennsylvania

The History and Early Pioneers of Victimology

An overview of early criminological works, particularly before the 20th century, shows a notable dearth of information on victims of crime (Fattah, 2000; Viano, 1976). This is not to state that there was a complete *absence* of discussion about crime victims (Viano, 1983), but rather that scholarly activity focused on perpetrators of crime. A review of early criminological works reveals some discussion of crime victims as seen through the writings of Beccaria (1764) and Lombroso (1876) (as cited in Dussich, 2006; Schafer, 1977), but, again, many criminology studies during this time focused on understanding the origins of crime through examining only the actions of the offender (Schneider, 2001). However, interest in the suffering of victims accelerated in the aftermath of World War II, and victimology began emerging from the broader field of criminology (Fattah, 2000).

Activity 1.1: Criminology and Victimology—Related but Different

Students should spend a few moments reviewing an area of criminal research that is of interest to them. After researching their selected area, students should construct three research questions related to that field from a *criminological* perspective. After sharing a few examples and parsing out the elements of the questions that center the lines of inquiry within criminology, students should then rework their same research questions from a *victimological* perspective. After sharing a few examples, spend time parsing out the elements of the questions that center the lines of inquiry within victimology as opposed to criminology.

Table 1.1 *Mendelsohn's (1956) Victim Culpability Spectrum With Examples*

Level of Victim Culpability	Examples
Completely Innocent	An individual killed while sleeping at home
Victim With Minor Guilt	An individual robbed after displaying money
Victim as Guilty as Offender	An individual killed during a drug transaction
Victim More Guilty than Offender	An individual killed after initiating a physical altercation
Most Guilty Victim	An individual killed while committing a robbery
Imaginary Victim	An individual who pretends that he/she was victimized

(as cited in Schafer, 1977)

Several early pioneers in victimology made lasting impacts on the field, and, interestingly, many began their careers in the legal profession. For example, Benjamin Mendelsohn (1900–1998) was an Israeli criminal law scholar (van Dijk, 1999) who coined the term *victimology* in a paper presentation in Bucharest, Romania, in 1947 and used it in a paper entitled "A New Branch of Bio-Psycho-Social Science: Victimology" in 1946 (Mendelsohn, 1963; The Victimologist, 1998). As a criminal defense lawyer, Mendelsohn, like many victimologists of the day, was interested in understanding how victims' actions contributed to criminal activity (van Dijk, 1999; Viano, 1976). Although there is some disagreement about whether he was the first to use the term or whether it was an American psychiatrist named Frederick Wertham in 1949 (Fattah, 2000), Mendelsohn continued to shape the field with his writings until his death in January 1998 (The Victimologist, 1998). Indeed, one of his lasting contributions to the field was the creation of a typology (see Table 1.1) delineating the responsibility of the victim versus the offender in criminal events, which ranged from completely innocent to completely guilty.

Although Mendelsohn was a pivotal member of the victimology field, the contributions made by Hans von Hentig, whom Mendelsohn himself cites (1963), were equally as important. Unlike many victimologists, Hans von Hentig (1887–1974) began his career as an academic and scholar with a keen focus on the role of victims in criminal activity (Viano, 1976). In his pursuit to understand the etiology of victimization, von Hentig was especially concerned about the interaction between victims and offenders and the exchanges that led to criminal events (Mendelsohn, 1963). Von Hentig's interest resulted in one of the most influential works in the field, *The Criminal and His Victim* (1948), in which he identified several victim risk factors that were important for understanding the genesis of crime (see Table 1.2). His seminal work, along with similar works of other victimologists of the period (e.g., Fattah,

Table 1.2 *Von Hentig's Victim Risk Factors*[1]

Victim Characteristics	Proneness to Crime Stems From
1. The Young	Emotional and Physical Vulnerability
2. Females	Physical Vulnerability
3. The Old	Mental and Physical Vulnerability; Access to Wealth
4. The Mentally Defective or Deranged	Vulnerability From Defect or Through Substance Use
5. Immigrants	Challenges in Assimilation into a New Culture
6. Minorities	Discrimination and Prejudice From Inequality
7. Dull Normal	Lack of Awareness and General Naïvete
8. The Depressed	Failing to Exercise Due Care
9. The Acquisitive	Greed and Recklessness
10. The Wanton	Lack of Appropriate Sensibilities
11. The Lonesome and Heartbroken	Desire for Companionship and Recklessness
12. Tormentor	An Abusive Environment That Often Spans Years
13. The Blocked, Exempted, Fighting	The Inability to Defend Against Attacks

(Von Hentig, 1948; Schafer, 1977)

Mendelsohn), also contributed to later debates surrounding whether victims were responsible, in whole or in part, for their own victimization (van Dijk, 1999).

Similar to Mendelsohn, Ezzat A. Fattah (b. 1929) began his career as a lawyer. In that capacity he witnessed the inhumane treatment of incarcerated offenders (Viano, 1976). It was through this position, and the reading of notable works like von Hentig's *The Criminal and His Victim*, that Fattah realized that systemic change in terms of crime prevention would occur only after researchers developed a holistic understanding of the origins of criminal activity (Viano, 1976). This holistic understanding required the consideration of the interactions and relationships between offenders and victims as well as the contributions of each to the criminal event itself (Viano, 1976). In pursuit of this goal, Fattah studied homicides committed during robberies in order to understand what contributed to the criminal event—including the victim's own actions (Viano, 1976). He, like many other eminent victimologists, also attempted to construct a way of understanding victimization risks along a type of continuum (see Table 1.3).

Table 1.3 *Fattah's Victim Classification Scheme*

Victim Classes	Characterized By
Non-Participating Victims	A lack of contribution or participation in the crime
Latent or Predisposed Victims	Presence of risk factors that increase the likelihood of crime
Provocative Victims	Engaging in actions that lead to the genesis of a crime
Participating Victims	Engaging in actions that facilitate the genesis of a crime
False Victims	The lack of actual victimization perpetrated by another individual

(as cited in Schafer, 1977)

Textbook Author Spotlight

***Dr. Jordana N. Navarro,* The Citadel**

Biography: Dr. Navarro grew up in south Florida where she aspired to a career in law enforcement. After studying sociology at the University of Central Florida, Dr. Navarro developed a passion for understanding victimization perpetrated both offline and online. She currently lives in Charleston with her husband and two young sons.

Favorite Part of Teaching: My favorite part of teaching is seeing how my students apply class material to their everyday world. This is one of the best things about teaching in the social sciences—there is a constant stream of relevant media to use in the classroom.

Research Interests and Areas: cybercrime, Geographic Information Systems, intimate partner violence, victimology and sexual violence

Education:
Ph.D.   Sociology, University of Central Florida
M.S.   Criminal Justice, University of Central Florida
B.A.   Political Science, Pre-Law, University of Central Florida

Sara Margery Fry (1874–1958) was particularly progressive for the period in which she lived. Similar to Fattah, her passion stemmed from witnessing the inhumane treatment of incarcerated offenders, and she worked throughout her life to improve the criminal justice system for both offenders and victims (Viano, 1976). Perhaps most importantly, Fry advocated for improved treatment of offenders without de-emphasizing the harm victims experienced in the aftermath of crime (Viano, 1976). After experiencing a crime herself, Fry worked tirelessly in England to encourage the establishment of a compensation fund for crime victims, which ultimately occurred in 1964 (Dussich, 2006; Viano, 1976). Additionally, her efforts led to the development of similar programs around the world—including in the United States (Viano, 1983).

Activity 1.2: Crime Victims Compensation Fund

Students should review the process of applying for funding through their state's crime victim compensation program. After locating the program, students should review what the funds can and cannot be used for. In this review, students should pay particular attention to what gaps may exist in victim services and whether these gaps can be filled. Aside from these areas of inquiry, students should answer the following questions either as an individual assignment or as a group:

1. What are the eligibility rules to apply for reimbursement?
2. If a sexual assault victim does not want to formally report the attack to law enforcement, is he/she still eligible to receive assistance?
3. Who should complete this application?
4. If you are a spouse or family member of a crime victim, are you able to apply to have compensation for counseling as well?
5. What types of lost earnings are reimbursable?
6. If you are the spouse of the victim, are you able to receive compensation for lost wages?
7. What type of funeral and death benefits may you apply for?
8. Can anyone apply for reimbursement due to pain and suffering?
9. Is travel to/from doctor appointments covered?

As these profiles illustrate, awareness of victims as important components of criminal events was occurring across the globe. This interest eventually led to the founding of the Institute for Victimology at Keio University (Tokyo, Japan) in 1969, which was largely the result of efforts by Koichi Miyazawa (b. 1930) (Viano, 1976). Miyazawa's interest in victimology originated during his early studies in criminology, when he realized that the role of victims in the genesis of criminal events was an underresearched area ripe for investigation (Viano, 1976). However, at that time, many of the works by early victimologists were not accessible to Japanese scholars (Viano, 1976). Therefore, Miyazawa's text *Basic Problems and Concepts in Victimology*, in which he synthesized the essential and important victimological works of the time in Japanese, was particularly significant (Viano, 1976). Aside from creating this accessibility, Miyazawa's *Basic Problems* also presented a theoretical framework for understanding victimization (Viano, 1976).

Textbook Author Spotlight

Dr. Catherine D. Marcum, Appalachian State University

Biography: Dr. Marcum grew up in West Virginia and aspired to a career in academia. As of this writing, she has authored or coauthored over 45 peer-reviewed journal articles and 10 books in her areas of expertise. She lives in North Carolina with her husband and two children.

Favorite Part of Teaching: I love watching my students succeed. The best part of my job is hearing from current and former students about achieving their professional and personal goals.

Research Interests and Areas: cybercrime victimization and offending, sexual victimization, correctional issues

Education:
Ph.D.   Criminology, Indiana University of Pennsylvania
M.S.   Criminal Justice, Marshall University
B.S.   Criminal Justice, West Virginia State University

Stephen Schafer (1911–1976) also began his career as a lawyer and pivoted toward academia after escaping persecution during World War II (Viano, 1976). His interest in victimology first arose during late adolescence, when he noticed that victims were largely overlooked in the administration of justice despite the harm these individuals experienced (Viano, 1976). Years later, he spent considerable time parsing out the "functional responsibility" victims had in criminal events (Viano, 1976, p. 224). Indeed, in his seminal work, *Victimology: The Victim and His Criminal*, Schafer (1977) criticized victimization studies for the lack of attention placed on the criminal-victim relationship, which he emphasized should be a central line of inquiry in the field.

Aside from calling attention to the perceived misdirection in the field, Schafer (1977) also proposed a typology that sought to overcome some of the challenges associated with previous frameworks that he noted were largely "speculative guesswork" (p. 45). In contrast to previous frameworks, Schafer's (1977) typology (see Table 1.4) accounted for both behavioral and social characteristics that contributed to the genesis of crime. Moreover, he sought to ensure that his framework was applicable and transferable to various types of crimes (Schafer, 1977). According to Schafer (1977), his ultimate goal in constructing this typology was to provide an instrument by which the responsibility of both the offender and the victim could be assessed in the criminal-victim relationship.

Table 1.4 *Schafer's Victim Responsibility Typology*

Type	Responsibility Determination
Unrelated Victims	Criminal is solely responsible; there is no relationship to the victim
Provocative Victims	Shared responsibility between criminal and victim because of victim's provocation
Precipitative Victims	Shared responsibility between criminal and victim because of victim's carelessness
Biologically Weak Victims	Shared responsibility between criminal and larger society, which failed to protect the victim despite his/her inherent vulnerabilities
Socially Weak Victims	Shared responsibility between criminal and larger society, which failed to protect the victim despite his/her socially vulnerable position
Self-victimizing Victims	The victim is completely responsible and is considered a criminal-victim
Political Victims	Victim is not responsible, because of his/her lack of socio-political capital

Although the previously noted scholars contributed to the rapid evolution of victimology, over time their work has drawn substantial criticism and debate given the victim-blaming nature of their typologies. In order to understand the origin of this debate and how these discussions continue to shape the field today, the next section of this chapter discusses the different areas of victimological thought beyond any particular scholar's work. In this discussion, we also explain and explore important concepts regarding the victim's role in criminal events (e.g., victim-precipitation, victim-provocation, and victim-facilitation) that largely developed because of these scholars' works.

Activity 1.3: Who Is Responsible for Crime?

Students should form teams, read the following widely shared (unattributed) vignette, and assign responsibility to each individual accordingly. The group must reach a consensus in order to complete this assignment.

There is a river with a bridge over it, and a WIFE and her HUSBAND live in a house on one side. The WIFE has a LOVER who lives on the other side of the river, and the only way to cross the river is to walk across the bridge or ask the BOATMAN to take her. One day, the HUSBAND tells his WIFE that he is leaving on a business trip. The WIFE pleads for him to take her because she knows if he does not, she will cheat on him. The HUSBAND refuses; he thinks she will get in the way of business. When he is gone, the WIFE goes over the bridge and stays with her LOVER. The night passes, and the sun is almost up when the WIFE leaves because she has to get home before her HUSBAND. She starts to cross the bridge but sees an ASSASSIN waiting for her on the other side. She knows if she crosses, she will die. She runs to the BOATMAN to get a ride, but he wants fifty cents. The WIFE has no money, so he refuses to take her. The WIFE runs back to the LOVER's house and explains her problem, asking for fifty cents to pay the boatman. The LOVER refuses, telling her it is her fault for getting into the situation. Dawn arrives, and in a fit of terror, she dashes across the bridge. When she faces the ASSASSIN, he takes out a large knife and stabs her until she is dead.

Rank the following in order of who is MOST responsible for these events:

___Assassin
___Boatman
___Husband
___Lover
___Wife

After completing this assignment, students should provide a detailed explanation of how they assessed responsibility in this case.

Areas of Victimological Thought

Penal Victimology

The focus on the understanding of victims as dynamic components of crime with varying degrees of responsibility dominated many early works in victimology, and, because of the nature of these studies, these lines of inquiry are referred to as penal victimology (van Dijk, 1999). Penal victimology, sometimes also known as interactionist victimology (van Dijk, 1999), broadly describes studies that focus on the interaction and relationship between offenders and victims within the confines of criminal law (van Dijk, 1999). In addition to these terms, some have referred to this field as positivist victimology given these scholars' heavy utilization of crime surveys in early studies (Walklate, 1990). Although the chief criticism of penal victimology has been the victim-blaming nature of the research, van Dijk (1999) notes that early works in this area were important attempts to improve crime prevention efforts through the greater understanding of criminal events. Moreover, studies in this area of victimology led to the development of three important concepts meant to provide an understanding of the victim's role in criminal events: victim-precipitation, victim-facilitation, and victim-provocation.

Marvin Wolfgang was the first scholar to empirically evaluate the concept of *victim-precipitation* in his study of homicides (1957). Although he focused his investigation on homicide, Wolfgang's (1957) description of victim-precipitation is easily applicable to all crimes: "The term *victim-precipitated* is applied to those criminal homicides in which the victim is a *direct, positive precipitator* in the crime" (p. 2; emphasis added). In other words, victim-precipitation broadly refers to a victim's actions or behaviors that prompted the crime itself (Meier & Miethe, 1993). Ultimately, Wolfgang (1957) found that out of 588 criminal homicide cases, 26% were victim-precipitated. Aside from this finding, Wolfgang (1957) also identified several characteristics that were important in the comparison of victim-precipitated homicides to non-victim-precipitated homicides: biological sex, race, relationship status, substance use.

Victim-provocation is similar to victim-precipitation, but the former arguably carries the most culpability in terms of assessing victim-responsibility. The greater culpability stems from the victim engaging in some *provocation* that leads to the onset of crime (Daigle & Muftic, 2015). For example, a patron at a bar becomes enraged and extremely hostile toward the establishment's management at closing time. In the course of the exchange, the patron grabs a knife and charges at one of the managers.

The manager responds by shooting the patron. Victimologists would likely agree that this case illustrates victim-provocation, because the patron would have left unharmed if it were not for his own actions.

In terms of gauging responsibility, victim-facilitation is associated with the least amount of culpability compared to victim-precipitation or victim-provocation. Victim-facilitation describes situations in which a crime occurs because of victim carelessness in safeguarding themselves or their property (Daigle & Muftic, 2015). For example, a home that is burglarized after the homeowner neglects to lock the front door certainly does not excuse the offender, but the crime was easier for the perpetrator to commit given the lack of security.

The previous categories, largely derived from early works in penal victimology, continue to provide ways of understanding the victim's role in the genesis of crime. However, distinctions between these categories are far from absolute and can be difficult to parse out. Moreover, each of these concepts entails assigning some level of responsibility to the victim for his/her own victimization, which is widely referred to as victim-blaming. Perhaps the most infamous penal victimological study, one that spurred great debate regarding the appropriateness of assigning responsibility for victimization to victims themselves, was Menachem Amir's (1967) study titled *Victim Precipitated Forcible Rape.*

Amir, a student of Wolfgang, essentially followed his mentor's prior work, but focused on victim-precipitated forcible rape instead of on victim-precipitated homicide. To conduct his study, he also looked at data from the Philadelphia Police Department comprising 646 forcible rapes (Amir, 1967). He defined victim-precipitation as "those rape situations in which the victim actually, or so it was deemed, agreed to sexual relations but retracted before the actual act or did not react strongly enough when suggestion was made by the offender" (1967, p. 495). He ultimately found that 122 cases of forcible rape were victim-precipitated (Amir, 1967). In terms of differences between victim-precipitated forcible rape and non-victim-precipitated forcible rape, Amir (1967) noted a greater proportion of victim-precipitated forcible rapes involved the use of alcohol and victims with "bad reputations" among other characteristics.

Amir's (1967) overall study, as well as some of the specific risk factors he reports on (i.e., "bad reputation"), was immediately attacked both in and outside academia as a flawed and ill-conceived study (Meier & Miethe, 1993; van Dijk, 1999). To understand this response to Amir's study, it is important that readers are familiar with the socio-political climate of that day. During the 1970s, the women's rights movement (see Chapter 3) was advocating for an end to systemic forms of gender oppression as well as greater recognition of crimes against women in the criminal justice system. In this movement, feminists, or individuals who advocated for gender equality, both in and outside of academia, were also increasingly calling attention to the idea that crimes against women (e.g., domestic abuse, rape, and other forms of sexual violence) were a result of systemic gender inequality. Given this context, opponents of Amir's research, which suggests that (at least a portion) of forcible rapes were *caused by the victim*, strongly challenged his findings by arguing that he had ignored the larger cultural and structural systems of oppression that also contributed to violence against women (van Dijk, 1999).

The controversy surrounding Amir's study led to important conversations in the nascent victimology field. As van Dijk noted (1999), whereas early pioneers in victimology approached the study of criminal-victim relationships with balanced concern for offenders and victims, a new generation of victimologists recognized that cultural and structural constraints were important factors in considering the victim's role in the genesis of crime. Moreover, concerns surrounding the appropriateness of assigning responsibility to victims for their own victimization persisted, and likely led to an overall pivot in victimology such that the field became a platform to advocate for victims (Fattah, 2000). Related to this pivot were conversations regarding the scope of victimology and whether the field should be bounded by criminal law or involve all types of victimization (van Dijk, 1999). Those who follow the latter precept are called general victimologists.

Activity 1.4: Victim-Blaming and Portrayals in Popular Media

Research indicates that what the media laypersons consume often contributes to their beliefs about crime—including about offenders and victims (Surett, 1998). While personal experiences with crime undoubtedly have a greater impact on individuals, crime dramas are powerful vehicles for shaping the perceptions of those who lack knowledge of the criminal justice system. It is in the latter case where crime victims are especially hurt by crime dramas, particularly those who engage in victim-blaming. In this activity, students should watch the *Law & Order: Special Victims Unit* episode from season 14 entitled "Funny Valentine." During the episode, students should pay particular attention to victim-blaming actions or statements and document accordingly. Students should also be cognizant that victim-blaming can be very indirect and subtle, but it carries the same intention and meaning as any other form of shaming.

1. Briefly summarize the plot of the episode.
2. What characteristics describe the victim? The perpetrator?
3. Describe instances of racism, sexism, or any other type of discrimination or prejudice seen in the episode.
4. Describe all instances of victim-blaming, including who engages in it.
5. Describe how the documented instances of victim-blaming affect the victim.
6. Describe how the documented instances of victim-blaming might affect a real victim of domestic abuse.

General Victimology

Although Mendelsohn's (1963) early work in victimology was oriented toward understanding the genesis of crime, he later advocated that all forms of victimization were rightfully within the purview of victimology (1976). In other words, Mendelsohn (1976) envisioned that victimology was rightfully considered as a separate area of social science focused on victimization broadly and not as a subfield within criminology. Included in this broad field were harms that resulted from crime, but also the environment, technology, and social trends (Mendelsohn, 1976). In the course of advocating for this expanded scope, Mendelsohn (1976) also called for formal organizations as well as clinics designed to promote a holistic understanding of victimization as a global problem. Given this shift in focus to understand all forms of victimization, as well as potential remedies for harm, general victimology is also known as assistance-oriented victimology (van Dijk, 1999). Others have referred to this branch of victimology as radical victimology, particularly in instances of state violence toward citizens (Mawby & Walklate, 1994).

The potential broadening of victimology to include all types of victimization was not an idea supported by all pioneers in the field. Fattah (2000) notes that the shift in victimology resulted in scholars assuming the role of activists, and the academic discipline itself morphing into a "humanistic movement" (p. 25). Another consequence of this pivot, according to Fattah (2000), is that there is an emphasis on assisting identifiable victims, which means there is less attention given to serious crimes without identifiable victims, such as white-collar crime (Fattah, 2000). Finally, by emphasizing harms stemming from victimization and advocating for increased victim remedies, some have suggested that conservative ideologues have been emboldened to pursue increasingly punitive crime policies (Fattah, 2000; McEvoy & McConnachie, 2012). Concerns expressed by Fattah and others arguably led to the development of the most recent branch of victimology: critical victimology.

Critical Victimology

According to Chouliaris (2011; as cited in Walklate, 2015), "critical victimology . . . engages in a twofold task: to cast light on the institutions and structural relations that favor specific images of victimization at the expense of others (contextualization); and to draw attention to situations that, despite producing serious victimization, are not designated as such." In other words, critical victimologists question how the wider societal structure influences our conception of victimization and the conditions under which the label "victim" is applied (Mawby & Walklate, 1994; Walklate, 1989, 1990, 2015). Relatedly, critical victimologists criticize the heavy utilization of national crime surveys by positivist victimologists as limiting the ability to capture complex contextual details about victims' choices and lives that are intrinsically tied to class, gender, and race (among other things) (Walklate, 1989, 1990, 2015). Critical victimologists have also been especially disapproving of positivist victimology because of its failure to question how the socio-political undertones of criminal law, which is crafted and shaped by the most powerful in society, influence broader understandings of victimization (Walklate 1989, 1990, 2015). Put broadly, critical victimology attempts "to examine the wider social context in which some versions of victimology have become more dominant than others and how those versions of victimology are interwoven with questions of policy response and service delivery to victims of crime" (Mawby & Walklate, 1994, p. 21).

Textbook Author Spotlight

Dr. George E. Higgins, University of Louisville

Biography: Dr. Higgins received his Ph.D. in Criminology at Indiana University of Pennsylvania in 2001. His research focuses on testing criminological theories. Dr. Higgins publishes consistently with students and colleagues from around the world.

Research Interests and Areas: Testing criminological theory

Education:

Ph.D.	Criminology, Indiana University of Pennsylvania
M.P.A.	Public Administration, University of Kentucky
B.A.	Criminal Justice, Kentucky State University

Summary and Future Directions

The victimology field continues to advance in terms of bringing additional understanding to the genesis of crime as well as the experiences of victims in navigating the criminal justice system. Relative to the broader criminology field, the victimology field is still young and continues to be shaped by its historical pioneers (e.g., Mendelsohn, von Hentig, Schafer) as well as contemporary trailblazers. As the field has grown, it has addressed and debated various controversies within it—such as balancing concern between offenders and victims, victim-blaming, and challenging various myths associated with victimization and crime victims themselves (Moriarty, 2008). As the nature of victimization changes, the field will continue to develop and expand. For example, one emerging area of the victimology field is cyber-victimology, which developed in reaction to the exploding field of cybercriminology. In the next chapter, we present an overview of the theoretical perspectives used in victimology.

Discussion Questions

1. Explain which branch of victimology you most identify with in terms of providing the best approach to understanding victimization. Be sure to justify your answer.
2. Explain whether you believe victimology should be "value-free," not a field that advocates for social change. Be sure to justify your answer.
3. Explain why victimology is important to the understanding of criminal activity based on information in this chapter. Be sure to justify your answer.

References

Amir, M. (1967). Victim precipitated forcible rape. *The Journal of Criminal Law, Criminology, and Police Science, 58*(4), 493–502.

Daigle, L. E., & Muftić, L. R. (2015). *Victimology*. Thousand Oaks, CA: Sage Publications.

Dussich, J. P. (2006). *Victimology—past, present and future*. 131st International Senior Seminar. Retrieved from www.researchgate.net/profile/John_Dussich/publication/242078160_VICTIMOLOGY_-_PAST_PRESENT_AND_FUTURE/links/55fc374308ae07629e09aef3/VICTIMOLOGY-PAST-PRESENT-AND-FUTURE.pdf

Fattah, E. A. (1989). Victims and victimology: The facts and the rhetoric. *International Review of Victimology, 1*, 43–66.

Fattah, E. A. (2000). Victimology: Past, present and future. *Criminologie*, 17–46.

Friedrichs, D. O. (1983). Victimology: A consideration of the radical critique. *Crime Delinquency, 29*, 283–294.

Hinduja, S., & Patchin, J. W. (2010, March 2). *Victimology in cyberspace* [Blog post]. Retrieved from http://cyberbullying.org/victimology-in-cyberspace

In memory of Benjamin Mendelsohn, founder of victimology. (1998, April). *The Victimologist*. Retrieved from www.worldsocietyofvictimology.org/wp- content/uploads/2014/12/wsv21.pdf

Mawby, R. I., & Walklate, S. (1994). *Critical victimology: International perspectives*. Thousand Oaks, CA: Sage Publications.

McEvoy, K., & McConnachie, K. (2012). Victimology in transitional justice: Victimhood, innocence and hierarchy. *European Journal of Criminology, 9*(5), 527–538.

Meier, R. F., & Miethe, T. D. (1993). Understanding theories of criminal victimization. *Crime and Justice, 17*, 459–499.

Mendelsohn, B. (1937, August–October). Methods to be used by counsel for the defense in the researches made into the personality of the criminal. *Revue de Droit Penal et de Criminologie*. France.

Mendelsohn, B. (1956, July–September). Une nouvelle branche de la science bio-psycho-sociale, la victimologie. *Etudes Internationales de Psycho-Sociologie Criminelle*. France.

Mendelsohn, B. (1963). The origin of the doctrine of victimology. *Excerpta Criminologica, 3*, 239–244.

Mendelsohn, B. (1976). Victimology and contemporary society's trends. *Victimology: An International Journal, 1*(1), 8–28.

Moriarty, L. J. (2008). *Controversies in victimology*. Cincinnati, OH: Anderson Publishing.

Schafer, S. (1977). *Victimology: The victim and his criminal*. Reston, VA: Reston Publishing Company.

Schneider, H. J. (2001). Victimological developments in the world during the past three decades (I): A study of comparative victimology. *International Journal of Offender Therapy and Comparative Criminology, 45*(4), 449–468.

Surette, R. (1998). *Media, crime and criminal justice: Images and realities*. Belmont, CA: Wadsworth Publishing.

Van Dijk, J. J. (1999, August). *Introducing victimology*. Caring for crime victims: selected proceedings of the Ninth International Symposium on Victimology. Monsey, NY: Criminal Justice Press/Willow Tree Press.

Viano, E. C. (1976). Victimology and its pioneers. *Victimology: An International Journal*, *1*(2), 189–192.

Viano, E. C. (1983). Victimology: The development of a new perspective. *Victimology: An International Journal*, *8*(1–2), 17–30.

Von Hentig, H. (1940). Remarks on the interaction of perpetrator and victim. *Journal of Criminal Law and Criminology*, *31*(3), 303–309.

Von Hentig, H. (1948). *The criminal & his victim: Studies in the sociobiology of crime*. New Haven, CT: Yale University Press.

Walklate, S. (1989). *Victimology*. New York, NY: Routledge Publishers.

Walklate, S. (1990). Researching victims of crime: Critical victimology. *Social Justice*, *17*(3), 25–42.

Walklate, S. (2015). Jock Young, left realism and critical victimology. *Critical Criminology*, *23*, 179–190.

Wertham, F. (1949). *The show of violence*. Garden City, NY: Doubleday.

Wolfgang, M. (1957). Victim precipitated criminal homicide. *Criminal Law, Criminology, and Police Science*, *48*(1), 1–11.

Chapter 2

Theories of Victimization

Introduction

Recall in Chapter 1, "Introduction to Victimology," that we spent considerable time noting the works of pioneers in the victimology field and the contributions made by each in the understanding of the genesis of crime. In many of these early studies, risk factors like age and gender, among others, were identified as affecting the odds of experiencing a criminal event. However, without utilizing a theoretical perspective to *frame* these risk factors, scholars have asserted that is all these findings remain—a list of variables not grounded in any broader understanding of *why* these events happen (Higgins, 2004). Thus, framing risk factors within a theoretical perspective in order to present a holistic understanding of victimization is arguably as important as conducting the research itself.

According to the dictionary, theory is "a plausible or scientifically acceptable general principle or body of principles offered to explain phenomena" (Theory [Def. 1], n.d.). Before discussing several theoretical perspectives utilized to understand the genesis of crime, it is important to note that no one framework is universally agreed upon by all scholars. Each perspective noted below has strengths as well as weaknesses. In this chapter, we present several perspectives in victimology, some of which focus on the offender and victim selection while others focus purely on victim behaviors.

Biosocial Criminology Theory

One of the earliest pioneers of biosocial criminology theory was Dr. Lee Ellis, who utilized this perspective in the understanding of rape (1991). According to the Biosocial Criminology Association, biosocial criminology seeks to "understand the biological and environmental influences on the development of antisocial behavior." In other words, biosocial criminologists investigate the perpetration and/or experiencing of criminal activity from a vantage point that accounts for biological as well as social factors. As mentioned, some of the earliest work utilizing this perspective focused on rape.

In his seminal (1991) article entitled "A Synthesized (Biosocial) Theory of Rape," Ellis attempted to integrate and merge other perspectives on the topic into one all-inclusive framework. At the time, many scholars utilized the following approaches to understand this crime: (1) feminist perspective, (2) evolutionary theory, and (3) social learning theory (Ellis, 1991). In order to understand Ellis' attempt to integrate and merge these theories into a biosocial criminology framework, it is necessary to discuss each of these perspectives separately.

In terms of the feminist perspective, scholars in this field theorize that violence against women, including rape, is ultimately an expression of power and control originating from a system of oppression and patriarchy (Ellis, 1991). From this perspective, rape is a symptom of the larger systemic issue of gender inequality—it is not grounded in sexual attraction or gratification (Ellis, 1991). From an evolutionary theory perspective, rape stems from an internal motivation among males to ensure the production of offspring (Ellis, 1991). Finally, from a social learning theory perspective, rape is the result of individuals internalizing sexist attitudes and beliefs, such as those depicted through mass media, and then acting on those antisocial norms (Ellis, 1991). Given that these perspectives speak to both biological (e.g., evolutionary theory) and social (e.g., feminist perspective; social learning theory) causes of violence, Ellis (1991) leveraged each of their respective strengths in his construction of a biosocial theory of rape.

From Ellis' (1991) biosocial criminology perspective, rape occurs as a result of the following four biosocial factors: (1) men's biological drive as well as social drive to "possess" another person; (2) men's desire to continue their lineage through the production of multiple offspring, which for men generally does not require the same level of investment as it does for women; (3) men's learned and internalized attitudes and beliefs about sexual activity perpetrated through mass media; and (4) men's hormonal differences compared to women's. In a later study focused on revisiting the biosocial criminological perspective on rape, Ellis and Widmayer (2008) found support for applying this perspective to sexual violence. In that study, the scholars found that non-rapists had fewer sexual partners than rapists, because, arguably, offenders sought to ensure the continuance of their lineage (Ellis & Widmayer, 2008). Moreover, findings indicated that the relationship between an offender and a survivor post-victimization varied depending on whether an offspring might be produced (Ellis & Widmayer, 2008). In addition to applying biosocial criminology to rape, scholars in the field have also used this perspective in understanding father-daughter incest.

In the 1986 study by Parker and Parker, the scholars used biosocial criminology to explain the etiology of father-daughter incest. The scholars hypothesized that humans are incest-avoidant given biological issues that arise in the resulting offspring (Parker & Parker, 1986). To support this claim, the authors cite historical records of early human settlements where individuals who shared intimate and prolonged interactions with others during childhood avoided later copulation with these individuals as adults (Parker & Parker, 1986). The scholars also ground their beliefs in incest-avoidance by noting that animals rarely mate with family members as well (Parker & Parker, 1986). Ultimately, the scholars found support for applying a biosocial criminological perspective to father-daughter incest in that this crime was more likely to occur when there was both *physical* and *psychological* distance between the father and the daughter (Parker & Parker, 1986). The biosocial criminology perspective continues to be utilized within the field, although it has received a substantial amount of criticism—particularly in light of the actions of the Nazis during World War II.

Wright and Cullen (2012, p. 237) summarize succinctly the main criticism put to biosocial criminology when they say it is "a dangerous idea, because it created Nazism, was used to justify racism and sexism, and led to the eugenics movement in the United States." Indeed, eugenics, or the practice of selective breeding for the purposes of improving the overall race (Eugenics [Def. 1], n.d.), was an unforeseen outcome of early biological criminological research like Cesare Lombroso's work on identifying physical and mental characteristics that were indicative of criminality (Lombroso, 1911). However, as Wright and Cullen (2012) assert, biosocial criminology has since evolved to take into account both the biological and social roots of crime. This field of study is especially important because evidence suggests that antisocial behavior as well as other psychological disorders is somewhat biologically driven, that a relationship exists between certain developmental delays and engagement in aggressive behaviors, and that one's environment affects genetic dispositions relevant for later criminality (Wright & Cullen, 2012).

Activity 2.1: Biosocial Criminology—Where is the field now?

Pick one of the following prominent biosocial criminologists and look up two of their most recent studies through your institution's library. After reading both studies, summarize the research objective and the investigation outcomes in 250 words each (500 words total). After summarizing these investigations, connect what you just read about biosocial criminology to your selected scholar's work. How does his/her research relate to biosocial criminology? Be prepared to share this information with your peers if called on by the instructor.

J. C. Barnes
Kevin M. Beaver
Danielle Boisvert
Brian Boutwell
Callie H. Burt
Matt DeLisi
Ryan Charles Meldrum
Adrian Raine
Anthony Walsh
John Paul Wright

Control Balance Theory

Charles Tittle proposed control balance theory (CBT) in 1995 and asserted that deviance resulted from an imbalance in control among individuals and, specifically, *control deficits* and *control surpluses* (Tittle, 2004). According to Tittle (2004), control is the degree to which individuals can influence a course of action or outcome. All individuals seek control, but are also subjected to it as well (Tittle, 2004). Those experiencing a *control balance* can influence outcomes, but are subjected to control themselves in proportional measure (Tittle, 2004). In contrast, those experiencing a *control deficit* experience more control than they exert, whereas those experiencing a *control surplus* can exert great control over outcomes (Tittle, 2004). In terms of the latter two situations of control, if someone is given the opportunity to engage in deviance, Tittle (2004) notes, criminal activity becomes more likely.

In instances of a control imbalance, Tittle (2004) theorized engagement in crime was more likely but that the *type* of crime would differ. For individuals experiencing a lack of control (i.e., control deficit), crimes of a *repressive* nature would dominate their criminal activity such as violence and sexual assault (Braithwaite, 1997) after there was recognition within the individual of their position (Tittle, 2004). Braithwaite (1997) provides the example of an individual who, upon recognizing his/her lack of autonomy, experiences humiliation and engages in deviance. Contrasting to the former, individuals experiencing great control are likely to engage in crimes of an *autonomous* nature such as bribery, extortion, and price-fixing (Braithwaite, 1997). Braithwaite (1997) provides the example of a powerful individual who, upon sensing dissension within his/her social circle, experiences anger and engages in deviance.

Given that CBT was not proposed until 1995, work in this area remains in its infancy relative to other criminological perspectives. However, scholars have explored the utility of this perspective and uncovered interesting findings. For example, in a study utilizing CBT in the investigation of youth relationships, findings indicated that individuals experiencing control deficits engaged in acts of defiance and predation (Delisi & Hochstetler, 2002). However, the findings surrounding control surpluses were less consistent (Delisi & Hochstetler, 2002). These results led Delisi and Hochstetler (2002) to conclude that there was some support for CBT in the examination of repressive forms of deviance, but that additional investigations were needed to focus on autonomous forms of deviance. Similarly, Piquero and Hickman (1999) found that their results aligned with CBT in that a control surplus explained autonomous forms of deviance, but a control surplus also explained defiance as well, which instead should align with control deficits. Therefore, like Delisi and Hochstetler (2002), the scholars called for additional research utilizing CBT (Piquero & Hickman, 1999).

Feminist Criminology

Feminist criminology grew out of the larger women's movement that gained momentum in the 1970s (Sharp, 2009). During the women's movement, criminological scholars began calling attention to the dearth of information in existence about female offenders and the inadequate responses by the criminal justice system to these events (Sharp, 2009). This gap in the literature was particularly important to address, because some suspected that women's involvement in crime would increase given the liberation propelled forward by the women's movement (Sharp, 2009). Along with calling for greater recognition of the female offender, scholars in the feminist criminology movement advocated for greater awareness of how women's crime experiences, whether as an offender or survivor, varied given their demographic backgrounds (Sharp, 2009). Indeed, a main line of inquiry within feminist criminology is how women's involvement in crime traces back to larger, systemic forms of oppression like racism and sexism (Sharp, 2009). In terms of understanding crime and victimization, particularly from the vantage point of females, one significant outgrowth of the feminist criminology movement was the feminist pathways theory (Sharp, 2009).

Feminist pathways theory (Pasko & Chesney-Lind, 2016) essentially frames women's engagement in crime as stemming from the negative impacts of prior victimization as well as their interactions with the criminal justice system. Similar in thought to the life course development perspective, which is discussed below, feminist pathways theory asserts that one cannot understand the origins of female-perpetrated crimes unless the impact of prior life experiences is also taken into account (Sharp, 2009). Sharp (2009) notes that scholars have found that young girls are often punished more harshly than their male counterparts for status offenses, which forces them into the criminal justice system at a pivotal time of their development. A scholar utilizing the feminist pathways theoretical perspective would argue that this early interaction between the female youth and the criminal justice system likely increases the chances of her engaging in later criminal activity.

Activity 2.2: Feminist Criminology—Applying Theory to Data

Read "Women Offenders" (www.bjs.gov/content/pub/pdf/wo.pdf), composed by statisticians at the Bureau of Justice Statistics (BJS). In this "think-pair-share" activity, pair up with a classmate and answer the following questions (3–4 sentences each). Be prepared to share your answers in class if called on by the instructor.

1. After reading the report, explain whether there is evidence to indicate that women's involvement in crime has increased.
2. Compare and contrast female offenders with male offenders in terms of incident and victim characteristics.
3. Compare and contrast female offenders with male offenders in terms of their typical demographic backgrounds.
4. Compare and contrast female offenders with male offenders in terms of their prior involvement in the criminal justice system—particularly during their youth.
5. Finally, using the information above, apply feminist criminology *or* pathways theory to these results. In other words, explain women's seemingly increasing involvement in criminal activity using one of those perspectives.

Life Course Development

Scholars in the life course development (LCD) field, such as Glen H. Elder, assert that this framework addresses a long-standing dearth of understanding within the academic community of how an individual's development and experiences from childhood to death affect their decisions (Elder, Johnson, & Crosnoe, 2003). The introduction of longitudinal surveys aided in the growth of LCD, because scholars could follow individuals for extended periods to monitor onset, persistence, and desistance from criminal activity (Jennings & Piquero, 2009). For example, using a longitudinal research methodology, the Gluecks (1930) conducted a seminal LCD study in which they followed the lives of 500 Boston youth to monitor their involvement in criminal activity (as cited in Jennings & Piquero, 2009).

The growth and utility of LCD is not restricted to criminology. It developed across various social science disciplines (Jennings & Piquero, 2009). To put the theory in broad terms, LCD scholars are concerned with how normative *social pathways* are altered by life events, referred to as *transitions*, that then lead to different *trajectories* (i.e., a long-term change in roles and expectations) (Elderet al., 2003). For example, the development and progression of a young man's life may dramatically change if he is diagnosed with a serious illness (change in trajectory) that requires him to completely change his life (transition). In another example more specific to criminology, the development and progression of a young woman's life may dramatically change if she is arrested on a serious charge (change in trajectory) that results in her incarceration (transition). In his discussion of LCD, Elder and his colleagues (2003; pp. 10–14) identified five general principles that drove this field of inquiry:

1. Human development and aging are lifelong processes
2. Individuals construct their own life course through the choices and actions they take within the opportunities and constraints of history and social circumstance
3. The life course of individuals is embedded in and shaped by historical time and places they experience over a lifetime
4. The developmental antecedents and consequences of life transitions, events, and behavioral patterns vary according to their timing in a person's life
5. Lives are lived interdependently and socio-historical influences are expressed through this network of shared relationships.

In terms of its applicability to criminology, Jennings and Piquero (2009) note that LCD scholars utilize the framework to understand the factors that contribute to, as well as deter from, the onset of criminal activity. Thinking back to earlier discussion on the feminist pathways theory, LCD scholars are also concerned with the effect victimization has on the onset of crime. For example, in a synthesis of the literature, Macmillian (2001) found that violent victimization has a profound, lasting impact on an individual's life. Macmillian (2001) notes that this profound impact stems from victimizations challenging an individual's sense of autonomy, safety, and security.

Lifestyle Exposure Theory

Unlike previous theoretical frameworks, lifestyle exposure theory (LET) centers on the actions and behaviors of potential victims that increase their vulnerability to experiencing a crime. LET was proposed by Hindelang, Gottfredson, and Garofalo in 1978 and is very similar to routine activities theory (RAT), which is the work of Cohen and Felson that is discussed later in this chapter. In fact, scholars have claimed that RAT is "merely an expansion" of LET (Choi, 2008, p. 308). In terms of its applicability to understanding victimization, LET essentially asserts that the risk of experiencing crime varies across society given the differences in how individuals are structurally situated (e.g., age, class, gender, race) (Choi, 2008).

Santana (2010) notes that LET originated in work devoted to understanding why certain segments of the population, such as young men, are more vulnerable to experiencing crime versus other groups. Santana (2010) continues, explaining that individuals' activities and *lifestyles* are intertwined with the roles and expectations they hold in society. Thus, a young bachelor is likely at greater risk of experiencing a crime by the sheer nature of leading a more active lifestyle that exposes him to potential offenders. In another example, a woman who engages in survival sex as a means to acquire life's necessities is at greater risk of experiencing crime by the sheer nature of that role. Reflecting on Chapter 1 and the concept of victim-blaming, these examples are not intended to assign responsibility but rather to identify vulnerabilities in the explanation of the genesis of crime.

In contrast to previously noted theoretical frameworks, LET is also one of the perspectives that is applicable to cybercrime victimization. Indeed, in their study on cyberstalking victimization Reyns and colleagues (2011) successfully applied LET and found that greater target attractiveness (e.g., risky online behaviors), when considered separately, are correlated to experiencing cyberstalking. This research supports similar studies, often utilizing the broader perspective referred to as RAT, that risky online behavior is important for assessing risk of victimization both offline and online (Navarro, Clevenger, Beasley, & Jackson, 2015; Navarro & Jasinski, 2012, 2013).

Media Byte 2.1: *Every F——ing Day of My Life*:
Applying Lifestyle Exposure Theory

Watch *Every F——ing Day of My Life* on YouTube (also available on Amazon for a fee). After watching the film, apply LET to the case to frame these events. In other words, what characteristics about the victim's lifestyle (Wendy) made her vulnerable to victimization? What structurally situated roles and expectations associated with Wendy's life made it difficult for her to escape the violence?

Warning: This film is extremely graphic and contains scenes of violence that may prompt painful memories for survivors. Please speak to your instructor privately if you are concerned about this assignment.

Low Self-Control

Low self-control (LSC) theory, also referred to as "self-control theory" or as the "general theory of crime," is unique in the sense that it is argued to be a general explanation of why individuals engage in crime regardless of the type of incident or surrounding cultural background (Gottfredson & Hirschi, 1990). The essential premise of the theory is that individuals engage in criminal activity because they cannot resist the opportunity for immediate gratification that it provides *and* they lack the barrier of self-control that law-abiding individuals develop during childhood (Gottfredson & Hirschi, 1990). This lack of self-control, which could be demonstrated by a volatile personality and/or substance use, is alleged to stem from inadequate parenting during childhood (Gottfredson & Hirschi, 1990).

Throughout the years, LSC has been applied to various types of crime, both online and offline. For example, Clevenger, Navarro, and Jasinski (2014) successfully applied LSC to their study on the differences between online sexual offenders who solely possess child pornography and online sexual offenders who possess as well as produce/distribute child pornography. Ultimately, the scholars found that both groups engaged in behaviors indicative of LSC, but that the latter group demonstrated a greater lack of self-control compared to those who only possessed the explicit material (Clevenger et al., 2014). Not only is LSC a unique perspective in that it is an alleged universal explanation for crime engagement (Gottfredson & Hirschi, 1990), but scholars have used this framework to explain victimization as well (Schreck, 1999).

In Schreck's (1999) study, he successfully utilized LSC to explain risk of victimization. As he notes, low self-control was important for assessing risk of experiencing both property and personal victimization, and remained a significant factor regardless of whether the victim had engaged in criminal activity him- or herself (Schreck, 1999). In other words, the relationship between low self-control and risk of experiencing victimization existed both for individuals who engaged in crime and those who abstained from these behaviors (Schreck, 1999). He ends his study by calling for more research on LSC to inform our understanding of risks of victimization (Schreck, 1999).

Routine Activities Theory

Cohen and Felson introduced routine activities theory (RAT) to academia in the 1970s at approximately the same time as LET (discussed earlier). Much like LET, RAT is an opportunity-driven theoretical understanding of victimization. According to Cohen and

Felson (1979), crime likely results from a convergence in time and space of the following three factors: a potential offender, a suitable target, and the lack of a capable guardian. This perspective, like LSC, is applicable across personal and property offenses; moreover, it has informed cybercrime research as well (Navarro et al., 2015; Navarro & Jasinski, 2012, 2013). While scholars conceptualize RAT's main components slightly differently across studies, the essential premise underlining each remains largely the same.

According to RAT scholars, potential offenders, formerly referred to as motivated offenders, are omnipresent in society (Mustaine & Tewksbury, 2009). Taking that into account, RAT scholars have rarely investigated this component until recently. In their 2015 study, Navarro and Jasinski investigated differences in demographics and motivations across three groups of online sexual offenders to discern factors that would assist law enforcement in identifying these perpetrator types before crime engagement. Ultimately, the scholars found that the mainstream media's characterization of online sexual offenders as "predators" did not align with these data (Navarro & Jasinski, 2015). Additionally, findings indicated that the demographic and background characteristics of online sexual offenders did vary across offense types (Navarro & Jasinski, 2015).

The second component of RAT is akin to the main premise of LET and takes into account target vulnerability to victimization. The target can be a person or property (Cohen & Felson, 1979), and vulnerabilities broadly range across studies. For example, in their 2015 study of cyberbullying on social networking sites (SNS), Navarro and colleagues assessed what behaviors on social media platforms like Facebook make users vulnerable to cybervictimization. Ultimately, the scholars found that using SNS daily increased the risk of experiencing cyberbullying (Navarro et al., 2015). Additionally, bullying others, posting status updates, and using private messages all increased the odds of experiencing cyberbullying (Navarro et al., 2015).

The third component, a capable guardian, counteracts the chance of victimization occurring (Cohen & Felson, 1979). Although scholars' conceptualization of the capable guardian widely varies across studies, this component was envisioned as someone who could keep a crime from happening by keeping "an eye on the potential *target* of crime" (Felson, 2006, p. 80). In other words, using an alarm system or bright lights may deter a burglary, but these items are not capable forms of guardianship in terms of understanding RAT. Instead, capable forms of guardianship are parents, police officers, teachers, and others who are in positions to both monitor potential targets of crime *and* act if a crime is likely to occur. Taking this into account, Cohen and Felson (1979) theorized that the *lack* of a capable guardian contributed to the genesis of crime when a potential offender and suitable target converged in time and space.

Activity 2.3: Situational Crime Prevention and Routine Activities Theory

Take a field trip to a densely populated area of campus (e.g., gym, library, or student union). Conduct observational research of your surroundings, but from the vantage point of a routine activities theorist. In other words, is it likely that there are potential offenders in the area given the number of people in that setting? Document your thoughts for your write-up. Next, watch the behaviors of individuals in that space and identify vulnerabilities. For example, are bags left unattended? Are individuals paying attention to their belongings? Again, document all the vulnerabilities you see for your write-up. Finally, are there any capable guardians present? Again, document all the capable guardians you see for your write-up. After conducting your observation, summarize your findings in a one-page write-up by addressing each component of RAT separately. Finally, at the end of the write-up, provide ideas—based on your findings—that campus leadership could implement in order to deter crime.

Social Disorganization Theory

Social disorganization theory (SDT) is perhaps one of the most influential theoretical perspectives in criminology. First introduced by Shaw and McKay (1942), the framework argues that victimization at the individual level is a product of disorganization at the community level. Indeed, the main premise of SDT is that all social problems that plague a community are ultimately a reflection of ecological factors (Sampson, 1992). When first introduced, SDT centered on the following three broad concepts: "physical status, economic status, and population status" (Walker, 2010, p. 313). However, after failed or inconsistent replication attempts, as well as a period of inactivity, SDT was revamped to focus on collective efficacy and various neighborhood factors (Walker, 2010).

Many studies have evaluated the utility of SDT in urban locations (Vélez, 2001) and rural locations (Osgood & Chambers, 2000) with interesting results. Broadly speaking, SDT scholars have found that various community-level factors, such as residential instability, family disruption, and ethnic heterogeneity affect juvenile delinquency (Osgood & Chambers, 2000; Sampson & Groves, 1989). More specifically, a community with residents frequently moving in and out (i.e., residential instability), that has unstable family dynamics (i.e., family disruption), and a population including individuals of various backgrounds and cultures (e.g., ethnic heterogeneity) is less likely to forge the collective bonds that curb juvenile delinquency (Osgood & Chambers, 2000; Sampson, 1992; Sampson & Groves, 1989; Vélez, 2001). The importance of these factors led Sampson (1992) to suggest that communities ranged from "disorganized" to "organized" and that the organized communities utilized strong formal and informal social controls that were essential to curbing juvenile delinquency. Although SDT is a macro-level theory that takes into account community-level factors rather than individual-level factors this perspective has framed various types of victimization.

Vélez (2001) used SDT to assess risk of victimization by primarily looking at the social capital in a community and its relationship to formal entities of social control. Social capital, as explained by Walker (2010), is a term that has particular relevance for SDT, because it describes the intangible yet extremely important relationships a community has established to guard against social problems. In Vélez's (2001) study, the impact of public social control on victimization risk was assessed by asking residents about the social capital they had garnered with their local government and law enforcement. Ultimately, the scholar found that communities that had stronger relationships with formal entities of social control (e.g., government and law enforcement) experienced less victimization (Vélez, 2001).

Social Interactionist Theory

Social interactionist (SI) theory, proposed by Felson and Tedeschi (1993), explains that victimization is the result of a conscious choice by offenders to utilize violence, or some other type of coercive action (e.g., bodily force, threat, or punishment), in order to achieve an important objective. Unlike frustration-aggression theory, where violence is an involuntary reaction to a perceived stressor, SI argues that perpetrators use violence in an instrumental and purposeful way (Felson & Tedeschi, 1993). According to Felson and Tedeschi (1993, p. 295), instrumental violence is often perpetrated with one or more of the following three goals in mind: "(1) gain compliance, (2) redress grievances, or (3) promote or defend valued identities." Perhaps what is most disturbing about this decision-making process, as Felson and Tedeschi (1993) note, is the fact that perpetrators of violence likely feel justified in their utilization of it.

Taking this into account, SI is easily applicable to various sorts of offenses, but particularly interpersonal abuse like domestic violence and sexual assault. Imagine an abuser who arrives home and finds dinner is not on the table yet (i.e., a perceived slight): the batterer may feel the need to reassert who controls the household and decide to physically assault the partner to redress this grievance. In another example, imagine a woman is trapped in a room with an aggressive male who is attempting to engage her in sexual activity. The male may decide to threaten her with great physical bodily harm unless she complies with his demands. Finally, imagine a group of young people is out at a social event. In the midst of having a good time, one individual hurls an insult at another. The targeted individual, feeling his very identity has just been challenged by the insult, may decide to defend himself by violent means.

Social Learning Theory

Social learning theory (Akers, 1973) argues that social behavior, regardless of whether it is prosocial or antisocial, is a learning process. Akers (1973) proposed SLT several decades ago and it has come to be referred to as a general theory of crime because, much like LSC, it has wide applicability across various offense types. As noted by Akers (1973), SLT comprises four important concepts: (1) differential association (e.g., association with deviant peers), (2) definitions (e.g., positive or negative beliefs about crime), (3) differential reinforcement (e.g., punishments or rewards), and (4) imitation. Depending on the effects of these four concepts, SLT theorists argue, individuals are socialized toward a path of prosocial behavior or antisocial behavior. To gain a greater understanding of SLT, further explanation of its key components is warranted.

Differential association, although considered as part of SLT here, is an important stand-alone concept in criminology first introduced by Sutherland (1939). The term essentially describes an association with deviant peers (Sutherland, 1939), which could then influence one's own engagement in deviance. Definitions are an important component of SLT, because engagement in delinquency is reliant on an individual believing criminal behaviors are acceptable (Akers, 1973). Next, differential reinforcement is critical for the potential replication of behavior. According to SLT, a behavior that is reinforced—either positively (e.g., something is added of value) or negatively (e.g., something is removed that is unwanted)—likely leads to a continuance of that behavior (Akers, 1973). In contrast, a behavior that results in punishment—either positively (e.g., something negative is added) or negatively (e.g., something of value is removed)—likely deters a continuance of that behavior (Akers, 1973). Finally, imitation occurs when the behavior is learned and repeated (Akers, 1973).

Strain Theory

Robert Agnew's general strain theory greatly expanded the understanding of criminal offending. According to Agnew (2001), engagement in criminal behavior ultimately stems from an individual encountering a source of adversity (i.e., strain), experiencing a negative emotion as a result (i.e., anger, frustration), and then reacting in an antisocial manner. It is important to note that Agnew identified several potential reactions from individuals, but engagement in deviance was most important for criminologists (Agnew, 2001). In terms of sources of strain, Agnew identified three broad groups: "loss of positive valued stimuli, presentation of negative stimuli, and goal blockage" (p. 319). Assessing whether an individual will react to strain or not is also dependent on whether "(1) these are seen as unjust, (2) are seen as high in magnitude, (3) are associated with low self-control, and (4) create some pressure or incentive to engage in crime" (Agnew, 2001, p. 320).

Agnew's (2001) sources of strain are easily applicable in the understanding of both offending and victimization. To consider the first source of strain, loss of positively valued stimuli, imagine a domestic abuser who becomes enraged after his partner threatens to terminate the relationship (i.e., loss of positively valued stimuli). The abuser may engage in or threaten violence to the partner in order to prevent the termination of the relationship, thus resolving the source of strain. Next, consider the second source of strain (i.e., the presentation of negative stimuli) and imagine the same situation as described above. After reconciling their relationship, the couple described above experience several horrific violent altercations. The partner, who fears for her life as her abuser continues to escalate in his violence (i.e., presentation of negative stimuli), kills him in a fit of rage. By killing her abuser, the victim resolved the source of strain confronting her. Finally, consider the final source of strain (i.e., goal blockage) and once again imagine the same couple as before, but with a different outcome. After reconciling their relationship, the abuser continues to escalate in his violence, because he blames his partner for his lack of success in his professional career (i.e., goal blockage). As a result, he becomes increasingly frustrated and kills his partner. While the aforementioned are gruesome examples, they illustrate how flexible general strain theory is in the application of criminal activity to understand why individuals perpetrate crime as well as experience it.

Structural Choice Theory

In order to leverage the strengths associated with lifestyle exposure theory and routine activities theory, Meier and Miethe (1993) proposed an integrated perspective referred to as structural choice theory. In their words, "proximity to motivated offenders, exposure to high-risk environments, target attractiveness, and absence of guardianship. . . [are]

necessary conditions for predatory crime" (p. 475). According to the scholars, structural choice theory (SCT) is uniquely suited to explain both offending and victimization, because it accounts for structural factors as well as micro-level factors (Meier & Miethe, 1993). Put another way, SCT asserts that risk of crime offending and victimization derives from patterned behavior that is both structurally driven (e.g., exposure to offenders and potentially risky situations) as well as offender "choice" driven (e.g., assessment of vulnerability of victim and presence of guardians) (Meier & Miethe, 1993).

Activity 2.4: The Green River Killer and Structural Choice Theory

Pair up with another student and conduct research on Gary Ridgway, the "Green River Killer." After researching his crimes, apply structural choice theory to these instances. In other words, identify each component of structural choice theory and apply it to the crimes of this infamous serial killer in order to explain how these crimes occurred.

Subculture of Violence Theory

The subculture of violence theory (SVT) is one of the few theoretical perspectives that explains both offending and victimization from a broad perspective. The theory originated from the work of Wolfgang and Ferracuti (1967) and is based on the premise of the existence of a violent subculture in which antisocial behavior becomes a normative response to certain affronts that, in turn, perpetuates the cycle (Kennedy & Baron, 1993). Kennedy and Baron (1993) reiterate that SVT does not claim that violence is *always* the reaction in this type of subculture, but rather that individuals in this subculture encounter situations in which violence is their normative response, in contrast to those socialized in the dominant culture (Kennedy & Baron, 1993). As noted by Kennedy and Baron (1993), adhering individuals likely experience praise for their conformity to these subculture norms, while those who fail to conform risk ostracization from the community.

SVT is therefore a useful perspective for understanding both why individuals engage in deviance as well as why individuals *experience* deviance. Examining various theoretical perspectives, not just SVT, shows that one of the most salient risk factors for experiencing victimization is the victim engaging in deviant activity. This is often referred to as the victim-offender overlap (Marcum, Higgins, Freiburger, & Ricketts, 2014; Schreck, 1999). It is easily applicable to SVT in the sense that individuals socialized to utilize violence as part of the normative culture are likely to also be met with violence, which can result in their own victimization. For example, imagine a gang member who engages in violence in order to maintain his/her status in the surrounding community and consider the likelihood of that gang member eventually experiencing violence him/herself.

Summary

The theoretical perspectives discussed in this chapter represent a large swath of the frameworks utilized in criminological and victimological research today. However, this chapter does not represent an inclusive list, as new ways of understanding crime and victimization are constantly proposed by scholars in the field. For example, as technology has advanced, scholars have explored whether traditional "offline" theoretical perspectives can apply to cybercrime victimization as well. Perhaps what is most important in the progression, though, is that the understanding of the genesis of criminal activity must remain focused on the individual making the choice to victimize another (i.e., the offender).

Discussion Questions

1. Identify the theoretical perspective you believe is *best* suited to explain criminal offending. Be sure to justify and support your decision.
2. Identify the theoretical perspective you believe is *best* suited to explain criminal victimization. Be sure to justify and support your decision.
3. Identify a type of crime that is of interest to you. Using one of the theoretical perspectives noted in this chapter, describe why that type of crime occurs.

References

Agnew, R. (2001). Building on the foundation of general strain theory. *Journal of Research in Crime and Delinquency, 38*(4), 319–361.

Akers, R. L. (1973). *Deviant behavior: A social learning approach*. Belmont, CA: Wadsworth.

Braithwaite, J. (1997). Charles Tittle's *control balance* and criminological theory. *Theoretical Criminology, 1*(1), 77–97.

Choi, K. (2008). An empirical assessment of an integrated theory of computer crime victimization. *International Journal of Cyber Criminology, 2*(1), 308–333.

Clevenger, S., Navarro, J. N., & Jasinski, J. L. (2014). A matter of low self-control? Exploring differences between child pornography possessors and child pornography producers/distributers using self-control theory. *Sexual Abuse: A Journal of Research and Treatment*, online first.

Cohen, L. E., & Felson, M. (1979). Social change and crime rate trends: A routine activity approach. *American Sociological Review, 44,* 588–608.

Delisi, M., & Hochstetler, A. L. (2002). An exploratory assessment of Tittle's Control Balance Theory: Results from the National Youth Survey. *The Justice Professional, 15*(3), 261–272.

Elder Jr., G. H., Johnson, M. K., & Crosnoe, R. (2003). The emergence and development of life course theory. In *Handbook of the life course* (pp. 3–19). New York: Springer.

Ellis, L. (1991). A synthesized (biosocial) theory of rape. *Journal of Consulting and Clinical Psychology, 59*(5), 631–642.

Ellis, L., & Widmayer, A. (2008). Perpetrators of sexual assault continuing to have sex with their victims following the initial assault: Evidence for evolved reproductive strategies. *International Journal of Offender Therapy and Comparative Criminology, 53*(4), 454–463.

Eugenics [Def. 1]. (n.d.). *Merriam-Webster Online*. Retrieved May 9, 2017, from www.merriam-webster.com/dictionary/eugenics

Felson, M. (2006). *Crime and nature*. Thousand Oaks, CA: Sage Publications.

Felson, R. B., & Tedeschi, J. T. (1993). A social interactionist approach to violence: Cross-cultural applications. *Violence and Victims, 8*(3), 295–310.

Gottfredson, M. R., & Hirschi, T. (1990). *A general theory of crime*. Palo Alto, CA: Stanford University Press.

Higgins, G. E. (2004). Can low self-control help with the understanding of the software piracy problem? *Deviant Behavior, 26*(1), 1–24.

Jennings, W. G., & Piquero, A. R. (2009). Life course criminology. In J. M. Miller (Ed.), *21st century criminology: A reference handbook* (pp. 262–270). Thousand Oaks, CA: Sage Publications.

Kennedy, L. W., & Baron, S. W. (1993). Routine activities and a subculture of violence: A study of violence on the street. *Journal of Research in Crime and Delinquency, 30*(1), 88–112.

Lombroso, C. (1911). *Crime, its causes and remedies* (Vol. 3). Boston, MA: Little, Brown, and Company.

Macmilliam, R. (2001). Violence and the life course: The consequences of victimization for personal and social development. *Annual Review of Sociology, 27*, 1–22.

Marcum, C. D., Higgins, G. E., Freiburger, T. L., & Ricketts, M. L. (2014). Exploration of the cyberbullying victim/offender overlap by sex. *American Journal of Criminal Justice, 39*, 538–548.

Meier, R. F., & Miethe, T. D. (1993). Understanding theories of criminal victimization. *Crime and Justice, 17*, 459–499.

Mustaine, E. E., & Tewksbury, R. (2009). Transforming potential offenders into motivated ones: Are sex offenders tempted by alcohol and pornography? *Deviant Behavior, 30*(7), 561–588.

Navarro, J. N., Clevenger, S., Beasley, M. E., & Jackson, L. (2015). One step forward, two steps back: Cyberbullying within social networking sites. *Security Journal*, online first.

Navarro, J. N., & Jasinski, J. L. (2012). Going cyber: Using routine activities theory to predict cyberbullying experiences. *Sociological Spectrum, 32*(1), 81–94.

Navarro, J. N., & Jasinski, J. L. (2013). Why girls? Using routine activities theory to predict cyberbullying experiences between girls and boys. *Women & Criminal Justice*, *23*, 286–303.

Navarro, J. N., & Jasinski, J. L. (2015). Demographic and motivation differences among online sex offenders by type of offense: An exploration of routine activities theories. *Journal of Child Sexual Abuse*, *24*(7), 753–771.

Osgood, D. W., & Chambers, J. M. (2000). Social disorganization outside the metropolis: An analysis of rural youth violence. *Criminology*, *38*(1), 81–115.

Parker, H., & Parker, S. (1986). Father-daughter sexual abuse: An emerging perspective. *American Journal of Orthopsychiatry*, *56*(4), 531–549.

Pasko, L., & Chesney-Lind, M. (2016). Running the gauntlet: Understanding commercial sexual exploitation and the pathways perspective to female offending. *Journal of Developmental and Life-Course Criminology*, *2*(3), 275–295.

Piquero, A. R., & Hickman, M. (1999). An empirical test of Tittle's control balance theory. *Criminology*, *37*(2), 319–342.

Reyns, B. W., Henson, B., & Fisher, B. S. (2011). Being pursued online: Applying cyberlifestyle-routine activities theory to cyberstalking victimization. *Criminal Justice and Behavior*, *38*(11), 1149–1169.

Sampson, R. J. (1992). Family management and child development: Insights from social disorganization theory. In J. McCord (Ed.), *Facts, frameworks, and forecasts: Advances in criminological theory* (pp. 63–93). Piscataway, NJ: Transaction Publishers.

Sampson, R. J., & Groves, W. B. (1989). Community structure and crime: Testing social-disorganization theory. *American Journal of Sociology*, *94*(4), 774–802.

Santana, S. A. (2010). Hindelang, Michael J., Gottfredson, Michael R., & Garofalo, James: Lifestyle theory. In F. T. Cullen & P. Wilcox (Eds.), *Encyclopedia of criminological theory* (Vol. 1). Thousand Oaks, CA: Sage Publications.

Schreck, C. J. (1999). Criminal victimization and low self-control: An extension and test of a general theory of crime. *Justice Quarterly*, *16*(3), 633–654.

Sharp, S. (2009). Feminist criminology. In J. M. Miller (Ed.), *21st century criminology: A reference handbook* (pp. 184–200). Thousand Oaks, CA: Sage Publications.

Shaw, C. R., & McKay, H. D. (1942). *Juvenile delinquency and urban areas*. Chicago, IL: The University of Chicago Press.

Sutherland, E. H. (1939). *Principles in criminology* (3rd ed.). Philadelphia, PA: Lippincott.

Theory [Def. 1]. (n.d.). *Merriam-Webster Online*. Retrieved May 9, 2017, from www.merriam-webster.com/dictionary/theory

Tittle, C. R. (2004). Refining control balance theory. *Theoretical Criminology*, *8*(4), 395–428.

Vélez, M. B. (2001). The role of public social control in urban neighborhoods: A multi-level analysis of victimization risk. *Criminology*, *39*(4), 837–864.

Walker, J. T. (2010). Social disorganization theory. In F. T. Cullen & P. Wilcox (Eds.), *Encyclopedia of criminological theory* (Vol. 1). Thousand Oaks, CA: Sage Publications.

Wolfgang, M. E., & Ferracuti, F. (1967). *The subculture of violence*. London, England: Tavistock.

Wright, J. P., & Cullen, F. T. (2012). The future of biosocial criminology: Beyond scholars' professional ideology. *Journal of Contemporary Criminal Justice*, *28*(3), 237–253.

Chapter 3

Victims' Rights and Remedies

- Identity Theft Assumption and Deterrence Act
- Identity Theft Enhancement and Restitution Act
- Ike Skelton National Defense Authorization Act
- International Parental Kidnapping Act
- James Zadroga 9/11 Health and Compensation Act
- Justice Assistance Act
- Justice for All Act
- Justice for Victims of Trafficking Act
- Kate Puzey Peace Corps Volunteer Protection Act
- Matthew Shepard and James Byrd Jr. Hate Crimes Prevention Act
- Missing Children's Act
- Missing Children's Assistance Act
- Parental Kidnapping Prevention Act
- Preventing Sex Trafficking and Strengthening Families Act
- Primary Survivors
- Prison Rape and Elimination Act
- PROTECT Act
- Secondary Survivors
- Student Right to Know and Campus Security Act
- Trafficking Victims Protection Act
- Victim Witness Protection Act
- Victims of Crime Act
- Victims' Rights Clarification Act
- Violence Against Women Act
- Violent Crime Control and Law Enforcement Act

Introduction

The previous chapters explored the development of the victimology field as well as theoretical frameworks utilized to inform understandings surrounding victimization. In this chapter, we will discuss how these two topics intersected to spur real-world change in the form of victims' rights and remedies. In other words, the victimology field is credited, in part, with promoting greater recognition of victims within the criminal justice system (Tobolowsky, Beloof, Jackson, Gaboury, & Blackburn, 2016). However, before considering where we are now, it is important to revisit the historical role of victims in the administration of justice.

The Historical Treatment of Victims

Although movements in the 1970s and 1980s spurred great social change in terms of the treatment of crime victims within the criminal justice system, this recognition has varied throughout history. For example, in early societies, crime was not a matter for state intervention, but was an interpersonal matter requiring resolution between offenders and victims directly (Tobolowsky et al., 2016). This type of system is best exemplified by ancient texts such as the Code of Hammurabi (i.e., "an eye for an eye") and the Torah (Tobolowsky et al., 2016), among others.

This method of resolution remained for a considerable amount of time. In early settlements in America, victims were responsible for virtually every aspect of the pursuit of justice (Tobolowsky et al., 2016). In order to hold offenders accountable, victims had to conduct their own investigations, hire a third party to capture the offenders, and then essentially litigate matters on their own behalf (Tobolowsky et al., 2016). While the foundation of the criminal justice system is readily apparent in these early processes, it is important to reiterate that during this period victims were on their own in the pursuit of justice.

As societies continued to evolve, various social factors led to the formalization of the criminal justice system. One such factor was how the conceptualization of crime shifted from an individual issue to a social issue (Tobolowsky et al., 2016). Put another way, criminal events were seen as affronts to the social system overall and thus warranted state action (Tobolowsky et al., 2016). While this shift lessened the burden on victims to investigate and pursue justice on their own, it also marginalized individuals who suffered the most during criminal events (Tobolowsky et al., 2016). Unfortunately, the victim remained on the sidelines of the criminal justice system for a considerable period until the 1970s.

As discussed in Chapter 1, the development of victimology began calling attention to the importance of understanding victims in the early to mid-1970s. Large-scale victimization surveys underscored this importance by indicating that many victims did not report offenses to law enforcement and current methods of collection (i.e., the Uniform Crime Report) were inadequate for understanding the complexities of crime. Finally, during this period, the women's movement gained national attention in their call for improved recognition and response by the criminal justice system to gender-based violence (e.g., domestic abuse, sexual violence) (Tobolowsky et al., 2016). Other victim groups dedicated to organizing for change, such as Mothers Against Drunk Driving (MADD) and Parents of Murdered Children, amplified this call for greater recognition of victim rights (Tobolowsky et al., 2016). Eventually, these social factors coalesced to spur sweeping systemic changes in terms of victims' rights and remedies that followed for the next few decades and continue today.

Given this chapter's space constraints, the following discussion will focus only on the legislative remedies that have occurred throughout the years, but readers should not infer that change was limited solely to legislation. As previously mentioned, change occurred on many fronts: through grassroots efforts, through legislation, and through wider public action following mass tragedies (e.g., the 1995 Oklahoma City bombing). Finally, it is important to note that most of the following bills have been reauthorized since their initial passage date, which is noted in parentheses. Therefore, readers should understand that the information presented in this chapter is a broad overview and further investigation is required for any in-depth analysis.

Victims' Rights and Remedies in the 1970s

Perhaps the earliest victims' rights legislation addressed violence committed against society's most vulnerable population: children. In 1974, the National Center for Child Abuse and Neglect, which is a resource for combating all forms of child abuse, began as part of the Child Abuse Prevention and Treatment Act (Office for Victims of Crime (OVC), 2017). This legislation and the subsequent founding of the center was likely spurred by Dr. Henry Kempe, who coined the term *battered child syndrome*, which raised awareness of child abuse (Kempe, Silverman, Steele, Droegemueller, & Silver, 2013). Despite this recognition, legislation aimed at combating partner violence would not materialize for several more years.

Victims' Rights and Remedies in the 1980s

The 1980s included a flurry of activity designed to address the long-standing marginalization of victims in the criminal justice system. Grassroots movements encouraged this effort by continuing to highlight that, not only had primary survivors been long overlooked in the criminal justice system, but secondary survivors had as well. Primary survivors, in contrast to secondary, are the individuals who directly experience the crime and resulting harm from criminal events (Clevenger & Navarro, 2017). While secondary survivors do not directly experience crimes themselves, these individuals suffer the resulting harm from criminal events given their intimate connection to the primary survivor (Clevenger & Navarro, 2017). In this section, we review the legislation that passed during the 1980s and drove the victims' rights movement forward.

Parental Kidnapping Prevention Act (PKPA) (1980)

Although many parents fear stranger-perpetrated abductions, research studies continue to note that children are at greatest risk of abduction from known relatives rather than strangers (Sedlack, Finkelhor, Hammer, & Schultz, 2002). Before the 1980s, noncustodial-parent-perpetrated abduction posed a significant legal challenge for the custodial parent in the retrieval process (Erickson, 1988; Schetky & Haller, 1983). The passage of the PKPA in 1980 addressed this problem and mandated that judges honor custody decisions whether or not the matter was resolved within that state or outside of it (Erickson, 1988; Schetky & Haller, 1983). Moreover, the act provided law enforcement resources to pursue abduction cases as well as federal resources in instances of felony kidnapping involving multiple states (Erickson, 1988; Schetky & Haller, 1983). The impetus of this act was expanded in the 1990s with the passage of the International Parental Kidnapping Act (1993), which sought to prevent and/or respond to the abduction of children by noncustodial parents to locations outside of the United States (OVC, 2017).

Victim Witness Protection Act (1982)

As conversation continued to swirl at the national level on victims' rights, President Ronald Reagan convened the Presidential Task Force on Victims of Crime in 1982 (Davis & Mulford, 2008; OVC, 2017; Young & Stein, 2004). The task force worked tirelessly to improve the overall system, and their efforts resulted in 68 recommendations (Davis & Mulford, 2008; OVC, 2017; Young & Stein, 2004). Although not all the recommendations were codified into law, several were implemented—such as the Victim Witness Protection Act.

In 1982, Congress began working toward correcting the absence of victims' voices in the justice process through the passage of the Victim Witness Protection Act. This act, like many that followed, granted victims crucial rights in the criminal justice system, such as the right to be heard during proceedings through victim impact statements and the right to restitution to offset victimization costs (Davis & Mulford, 2008; Young & Stein, 2004). While all of these rights are important, victim impact statements were particularly important, because it brought the harm experienced by the survivor and his/her family back into focus in the courtroom.

Missing Children's Act (1982)

The Missing Children's Act, passed in the wake of the Adam Walsh tragedy (see Media Byte 3.1), sought to aid families experiencing abductions whether they were perpetrated by a family member or an unrelated person. One essential purpose of the act was that it required greater information sharing between law enforcement entities and the Federal Bureau of Investigation's National Crime Information Center (Levesque, 2014; OVC, 2017). By sharing information about missing children through the national database, the act sought to expedite and improve the recovery of abducted children (OVC, 2017). Aside from this goal, the act required the development of procedures to guide law enforcement agencies in matters concerning missing children (such as disputes arising from custody decisions) (Levesque, 2014).

Media Byte 3.1: The Abduction and Murder of Adam Walsh

Adam Walsh, the son of John Walsh, disappeared from a Florida shopping mall in 1981 and was never seen alive again (Almanzar, 2008). His parents learned of his fate a few weeks later when his severed head was discovered in Vero Beach, Florida (Almanzar, 2008). Ultimately, a career criminal named Ottis E. Toole was convicted of the crime, and he died in prison in 1996 (Almanzar, 2008). John Walsh honored the memory of his son by using this tragedy as a call for greater awareness about missing children through the National Center for Missing and Exploited Children (Almanzar, 2008). He went on to champion many pieces of legislation centered on victims' rights, such as the Missing Children's Act of 1982. In addition, he hosted the TV show *America's Most Wanted* for a number of years (Almanzar, 2008).

Working with a partner, discuss how the Missing Children's Act could have aided in the recovery of Adam Walsh. After conducting your own research on the Missing Children's Act, identify two strengths of the legislation as well as two areas for improvement (as of that time). Be prepared to share your thoughts with the class.

Victims of Crime Act (1984)

The Victims of Crime Act (VOCA) continued to expand on the remedies provided to survivors by creating a victim compensation fund through the payment of offenders' fines (OVC, 2017; Tobolowsky et al., 2016). Readers should recall that Sara Margery Fry, an early pioneer of victimology, worked extensively to improve the criminal justice system and advocated for victim compensation funds for many years (Viano, 1976). After experiencing a crime herself, Fry reflected on how victims with few resources could recover in instances of financial or debilitating violent crime (Viano, 1976). This experience and reflection led her to advocate for a victim compensation fund generated by the state, which is widely available today. Aside from creating this funding, VOCA also led to the development of the Office for Victims of Crime (OVC, n.d.).

Activity 3.1: Victim Compensation Fund Activity

In this activity, imagine you have experienced a crime and need financial assistance to defer expenses. Locate the application for accessing the crime victim compensation fund in your state. After locating this information, complete the application with details of the incident that you imagined. Before you begin, be sure you understand the eligibility requirements. After completing the application, answer the following questions: (1) was the process of filing for compensation easy to understand and complete?, (2) what benefits does the fund provide to survivors?, and (3) what are the limitations of acquiring funding? After answering these questions, work with a partner and discuss your thoughts. Then, with your partner, think of 3–4 improvements to this program that would overcome its limitations.

Justice Assistance Act (1984)

New resources were provided to crime victims, as well as law enforcement charged with investigating crimes, through the passage of the Justice Assistance Act, which led to the creation of the Office of Justice Programs (Office of Justice Programs, n.d.b). Aside from aiding crime victims through working with law enforcement, the Office of Justice Programs assists in the development of effective prevention and intervention programs to combat crime (Office of Justice Programs, n.d.b). One mechanism by which to spur this innovation is the awarding of grants to law enforcement agencies and specialized victim services organizations (Civic Impulse, 2017a).

Missing Children's Assistance Act (1984)

The tireless work of the Walsh family to shine a light on child victims led to the passage of the Missing Children's Assistance Act of 1984, which resulted in the founding of the National Center for Missing and Exploited Children, which serves as a clearinghouse for the topic (Fernandes-Alcantara, 2014a; OVC, 2017). As knowledge increased about missing and exploited children, expanded services were built in through amendments to the act. For example, in later amendments, the legislation mandated increased coordination with the Runaway and Homeless Children Program (Fernandes-Alcantara, 2014a). Although these were significant steps forward in raising awareness and addressing violence against children, there remained a dearth of policies designed to address family violence as a whole until the mid-1980s.

Family Violence Prevention and Services Act (1984)

In 1984, family violence was formally recognized as a serious social problem through the Family Violence Prevention and Services Act (FVPSA) (Fernandes-Alcantara, 2014b). Before this time, despite the fact that family violence was gaining attention in the victims' rights movement, victims had few recourses to seek help. The FVPSA provided several important resources as first steps to combat violence in the home, such as establishing a national reporting hotline (Fernandes-Alcantara, 2014b). Additionally, funding was established for victim services agencies to provide critical resources to survivors (e.g., counseling, crisis services) as well as to create and promote prevention and intervention programs (Fernandes-Alcantara, 2014b).

Activity 3.2: The Burning Bed

In the 1970s domestic violence was largely seen as a "private trouble." Even if law enforcement were called to the scene, typically very little was done to halt any subsequent violence. Additionally, the sociocultural climate of the 1970s, when women were continuing their battle for greater equality in and outside of the home, left victims of domestic violence in extremely precarious positions as they were often dependent on their abuser. The struggle to escape that many women experienced is poignantly depicted in the film *The Burning Bed*, which is based on the real-life account of Francine Hughes. In this active-learning exercise, watch the film in class. After watching the film, work with a classmate to answer the following questions: (1) recalling information from Chapter 2, which theoretical perspective *best* frames Francine's continued victimization?, (2) what challenges did Francine experience in her multiple attempts to leave Mickey?, and (3) thinking about those challenges, describe legislation that could have aided her in leaving Mickey. Ensure you spend time explaining each answer and be prepared to share your work with the class.

Children's Justice Act (1986)

The Children's Justice Act of 1986 sought to improve the administration of justice in cases involving child victims (Children's Bureau, 2012). The act strengthened the processing of cases involving children by providing grants to qualifying states in order to encourage activities that improved victims' experiences within the criminal justice system (Children's Bureau, 2012). While specific activities varied across the country, states could utilize the funding to develop training programs for agencies involved in the processing of cases or to minimize the potential of revictimization through improving centers overall (Children's Bureau, 2012). For example, agencies could apply for funding to create specialized medical examination centers for children in lieu of conducting examinations in hospitals.

Drunk Driving Prevention Act (1988)

At the end of the 1980s, substantial progress had been made to address the marginalization of victims in the criminal justice system. However, secondary victims—particularly those who had lost loved ones due to drunk driving—continued to push for greater oversight of alcohol usage. This change finally materialized in the Anti–Drug Abuse Act of 1988, which contained the Drunk Driving Prevention Act (Civic Impulse, 2017b). Aside from establishing the minimum drinking age, the act also provided funding to encourage states to combat drunk driving through such actions as establishing legal thresholds for blood alcohol concentration during the operation of vehicles and outlawing open containers in vehicles (Civic Impulse, 2017b).

Victims' Rights and Remedies in the 1990s

In the 1990s, victims' rights continued to expand as new challenges confronted the criminal justice system in serving *all* victims of crimes. While several of the following acts built on progress that began in the 1970s and 1980s, other pieces of legislation included groups of survivors who remained marginalized (e.g., LGBTQ individuals). Perhaps one of the largest pieces of legislation of the decade, the Crime Control Act, addressed various forms of violence and was enacted after the turbulent 1980s.

Crime Control Act (1990)

The Crime Control Act (CCA) of 1990 addressed various crimes and was implemented after the surge in violence that dominated much of the 1980s. Crimes addressed in the act ranged from financial to violations perpetrated against children (Civic Impulse, 2017c). In terms of crimes against children, the CCA built on prior progress and strengthened the processing of these cases in the criminal justice system by providing alternatives to collecting testimony from children and implementing confidentiality standards to safeguard against unwanted disclosures (Civic Impulse, 2017c). Additionally, the act mandated access to guardian ad litem representatives for all child victims, and these representatives were empowered to advocate on the child's behalf (Civic Impulse, 2017c). Aside from these benefits, which minimized the potential re-traumatization of children in the criminal justice system, the act also mandated training for judicial personnel and required strict standards for those employed in a role that interacted with children (Civic Impulse, 2017c).

Activity 3.3: Mapping Hate Across the United States

The Southern Poverty Law Center (SPLC) tracks hate crimes and hate groups across the United States. Although SPLC was founded in the 1970s, hate crime statistics were not formally tracked in the criminal justice system until much later. Indeed, it was not until the passage of the Hate Crime Statistics Act (1990) that crimes motivated by prejudices were tracked at a national level (OVC, 2017). Despite the SPLC's work, hate crimes and groups remain a social problem throughout the country. In this exercise, access the map located at the following web address: www.splcenter.org/hate-map. After locating the map, select a state to reference and then select two different types of groups in that location. Summarize the information about each group and be prepared to share this information with the class.

Student Right to Know and Campus Security Act (1990)

Before the rise in university shootings, many laypersons largely assumed that crime occurring on college campuses was relatively minor compared to the street-level crime that dominated the evening news. However, several horrific victimizations, such as the rape and murder of Jeanne Clery, called attention to the need for greater protections in higher education institutions. In the aftermath of their daughter's murder, Jeanne's parents advocated for greater awareness and information sharing about crimes occurring on college campuses (Clery Center, n.d.). Eventually, the Student Right to Know and Campus Security Act (1990), otherwise known as the Clery Act, materialized from these efforts (Clery Center, n.d.). The Clery Act mandated that institutions of higher education publish campus crime statistics (Violence Against Women Act, 2014). Additionally, institutions of higher education were mandated to publicly communicate what policies and procedures existed to combat crimes on campus, which might include disciplinary interventions as well as prevention programming (Violence Against Women Act, 2014).

Battered Women's Testimony Act (1992)

As public awareness and knowledge about domestic abuse continued to increase, survivors were increasingly pursuing legal remedies through the criminal justice system. In order to ensure that domestic abuse, and all its complexities, were accurately described in legal proceedings, the Battered Women's Testimony Act (1992) was enacted. The act encouraged the inclusion, in relevant cases, of testimony from domestic abuse experts who could speak to the ramifications of violence on survivors (OVC, 2017). This development was particularly important given the growing awareness of topics like "the cycle of violence" and "learned helplessness" (see Chapter 7).

Child Sexual Abuse Registry Act (1993)

As the previous act demonstrates, the 1990s included legislation that aimed, not only to improve victims' experiences in the criminal justice system, but also to increase information sharing with the intention to *prevent* victimization. In order to prevent horrific child victimizations, such as the Adam Walsh case, the Child Sexual Abuse Registry Act of 1993 mandated the creation of a national sexual offender database (OVC, 2017).

Collecting information about sexual offenders in a comprehensive database then enabled law enforcement to increase monitoring and surveillance of these perpetrators.

Violence Against Women Act (1994)

The Violence Against Women Act (VAWA) greatly extended the protections and rights to survivors of gender-based violence, such as barring the admissibility of sexual history in legal cases in most circumstances (Hallock, 1993). Additionally, provisions in VAWA also aimed to combat abuse from a standpoint of prevention (i.e., before the crime happens) and intervention (i.e., after the crime happens) (Hallock, 1993). Methods to accomplish the latter included establishing several grants to help fund these efforts, such as the Services, Training, Officers, Prosecutors (STOP) grant, and the Grants to Encourage Arrest Policies (GTEAP) grant (NNEDV, n.d.). Since the initial passage of VAWA in 1994, the grant has expanded in scope to include LGBTQ survivors as well as male survivors (NNEDV, n.d.).

Violent Crime Control and Law Enforcement Act (1994)

The Violent Crime Control and Law Enforcement Act (VCC-LEA) surpassed the CCA as the largest bill of the 1990s aimed at combating and controlling crime. The act mandated substantial resources directed at preventing various crimes from both a perpetration (e.g., through restrictions placed on known offenders; targeting at-risk youth) and victimization (e.g., through improving public spaces for women; public access to sex offender information) standpoint (Civic Impulse, 2017d). More specifically, and in terms of placing restrictions on known offenders, the VCC-LEA mandated that certain types of offenders were barred from owning firearms given the documented risk to survivors of violence post-victimization (Civic Impulse, 2017d). Moreover, even though women are more likely to be harmed by an intimate partner versus a stranger, the act sought improvement to public and recreational spaces in order to ultimately deter gender-based crime (Civic Impulse, 2017d). Finally, following the tragic kidnapping and murder of Jacob Wetterling by a sexual offender living in the area, the act required that states create their own sexual offender registries that contained demographic and background information on sexual offenders, which could be disclosed if deemed necessary (Civic Impulse, 2017d). This act was amended following the murder of Megan Kanka (see Media Byte 3.2).

Media Byte 3.2: The Abduction and Murder of Megan Kanka

Before the implementation of the Community Notification Act of 1996, otherwise known as "Megan's Law," there was no requirement to alert communities about sexual offenders living in the neighborhood. However, after the kidnapping, rape, and murder of Megan Kanka, her parents lobbied for change (Schapiro, 2014). Megan disappeared on July 29, 1994, and her parents learned the next day that a sexual offender living in the neighborhood had assaulted and murdered her (Schapiro, 2014). The knowledge compounded the parents' grief, as they had no idea of the danger that existed a few yards away from their daughter (Schapiro, 2014). The outrage, which spread across the country, led to the Community Notification Act, which requires public disclosure of the whereabouts of dangerous sexual offenders (Schapiro, 2014).

In order to explore the impact of this mandate, navigate to your state's online sexual offender registration system. After locating the site, enter your home address and search. Review the sexual offenders that are within one mile of your address and summarize your findings (if no sexual offenders exist, continue to expand your search until there are results, or speak with the instructor). In addition to summarizing the sexual offenders situated around you, describe whether you believe the registry is a useful tool for preventing victimization.

Antiterrorism and Effective Death Penalty Act (1996)

On April 19, 1995, the United States experienced one of the most devastating domestic terror incidents of the time—the bombing of the Alfred P. Murrah Federal Building in Oklahoma City (History, 2016b). In contrast to the terrorist attacks of September 11, 2001, the Oklahoma City bombing was carried out by two U.S. citizens: Timothy McVeigh and Terry Nichols (Gorman, 2015). The perpetrators conducted their attack by detonating a van full of explosives that was parked outside the Murrah Building, an act that ultimately killed 168 people, including children (Gorman, 2015). In the wake of the bombing, legislation was passed to grant victims of this crime rights and remedies similar to those granted to other crime victims, such as the right to restitution

(Civic Impulse, 2017e). Additionally, funding was allocated to support counter-terrorism initiatives and to train law enforcement (Civic Impulse, 2017e).

Activity 3.4: Drug-Induced Sexual Assault

Rape and sexual assault remained an underresearched topic for a substantial amount of time, especially on college campuses. One of the first studies was conducted in the late 1950s, and the results indicated that nearly a quarter of respondents had experienced an attempted or completed sexual assault (Kirkpatrick & Kanin, 1957). Since that point, a substantial amount of research has been conducted on rape and sexual assault, and one finding in numerous studies is that perpetrators frequently utilize substances such as alcohol to facilitate victimizations (Combs-Lane & Smith, 2002; Schwartz & Pitts, 1995; Siegel & Williams, 2003; Ullman, Karabatsos, & Koss, 1999). This finding led, in part, to the passage in 1996 of the Drug-Induced Rape Prevention Act, which mandated stricter penalties for perpetrators and called for increased law enforcement training (Civic Impulse, 2017f). In this activity, work with a partner and select one of the following "date-rape" drugs to research: alcohol (the most widely used), GHB, ketamine, benzodiazepines including rohypnol, and zolpidem (a.k.a. Ambien). After selecting one, research the drug in terms of use, effects, and long-term consequences for survivors. After conducting your research, prepare a report of your findings and be prepared to share it with the class.

Victims' Rights Clarification Act (1997)

Following the Oklahoma City bombing, a controversy ensued during the trial of the perpetrators where victims were informed they could not observe the proceedings if they intended to testify in the sentencing phase (Thomas, 1997). The justification for the exclusion, according to Thomas (1997), was to prevent the influencing of victims' testimonies during the actual trial. This exclusion led to the Victims' Rights Clarification Act, which mandated that victims be allowed to attend trials regardless of whether they intend to testify in the sentencing phase (Civic Impulse, 2017g).

Child Protection and Sexual Predator Punishment Act (1998)

The advancement of technology has provided invaluable benefits to society, such as increased communication and rapid dissemination of information. However, perpetrators inevitably learn how to use the gains for malicious purposes. One example is the utilization of technology to engage in child sexual exploitation. In order to combat and deter online child sexual exploitation, as well as offline child sexual exploitation, the Child Protection and Sexual Predator Punishment Act imposed increased punishments for "offline" sexual offenders as well as "online" sexual offenders (OVC, 2017).

Crime Victims with Disabilities Awareness Act (1998)

As knowledge about interpersonal violence increased and victimologists continued to explore the different facets of victimization, studies indicated that individuals with disabilities were at an increased risk of victimization (Civic Impulse, 2017h). This knowledge, and the desire to provide remedy to these victims, propelled the Crime Victims with Disabilities Act of 1998 forward. The act mandated further research on this topic and that victimization surveys include questions on this topic in order to determine the scope of the problem (Civic Impulse, 2017h).

Identity Theft Assumption and Deterrence Act (1998)

The advancement of the Internet and technology, as previously described, also enabled perpetrators to engage in new identity theft schemes (Navarro & Jasinski, 2014). Until the Identity Theft Assumption and Deterrence Act of 1998, unfortunately, financial institutions were largely recognized as the sole victims of this type of crime (Navarro & Jasinski, 2014). The passage of this act was, therefore, critically important, because it defined and outlawed identity theft (Civic Impulse, 2017i). Moreover, the act mandated that individual victims, not solely financial institutions, be granted information on the crime and that this information be shared with relevant agencies in order to minimize the damage suffered by individual victims (Civic Impulse, 2017i).

Victims' Rights and Remedies in the 2000s

By the 2000s, the victims' rights movement had made significant gains to decrease the marginalization of victims in the criminal justice system. As previously noted, many states guaranteed core rights to victims that ensured their participation in the justice process. However, there were still areas for improvement. For example, modern-day slavery (i.e., human trafficking) remained a serious global social problem. In another example, while some victims of sexual assault gained rights and remedies, others fought for awareness and recognition (e.g., sexually assaulted prisoners).

Trafficking Victims Protection Act (2000)

Human trafficking remains a significant social problem that affects nations across the globe—including the United States (Department of State, 2016). Although it is difficult to assess the actual prevalence of this social problem, nearly 78,000 were trafficked across the globe in 2015 alone (Department of State, 2016). Moreover, from 2008 until 2015, the global total of identified victims was nearly 370,000 (Department of State, 2016). The magnitude of this problem led to the passage of the Trafficking Victims Protection Act of 2000 (TVPA), which used a multifaceted approach that addressed prevention and deterrence (Civic Impulse, 2017j). In terms of prevention, the TVPA included financial resources to combat and deter human trafficking through the funding of programs targeted at vulnerable populations: children and women (Civic Impulse, 2017j). In terms of deterrence, the TVPA mandated the global tracking of human trafficking occurrences and responses by countries that received financial assistance from the United States (Civic Impulse, 2017j). Additionally, TVPA implemented harsher penalties for those who engaged in human trafficking (Civic Impulse, 2017j).

Media Byte 3.3: 9/11 and the War on Terror

On September 11, 2001, the worst terrorist attack on U.S. soil perpetrated by an international organization—al Qaeda—resulted in the death of over 3,000 individuals: civilians, firefighters, and law enforcement (Bergen, 2017). The method utilized to carry out the attack was unexpected; the perpetrators hijacked commercial airplanes and flew two into the World Trade Center Towers and one into the Pentagon (Bergen, 2017). On the fourth plane, United Airlines flight 83, the passengers realized what was happening and fought back, forcing the plane down into a Pennsylvania field and preventing the terrorists from reaching the last target. The downed aircraft could have been heading for a number of government buildings in Washington, DC (Bergen, 2017).

Following the attacks, several pieces of legislation were passed to address the widespread victimization and security vulnerabilities that occurred on that horrific day. The Air Transportation Safety and System Stabilization Act (2001) was enacted near the end of September in an effort to buttress the aviation industry after the attack (Civic Impulse, 2017k). Among other mandates, the act sought to offset losses by the aviation industry from September 11 through the establishment of a financial compensation fund (Civic Impulse, 2017k). These financial resources were particularly important as the act sought to ensure that the aviation industry remained stable and capable of providing service to communities around the country—particularly small locations (Civic Impulse, 2017k). In terms of aiding individual victims who were injured or killed, the act also established a victim compensation fund (Civic Impulse, 2017k).

A decade following the attacks, the James Zadroga 9/11 Health and Compensation Act (2011) passed and addressed a long-neglected area of need among first responders who suffered serious health consequences because of breathing in materials near crash sites (Civic Impulse, 2017l). The act was named for James Zadroga, a former homicide detective who died at age 34 (Kahn, 2008). After his death, an autopsy revealed that Zadroga's lungs were irreparably damaged by tiny debris particles that he had breathed in while working at the World Trade Center crash site (Kahn, 2008). Zadroga's death served as a catalyst to expand victim's rights and benefits to 9/11 first responders (Kahn, 2008).

Thinking about 9/11, do you believe the security measures in place at airports are adequate to prevent a similar attack? If so, what procedures are most important to security? If not, what procedures are needed to prevent a similar attack? Thinking about these questions, identify some areas where security is strong and some outstanding weaknesses in the aviation industry. Be prepared to share your thoughts with the class.

Child Abuse Prevention and Enforcement Act (2000)

The Child Abuse Prevention and Enforcement Act (2000) sought to prevent child abuse by providing funding to increase the efficiency and expediency of the administration of justice in these cases (Civic Impulse, 2017m). The act also included a section entitled "Jennifer's Law," which mandated increased information gathering on all unidentified persons who interacted with the criminal justice system (Civic Impulse, 2017m). Then, following the gathering of identification information (dental records, DNA, etc.), the act called for these data to be entered into the FBI's National Crime Information Center database (Civic Impulse, 2017m). The ultimate goal of Jennifer's Law was to aid families of abducted and missing children in locating their loved ones (Civic Impulse, 2017m).

PROTECT Act (2003)

While response to suspected child abuse and abduction cases dramatically improved throughout the years, rapid communication of incidents remained a challenge. The need for rapid communication of information about missing children was never more evident than in the homicide case of young Amber Hagerman (Office of Justice Programs, n.d.a). As a response to the public outcry against another kidnapping and murder, the Prosecutorial Remedies and Other Tools to End the Exploitation of Children Today Act of 2003 was enacted (Civic Impulse, 2017n). Aside from increasing the penalties for engaging in various crimes against children, including sex tourism, the act also mandated the national coordination of the AMBER (America's Missing: Broadcast Emergency Response) Alert System—named for Amber Hagerman (Civic Impulse, 2017n; Office of Justice Programs, n.d.a).

Prison Rape Elimination Act (2003)

The Prison Rape Elimination Act (PREA) of 2003 was groundbreaking, because it was the first legislative action to address sexual violence in correctional institutions (Civic Impulse, 2017o). Recognizing that prison rape was likely an underreported occurrence, the act first called for the collection of data to understand the scope of the problem (Civic Impulse, 2017o). In-depth analyses of institutions with high and low occurrences of rape was also mandated in order to learn about factors that aggravated and mitigated the risk of this type of crime (Civic Impulse, 2017o). Ultimately, this work would drive national standards for correctional institutions on preventing sexual violence, and the act specified that states were required to comply or risk losing a portion of their funding (Civic Impulse, 2017o).

Justice for All Act (2004)

The Justice for All Act (JAA) of 2004 mandated several important rights for victims. Perhaps most importantly, in section 3771, the act outlined several rights guaranteed to all victims (as quoted directly from Civic Impulse, 2017r):

(1) The right to be reasonably protected from the accused;

(2) The right to reasonable, accurate, and timely notice of any public court proceeding, or any parole proceeding, involving the crime or of any release or escape of the accused;

(3) The right not to be excluded from any such public court proceeding, unless the court, after receiving clear and convincing evidence, determines that testimony by the victim would be materially altered if the victim heard other testimony at that proceeding;

(4) The right to be reasonably heard at any public proceeding in the district court involving release, plea, sentencing, or any parole proceeding;

(5) The reasonable right to confer with the attorney for the government in the case;

(6) The right to full and timely restitution as provided in law;

(7) The right to proceedings free from unreasonable delay; and

(8) The right to be treated with fairness and with respect for the victim's dignity and privacy.

To ensure that victims were informed of these important rights, the JAA also earmarked funding to support resources within the criminal justice system that aided survivors (Civic Impulse, 2017r). Finally, as DNA and other forensic science testing grew in prominence and reliability, legislators recognized its power in aiding in the administration of justice. Thus, another large emphasis of the JAA was to encourage DNA and other forensic science testing to aid in the resolution of outstanding crimes and be used as a potential tool in post-conviction appeals (Civic Impulse, 2017r).

Adam Walsh Child Protection and Safety Act (2006)

The Adam Walsh Child Protection and Safety Act (AWCPSA) was a comprehensive and holistic bill that brought together previous pieces of legislation (e.g., Megan's Law) into one act. One of the most important parts of the act was the separation of sexual offenders into three tiers based on the seriousness of their offenses (Civic Impulse, 2017s). In order to communicate the risks posed by these offenders, particularly tier three offenders, the act also mandated that registries be placed online for public usage (Civic Impulse, 2017s). While all offenders were required to register, the amount of time they were on the registry was driven by their tier placement (Civic Impulse, 2017s). Aside from these provisions, the act also outlined multiple safeguards to combat and deter child victimization, such as grant programs, increased punishments for offenses, and mandatory reporting requirements, among others (Civic Impulse, 2017s).

Identity Theft Enhancement and Restitution Act (2007)

The widespread use of social networking sites by individuals as well as businesses, which in turn made them targets for identity thieves looking to wreak monetary or personal destruction (see Navarro & Jasinski, 2014), led to an expansion in how identity theft was defined in 2007. Indeed, until the passage of the Identity Theft Enhancement and Restitution Act of 2007, it was not possible to consider businesses as "victims" of identity theft (Civic Impulse, 2017t). As a result, a perpetrator could establish a fake Facebook profile page masquerading as a popular brand and engage in a variety of destructive behavior meant to hurt that brand's consumer base with little legal recourse possible. Aside from rectifying the aforementioned, the act also implemented increased punishments for various types of identity theft (Civic Impulse, 2017t).

Media Byte 3.4: The Murder of Matthew Shepard

The murder of Matthew Shepard in Laramie, Wyoming, galvanized a long-overdue conversation about the prevalence of hate crimes in the United States (Matthew Shepard Foundation, n.d.). The sheer brutality with which Matthew Shepard was treated—abducted, hog-tied to a fence, severely beaten, and left for dead—sent shock waves around the globe (Matthew Shepard Foundation, n.d.). This horrific crime, as well as hate crimes involving similarly appalling actions, like the dragging and murder of James Byrd Jr. (Biography, n.d.), led to the passage of the Matthew Shepard and James Byrd Jr. Hate Crimes Prevention Act (2009) as part of a larger defense bill (Civic Impulse, 2017u). One of the most significant parts of the act was the recognition of gender identity in the hate crime definition (Civic Impulse, 2017u). In addition to recognizing gender identity as a motivating factor in hate crimes, the legislation also enhanced punishments for engaging in these crimes as well as outlined federal resources available to states during the investigation of potential cases (Civic Impulse, 2017u).

> After considering these improvements to existing law, consider what other steps are necessary to combat hate crimes. Think of at least two ideas to aid in combating hate crimes and describe them briefly in a paragraph each. After you are done, be prepared to share your ideas with the class.

Coast Guard Authorization Act (2010)

Recently, sexual assaults in the military have gained increasing public attention, particularly following the Tailhook scandal (Winerip, 2013) and films like *The Invisible War*. In 2010, as part of a larger authorization act, the U.S. Coast Guard was mandated to start tracking instances of sexual assault within the organization (Civic Impulse, 2017v). In addition to tracking such instances, the Coast Guard was also required to report the outcomes of these incidents and develop policies and procedures to combat the problem (Civic Impulse, 2017v). This act was one of the earliest pieces of legislation designed to address sexual violence within a branch of the military until a more comprehensive mandate was enacted, with similar requirements, that covered the entire armed forces: the Ike Skelton National Defense Authorization Act (2011) (Civic Impulse, 2017w).

Cruise Vessel Security and Safety Act (2010)

In order to address victimization that occurs on cruise ships, the Cruise Vessel Security and Safety Act of 2010 was enacted. It required vessels to take several proactive and reactive steps regarding interpersonal crime (Civic Impulse, 2017x). In terms of proactive steps, the act mandated the outfitting of cruise ships with several safety features, such as peepholes in doors and security cameras (Civic Impulse, 2017x). In terms of reactive steps, the act mandated that cruise ships establish policies and procedures for responding to crimes onboard—particularly when the collection and preservation of evidence is time-sensitive (e.g., sexual assault) (Civic Impulse, 2017x). Finally, the act called for cruise ships to disclose information on reported victimization incidents to the public (Civic Impulse, 2017x).

Kate Puzey Peace Corps Volunteer Protection Act (2012)

The Kate Puzey Peace Corps Volunteer Protection Act of 2012 was named for Kate Puzey, a young Peace Corps worker who was murdered while stationed at Benin, West Africa (Kate's Voice, n.d.). While on assignment teaching English to local school-children, Kate learned that a fellow Peace Corps worker was sexually abusing young women (Kate's Voice, n.d.). After reporting the disturbing news to the central Peace Corps office in the area, Kate was murdered following that employee's dismissal (Kate's Voice, n.d.).

To address this horrible event, as well as in recognition of the other crimes that have occurred in the Peace Corps, this act sought to improve the Peace Corps' tracking and response to sexual violence (Civic Impulse, 2017y). In order to accomplish this overall goal, the act mandated that the Peace Corps develop programs to aid employees in their placements, such as cultural competency and risk reduction (Civic Impulse, 2017y). Taking into account that Kate Puzey's murder is suspected to have stemmed from a breach in the confidential report she provided to the Peace Corps, which subsequently enraged the dismissed employee upon learning of her involvement in his firing, the act also outlines confidentiality protections for Peace Corps volunteers who report abuse (Civic Impulse, 2017y). Aside from these provisions, the act also mandated that potential Peace Corps workers be notified of the risks associated with each placement (Civic Impulse, 2017y).

Preventing Sex Trafficking and Strengthening Families Act (2014)

Unfortunately, research continues to indicate that children are most at risk of victimization by caretakers rather than strangers, and foster children are particularly vulnerable to abuse (Fong & Cardoso, 2010). Until this point, however, there was a dearth of attention placed on children in foster care and the potentiality of abuse suffered at the hand of their caretakers—including sex trafficking. The Preventing Sex Trafficking and Strengthening Families Act of 2014 sought to remedy that gap by mandating the tracking of sexual victimization among children in foster care placements (Civic Impulse, 2017z). In order to prevent sex trafficking from occurring, the act also mandated the identification, monitoring, and support of youth deemed to be at risk of becoming sex trafficking victims (Civic Impulse, 2017z).

Justice for Victims of Trafficking Act (2015)

The Justice for Victims of Trafficking Act of 2015 was a very comprehensive legislation designed to combat human trafficking from a prevention (e.g., through the establishment of various grants, outreach events, and training programs) and intervention (e.g., through calling for expedited and efficient investigations) standpoint. Aside from addressing human trafficking broadly, the act delved into crimes that have a nexus to human trafficking, such as child pornography and runaway youth (Civic Impulse, 2017aa). The act also outlined several rights and resources for human trafficking survivors, such as the right to be notified of sentencing outcomes and the right to notification about various resources to aid in their recovery (Civic Impulse, 2017aa). For example, one of the main resources provided through the passage of the act was the establishment of a compensation fund to aid survivors of human trafficking in their medical expenses (Civic Impulse, 2017aa).

Summary

The preceding paragraphs broadly describe much of the victims' rights legislation that has passed since the early 1970s, but even this chapter does not present an exhaustive list. Given the breadth of change, it is important to reiterate that victimologists drove forward much of the conversation about victims' rights and called attention to the need for greater remedies by the criminal justice system. This progress has not slowed, as new pieces of victims' rights legislation are constantly proposed to further improve the responsiveness of the criminal justice system. The constant addition and/or editing of victims' rights legislation likely stems from the changing nature of victimization, particularly due to the advancement of technology, as discussed in the next chapter.

Discussion Questions

1. In your opinion, what is the most important piece of victims' legislation from the aforementioned? Describe what led to your opinion.
2. In your opinion, what area of victimization is not adequately addressed in any of the aforementioned legislation? Describe what you would do differently and why.

References

Almanzar, Y. (2008, December 16). 27 years late, case is closed in slaying of abducted child. *The New York Times*. Retrieved from www.nytimes.com/2008/12/17/us/17adam.html

Bergen, P. L. (2017). September 11 attacks. *Encyclopaedia Britannica Online*. Retrieved from www.britannica.com/event/September-11-attacks

Biography. (n.d.). *James Byrd Jr*. Retrieved from www.biography.com/people/james-byrd-jr-092515

Children's Bureau. (2012). *Children's Justice Act*. Retrieved from www.acf.hhs.gov/cb/resource/childrens-justice-act

Civic Impulse. (2017a). *H.J.Res. 648–98th Congress: A joint resolution making continuing appropriations for the fiscal year 1985, and for other purposes*. Retrieved from www.govtrack.us/congress/bills/98/hjres648

Civic Impulse. (2017aa). *S. 178–114th Congress: Justice for Victims of Trafficking Act of 2015*. Retrieved from www.govtrack.us/congress/bills/114/s178

Civic Impulse. (2017b). *H.R. 5210–100th Congress: Anti-Drug Abuse Act of 1988*. Retrieved from www.govtrack.us/congress/bills/100/hr5210

Civic Impulse. (2017c). *S. 3266–101st Congress: Crime Control Act of 1990*. Retrieved from www.govtrack.us/congress/bills/101/s3266

Civic Impulse. (2017d). *H.R. 3355–103rd Congress: Violent Crime Control and Law Enforcement Act of 1994*. Retrieved from www.govtrack.us/congress/bills/103/hr3355

Civic Impulse. (2017e). *S. 735–104th Congress: Antiterrorism and Effective Death Penalty Act of 1996*. Retrieved from www.govtrack.us/congress/bills/104/s735

Civic Impulse. (2017f). *H.R. 4137–104th Congress: Drug-Induced Rape Prevention and Punishment Act of 1996*. Retrieved from www.govtrack.us/congress/bills/104/hr4137

Civic Impulse. (2017g). *H.R. 924–105th Congress: Victim Rights Clarification Act of 1997*. Retrieved from www.govtrack.us/congress/bills/105/hr924

Civic Impulse. (2017h). *S. 1976–105th Congress: Crime Victims With Disabilities Awareness Act*. Retrieved from www.govtrack.us/congress/bills/105/s1976

Civic Impulse. (2017i). *H.R. 4151–105th Congress: Identity Theft and Assumption Deterrence Act of 1998*. Retrieved from www.govtrack.us/congress/bills/105/hr4151

Civic Impulse. (2017j). *H.R. 3244–106th Congress: Victims of Trafficking and Violence Protection Act of 2000*. Retrieved from www.govtrack.us/congress/bills/106/hr3244

Civic Impulse. (2017k). *H.R. 2926–107th Congress: Air Transportation Safety and System Stabilization Act*. Retrieved from www.govtrack.us/congress/bills/107/hr2926

Civic Impulse. (2017l). *H.R. 847–111th Congress: James Zadroga 9/11 Health and Compensation Act of 2010*. Retrieved from www.govtrack.us/congress/bills/111/hr847

Civic Impulse. (2017m). *H.R. 764–106th Congress: Child Abuse Prevention and Enforcement Act*. Retrieved from www.govtrack.us/congress/bills/106/hr764

Civic Impulse. (2017n). *S. 151–108th Congress: Prosecutorial Remedies and Other Tools to End the Exploitation of Children Today Act of 2003*. Retrieved from www.govtrack.us/congress/bills/108/s151

Civic Impulse. (2017o). *S. 1435–108th Congress: Prison Rape Elimination Act of 2003*. Retrieved from www.govtrack.us/congress/bills/108/s1435

Civic Impulse. (2017p). *H.R. 2622–108th Congress: Fair and Accurate Credit Transactions Act of 2003*. Retrieved from www.govtrack.us/congress/bills/108/hr2622

Civic Impulse. (2017q). *H.R. 1731–108th Congress: Identity Theft Penalty Enhancement Act*. Retrieved from www.govtrack.us/congress/bills/108/hr1731

Civic Impulse. (2017r). *H.R. 5107–108th Congress: Justice for All Act of 2004*. Retrieved from www.govtrack.us/congress/bills/108/hr5107

Civic Impulse. (2017s). *H.R. 4472–109th Congress: Adam Walsh Child Protection and Safety Act of 2006*. Retrieved from www.govtrack.us/congress/bills/109/hr4472

Civic Impulse. (2017t). *S. 2168–110th Congress: Identity Theft Enforcement and Restitution Act of 2007*. Retrieved from www.govtrack.us/congress/bills/110/s2168

Civic Impulse. (2017u). *H.R. 2647–111th Congress: National Defense Authorization Act for Fiscal Year 2010*. Retrieved from www.govtrack.us/congress/bills/111/hr2647

Civic Impulse. (2017v). *H.R. 3619–111th Congress: Coast Guard Authorization Act of 2010*. Retrieved from www.govtrack.us/congress/bills/111/hr3619

Civic Impulse. (2017w). *H.R. 6523–111th Congress: Ike Skelton National Defense Authorization Act for Fiscal Year 2011*. Retrieved from www.govtrack.us/congress/bills/111/hr6523

Civic Impulse. (2017x). *H.R. 3360–111th Congress: Cruise Vessel Security and Safety Act of 2010*. Retrieved from www.govtrack.us/congress/bills/111/hr3360

Civic Impulse. (2017y). *S. 1280–112th Congress: Kate Puzey Peace Corps Volunteer Protection Act of 2011*. Retrieved from www.govtrack.us/congress/bills/112/s1280

Civic Impulse. (2017z). *H.R. 4980–113th Congress: Preventing Sex Trafficking and Strengthening Families Act*. Retrieved from www.govtrack.us/congress/bills/113/hr4980

Clery Center. (n.d.). *About*. Retrieved from https://clerycenter.org/about-page/

Clevenger, S., & Navarro, J. N. (2017). Expanding the conceptualization of "Survivor": Examining sexual assault victims' families and loved ones as secondary victims. In C. Roberson (Ed.), *Handbook on victims issues in criminal justice* (pp. 63–70). New York, NY: Routledge Handbooks.

Combs-Lane, A. M., & Smith, D. W. (2002). Risk of sexual victimization in college women: The role of behavioral intentions and risk-taking behaviors. *Journal of Interpersonal Violence*, *17*(2), 165–183.

Davis, R., & Mulford, C. (2008). Victim rights and new remedies: Finally getting victims their due. *Journal of Contemporary Criminal Justice*, *24*(2), 198–208.

Department of State. (2016). *Trafficking in persons report*. Washington, DC: United States of America. Retrieved from www.state.gov/documents/organization/258876.pdf

Erickson, N. S. (1988). The parental kidnapping prevention act: How can non-marital children be protected? *Golden Gate University Law Review*, *18*(3), 529–537.

Fernandes-Alcantara, A. L. (2014a). *Missing and exploited children: Background, policies, and issues*. Washington, DC: Congressional Research Service. Retrieved from https://digital.library.unt.edu/ark:/67531/metadc627104/

Fernandes-Alcantara, A. L. (2014b). *Family violence prevention and services act (FVPSA): Background and funding*. Washington, DC: Congressional Research Service. Retrieved from https://digital.library.unt.edu/ark:/67531/metadc795432/

Fong, R., & Cardoso, J. B. (2010). Child human trafficking victims: Challenges for the child welfare system. *Evaluation and Program Planning, 33*(3), 311–316.

Gorman, R. (2015, April 19). *20 years after the Oklahoma City Bombing, Timothy McVeigh remains the only terrorist executed by US*. Retrieved from www.businessinsider.com/20-years-after-the-oklahoma-city-bombing-timothy-mcveigh-remains-the-only-terrorist-executed-by-us-2015-4

Hallock, W. H. (1993). The violence against women act: Civil rights for sexual assault victims. *Indiana Law Journal, 68*(2), 577–619.

Kahn, J. (2008, September 15). A cloud of smoke: The complicated death of a 9/11 hero. *The New Yorker*. Retrieved from www.newyorker.com/magazine/2008/09/15/a-cloud-of-smoke-jennifer-kahn

Kate's Voice. (n.d.). *About Kate*. Retrieved from www.katesvoice.net/about-kate/

Kempe, C. H., Silverman, F. N., Steele, B. F., Droegemueller, W., & Silver, H. K. (2013). The battered-child syndrome. In C. Henry Kempe (Ed.), *A 50 year legacy to the field of child abuse and neglect* (pp. 23–38). Netherlands: Springer.

Kirkpatrick, C., & Kanin, E. (1957). Male sex aggression on a university campus. *American Sociological Review, 22*(1), 52–58.

Langton, L. (2011). *Identity theft reported by households, 2005–2010*. Washington, DC: U.S. Department of Justice, Office of Justice Programs, Bureau of Justice Statistics.

Levesque, R. J. (2014). Missing Children Act. In *Encyclopedia of adolescence* (Vol. 2, pp. 1747–1748). New York, NY: Springer Science+Business Media.

Matthew Shepard Foundation. (n.d.). *About us*. Retrieved from www.matthewshepard.org/about-us/

National Network to End Domestic Violence. (n.d.). *The Violence Against Women Act (VAWA) renewal passes the House and Senate and signed into law*. Retrieved from http://nnedv.org/policy/issues/vawa.html

Navarro, J. N., & Jasinski, J. L. (2014). Identity theft. In C. D. Marcum & G. E. Higgins (Eds.), *Social networking as a criminal enterprise*. Boca Raton, FL: CRC Press/Taylor & Francis Group.

Office for Victims of Crime. (2017). *National crime victims' rights week resource guide*. Retrieved from https://ovc.ncjrs.gov/ncvrw2017/landmarks.html

Office of Justice Programs. (n.d.a). *About AMBER alert*. Retrieved from www.amberalert.gov/about.htm

Office of Justice Programs. (n.d.b). *Organization, mission and functional manual: Office of justice programs*. Retrieved from www.justice.gov/jmd/organization-mission-and-functions-manual-office-justice-programs

Office for Victims of Crime. (n.d.). *About OVC*. Retrieved from https://ojp.gov/ovc/about/index.html

Schapiro, R. (2014, July 27). Exclusive: Parents of little girl who inspired Megan's Law recall brutal rape, murder of their daughter 20 years later. *New York Daily News*. Retrieved from: www.nydailynews.com/news/crime/parents-girl-inspired-megan-law-recall-tragedy-article-1.1881551

Schetky, D. H., & Haller, L. H. (1983). Parental kidnapping. *Journal of the American Academy of Child Psychiatry, 22*(3), 279–285.

Schwartz, M. D., & Pitts, V. L. (1995). Exploring a feminist routine activities approach to explaining sexual assault. *Justice Quarterly, 12*(1), 9–31.

Sedlack, A. J., Finkelhor, D., Hammer, H., & Schultz, D. (2002). National estimates of missing children: An overview. *NISMART Series Bulletin*. Chicago.

Siegel, J. A., & Williams, L. M. (2003). Risk factors for sexual victimization of women: Results from a perspective study. *Violence Against Women, 9*(8), 902–930.

Thomas, J. (1997, March 26). New law forces a reversal in Oklahoma bombing case. *The New York Times*. Retrieved from www.nytimes.com/1997/03/26/us/new-law-forces-a-reversal-in-oklahoma-bombing-case.html

Tobolowsky, P. M., Beloof, D. E., Jackson, A. L., Gaboury, M. T., & Blackburn, A. G. (2016). *Crime victim rights and remedies*. Durham, NC: Carolina Academic Press.

Ullman, S. E., Karabatsos, G., & Koss, M. P. (1999). Alcohol and sexual assault in a national sample of college women. *Journal of Interpersonal Violence, 14*(6), 603–625.

Viano, E. C. (1976). Victimology and its pioneers. *Victimology: An International Journal, 1*(2), 189–192.

Violence Against Women Act, 79 Fed. Reg. 62752 (October 20, 2014) (to be codified at C.F.R. pt. 668).

Winerip, M. (2013, May 13). Revisiting the Military's Tailhook Scandal. *The New York Times*. Retrieved from www.nytimes.com/2013/05/13/booming/revisiting-the-militarys-tailhook-scandal-video.html

Young, M., & Stein, J. (2004). *The history of the crime victims' movement in the United States*. Washington, DC: US Department of Justice, Office of Justice Programs, Office for Victims of Crime.

Chapter 4

Hybrid and Online Victimization

Keywords

- Hybrid Crime Victimization
- Online Victimization
- Revenge Pornography
- Bullying
- Cyberstalking
- Identity Theft
- Malware Victimization
- Sexting
- Hacking Victimization

Introduction

Crime is an important facet of society. Crime is often defined as an act of force or fraud that someone pursues in their interest (Gottfredson & Hirschi, 1990). The acts of force or fraud can have a vast range. For instance, some criminal behaviors may include violent acts as well as theft. Crime may also encompass activities such as pornography (i.e., child pornography), bullying, stalking, and identity theft.

Traditional crime behaves in a number of ways. Generally, crime requires a first party, and this is someone who harbors an intention and ultimately perpetrates the action. Next, crime often requires a second party, and this is often an object of a crime that could be a person or any tangible item. When the individual(s) that are harboring intention for crime encounters a desirable object for a crime, the crime action is likely to occur. This creates interesting criminological issues.

Most relevant to this book, the interesting criminological issue is the second party of the crime—specifically, the object or person that has been victimized for crime. In many instances, the object of the criminal behavior is the computer. The information that is stored on the computer as well as the physical make-up of the computer may become compromised. This is an issue that will be discussed in a future chapter.

The person may be victimized in a myriad of ways. The victimization may occur in multiple locations. This is the essence of a hybrid crime. To clarify: hybrid crimes may occur in a cyber world (cybercrime), or they may occur in the real world. In another form, the person is the object of the criminal activity, and is subsequently the victim.

Hybrid crimes and cybercrimes that lead to victimization are boundless. These types of activities may have a perpetrator in one country and a victim in another country. The Internet provides a clear path for this type of interaction. The same type of activity may take place between people who are in closer proximity. A number of criminal acts may comprise hybrid crimes. In this chapter, specific behaviors are used to provide examples of hybrid crimes. These behaviors include the following: sexting, cyberstalking, and child pornography.

Sexting

Sexting behavior is relatively new to the cyber world. The recent introduction to sexting makes it difficult to understand a complete definition of this behavior. For instance, some indicate that sexting is the transmission of images including nude or semi-nude photographs. Others indicate that sexting is the transmission of text messages that include nude or semi-nude photographs. While these two definitions seem very similar to one another, the differences are substantial.

To understand these differences, we have to consider the medium and the term *nude*. The first definition of sexting—transmission of images including nude and semi-nude photographs—implies transmission of images using some other device than a mobile phone. Some of these devices may include a computer—this includes a tablet device. Transmitting these types of images using these devices involves the use of the Internet. The use of the Internet has major implications that will be discussed later. The second definition of sexting emphasizes the use of mobile phones and the transmission taking place through text messages. The transmission has important implications. The Internet and text messages use different mechanisms to transmit any data. For instance, the Internet uses the World Wide Web to move data between computers and other devices. Text messages do not require the Internet for data to be transmitted. Data in text messages moves as voice data does, through phone lines.

Further complicating the issue of sexting is the notion of the term *nude,* because most definitions of sexting include "nearly nude" or "semi-nude." These terms require a subjective interpretation by researchers, respondents, and government agencies, and this subjectivity makes comparisons between multiple studies and study subjects difficult. The difficulty results in an inability to provide accurate estimates of sexting rates. In other words, the definition of sexting does not provide a method of understanding the prevalence of the behavior.

While the definition precludes an accurate understanding of sexting, some estimates of sexting are available. The Pew Research Center indicates that nearly 4% of teenagers in the U.S. have sent sext messages (Lenhart, 2009). Other researchers have shown similar results in their sexting studies (Reyns, Henson, & Fisher, 2014). Some, however, have estimated the prevalence of sexting behavior from 7 to 27% (Dake, Price, Maziarz, & Ward, 2012; Ricketts, Maloney, Marcum, & Higgins, 2014). These estimates are not conclusive, but they do indicate that the behavior does occur.

The utility of different definitions has led to a number of issues in the research literature, but the vast majority of the literature seems to indicate mixed results, especially in the area of demographics. First, researchers tend to indicate a link between sexting behavior and age (Mitchell, Finkelhor, Jones, & Wolak, 2012; Strassberg, McKinnon, Sustaita, Rullo, 2013). Specifically, researchers show that there is a link between sexting behavior and increasing age (Ricketts et al., 2014). In the context of gender, the research on sexting is mixed. For instance, some research shows that sexting prevalence is equal between genders (Dake et al., 2012), but other studies show higher prevalence rates for males, and still others, show higher prevalence rates for females (Jonsson, Priebe, Bladh, & Svedin, 2014). This indicates a lack of clarity among researchers in the prevalence of sexting behavior.

Sexting seems to vary among racial and ethnic minorities. When studying adolescents (i.e., 12- to 17-year-olds), researchers show that sexting behaviors tend to be higher among African-Americans and Hispanics (Dake et al., 2012). For college students, researchers reveal that whites sext more often (Reyns et al., 2014). This indicates that the research literature is not conclusive on sexting behavior among racial and ethnic groups.

Activity 4.1: Teenage Sexting

Go to the following website http://abcnews.go.com/Technology/WorldNews/sexting-teens/story?id=6456834. Read the article. Then describe the potential issues that may arise from sexting issues. Do you have any suggestions to help prevent sexting? Please explain. What is your opinion regarding sexting?

While it is instructive to know who is sexting, it is just as important to understand why individuals engage in the activity. For instance, some will sext as a form of flirting or to gain attention. Research shows that this generally occurs among adolescents (Baumgartner, Sumter, Peter, Valkenburg, & Livingstone, 2014). Those who engage in this type of activity are likely to feel as though they are sexy, or sexting may provide a sense of thrill, or sexting may provide some sense of play (Strassburg et al., 2013). In any instance, sexting behavior provides a psychological benefit that encourages the behavior.

Sexting may not only provide a psychological benefit that encourages the behavior, but it may also provide a physical benefit, as when sexting may result in a sexual or romantic relationship (Lenhart, 2009). For instance, some may use sexting to initiate a relationship, and others may use sexting to enrich a sexual or romantic relationship. Researchers have shown that sexting behavior is becoming part of normal discourse in relationships (Renfrow & Rollo, 2014). Some have shown that people who sext do so for a myriad of reasons that could enrich their relationships (e.g., partner wanted a photo, to close a geographical distance gap between partners, or as a sexy present; Reynset al., 2014).

While this may have positive benefits, sexting behavior is usually fraught with a number of issues. Some may sext to enrich their relationships, but often individuals report that they sexted when they did not wish to sext. When these individuals did not wish to sext, they felt a substantial amount of pressure from their partner or friends to self-produce or produce at least one image. Research shows that some indicated they were given ultimatums: produce the image or lose the relationship (Walgrave, Heirman, & Hallman, 2013). This type of victimization is known as emotional abuse.

The individual who felt pressured to produce the image is placed in a "no win" situation. They either produce an image that they do not want to produce or they lose their relationship. The loss of the relationship for some outweighs the cost of their dignity. To make matters worse, research has shown in these situations that many of the images that are given to the partner do not stay private (Ringrose, Harvey, Gille, & Livingstone, 2013). These images are often tagged, sent, and shared with others as an expression of sexual activity. This further victimizes the unwilling participant: not only did the individual not want to participate, but they are now humiliated in front of others for whom the image was not intended.

A complication exists with tagging, sending, and sharing the images that creates long-lasting consequences (Ringroseet al., 2103). One complication is the permanence of the image. The image that is shared one time between partners may go on to be shared hundreds and sometimes thousands of times. In other words, it is possible for an image to take on a life of its own and live in the cyber world in infamy. Lenhart (2009) reported on a number of concerns for sexting behaviors. Some of these concerns included sharing the images outside of the consensual relationship. This can occur in multiple ways. For instance, some may share the images for fun or acceptance. The images may also be shared if mobile devices or computers are hacked and the images are taken.

A substantial amount of psychological distress and harm comes from this type of behavior. One way this occurs is that the images were taken consensually; however, the distribution of the images occurs without the depicted person's knowledge or consent. Often the distribution takes place following a relationship break-up. This is non-consensual distribution of sexual images. In the research literature, this has been referred to as "revenge porn" (Bates, 2017). Revenge porn is harmful because its distribution occurs in multiple formats (i.e., mobile phones and social media) (Bates, 2017; Lippman & Campbell, 2014). For some, the revenge may never end because the images may resurface later in life, harming opportunities (e.g., job searches or romantic relationships) (Wolak & Finkelhor, 2011).

Activity 4.2: Revenge Porn

Visit the following website: http://mashable.com/2017/05/07/revenge-porn-survey-australia/#h05lbx_Cdqqp. Read the article, then explain how marginalization may contribute to revenge porn. What do you think can be done to prevent this? What is your opinion regarding revenge porn?

Revenge porn is not the only form of victimization related to sexting. Cyberbullying, which will be discussed in a later chapter, is one mechanism that may occur. Another form of victimization is sextortion. Sextortion is where the individual is being abused online or offline as a result of their sexting behaviors. For instance, the object of the sextortion may experience threats or blackmail due to their sexting behaviors. These types of activities have led to a number of psychological issues that include anxiety, sadness, or depression (Livingstone & Smith, 2014).

Overall, sexting is a complex behavior that may create a number of victimization issues. The nature of the victimization may vary widely, and the result of victimization may be wider still.

Cyberstalking

Sexting behavior is not the only form of criminal activity that may result in victimization using electronic devices. Stalking behavior may occur offline as well as online. The online version is known as cyberstalking. Cyberstalking is another criminal activity that results in victimization.

Cyberstalking is a behavior that is gaining academic interest. Much like sexting, cyberstalking occurs using a computer, tablet, or other mobile device. All that is needed for cyberstalking to take place is access to someone else's personal contact information (e.g., email account or phone number). This information allows a perpetrator to consistently communicate threatening messages to another person over time (Durkin & Patterson, 2011). While this is the essence of cyberstalking, no universal definition of cyberstalking exists.

Activity 4.3: Comparison of Stalking and Cyberstalking

Compare and contrast stalking offline versus cyberstalking.
Which one do you believe is more dangerous? Why?
Which one do you think people fear more? Explain.

Currently there is some concern in the literature about the unclear definition of cyberstalking. The lack of clarity creates an issue because having no agreed-upon definition provides room for a debate over whether cyberstalking is different from offline stalking (i.e., physical stalking).

The two forms of stalking share a number of characteristics. One such characteristic is repetition of actions over time. For example, an individual may invade someone else's privacy repeatedly over time in "real life" by following them, or virtually via unwanted emails. Another shared characteristic is that the repetition of actions creates a perception of threat. The final shared characteristic is that neither form of stalking requires the victim and the perpetrator to know each other. The perception of threat creates a sense of vulnerability. The vulnerability leaves those who have been victimized psychologically traumatized and potentially physically fearful for their safety.

Cyberstalking does have some distinguishable characteristics from physical stalking. One unique characteristic of cyberstalking is that the behavior is not bounded by geography. This means that victim and perpetrator may be separated by thousands of miles or multiple countries. The nature of the Internet means the victim and perpetrator need not be in close proximity.

Another unique characteristic of cyberstalking is multiple motivations. Researchers have indicated that cyberstalkers' motivations differ from the motivations of offline stalkers. For instance, cyberstalkers are motivated by more than power and control over the victim (Navarro, Marcum, Higgins, & Ricketts, 2016).

The research literature indicates that cyberstalking rates are increasing. The National Crime Victimization Survey (NCVS) indicates that 21.5% of the people who reported that they were stalked also reported that they were cyberstalked (Reyns, Henson, & Fisher, 2012). People who report being cyberstalked indicate a number of methods were used. There are two main levels: lower and higher. The lower level methods include blogs, email, instant messaging, and text messages. The higher level methods include spyware, listening devices, and digital cameras.

While these national figures provide some insight into cyberstalking, no other national rates on other populations exist. Most research on cyberstalking has taken place using college students, in part because they are a technologically savvy age group. Many college students grew up during the Internet age, and they have used the Internet extensively for grade school and secondary education. Further, college students routinely take actions that put them at risk for cyberstalking. Researchers report that college students provide information that could be used for cyberstalking through social media and other means (Reyns et al., 2012). Researchers indicate that 1% to 40% of college students have experienced cyberstalking (Reyns et al., 2012), but it is important to note that these studies do not encompass the entire United States but are samples of students from individual universities. The research on cyberstalking indicates a number of demographic differences. For instance, females have been shown to be more at risk, and males are more likely to be perpetrators (Bates, 2017).

Case Study 4.1: Cyberstalking

Jenny is a senior at Finish High School, and she has been dating Johnny for most of the school year. The school year is coming to an end, and Jenny and Johnny have decided to attend colleges on opposite sides of the United States. Because of the distance between the two schools, Jenny has decided to end the relationship with Johnny. Johnny has difficulty with the break-up. Instead of accepting it, Johnny begins sending Jenny nasty and degrading text messages and emails. Then the messages change to threats. Jenny asks Johnny to stop, but he does not stop. Jenny changes her e-mail account and her phone number, but somehow Johnny finds her new information. With the new information, Johnny begins the threatening messages again.

Based on this information, is Jenny a victim of cyberstalking? Why or why not? How should she proceed?

Hacking Victimization

Hacking is an important form of computer abuse. Gaining an understanding of hacking involves defining the term. Many definitions of hacking exist. Taylor et al. (2010) argue that hacking is obtaining unauthorized access to and using a computer system for criminal purpose. The major issue with this definition is the idea that crime is involved. Many hackers do not consider themselves criminals because of the advanced level of skill and knowledge that is necessary to perform hacking activity (Holt, 2007; Jordan & Taylor, 1998; Loper, 2000). In addition, many hackers also see their behavior as exploratory because they are often perusing different operating systems to learn; thus, hacking is viewed as an achievement rather than a label (Wadeet al., 2008).

Hacking can take many forms: breaking into a computer system, developing or using viruses (i.e., malware), destroying or altering files, theft of services, credit card fraud, and infiltrating software (Rogerset al., 2005, as cited in Wadeet al., 2008). Rogers et al. (2005) made the argument that not all hacking behaviors are criminal, suggesting that a definition that includes crime should actually be used for a different individual known as a cracker. With this, a hacker is someone who is solely trying to gain unauthorized access to a computer system or file (Meyer, 1989; Holt, 2007).

Because of the lack of a social science or legal definition of hacking, some have defined hacking based on the methods that hackers use to access a computer system. For instance, a number of methods are often used to hack into computer systems that range from low technological to high technological. Low technological techniques include "brute-force attacks," "shoulder surfing," or "social engineering." Brute-force attacks involve system access purely by trying to guess passwords, while shoulder surfing is accomplished by watching a hacking victim use a personal identification number (PIN) (Marcum, Higgins, Ricketts, & Wolfe, 2014). Another low technological method is social engineering, and it involves the offender posing as a professional and requesting information about the victim's computer system (McDowell, 2009; Taylor et al., 2010). Higher technological methods include key-logging techniques (Holt, 2007).

Activity 4.4: Your Behavior

How often are you aware of shoulder surfing?
How will you reduce instances of shoulder surfing for your information?

Understanding a profile of a hacker is difficult because of the secrecy that occurs in the hacking subculture. This has limited the knowledge base of hackers, and to some degree it has limited the knowledge base of hacking victimization. To provide some perspective about hackers, Skinner and Fream (1997) used a sample of American college students from specific academic departments associated with a higher level of computer skills (i.e., engineering, business, and the sciences). Their study covered a number of computer crime behaviors that encompassed hacking. Skinner and Fream (1997) showed that males were more likely than females to participate in hacking behavior. Racially, they found whites and Asians were more likely than other racial or ethnic groups to perform hacking activity. Others have examined hacking behavior as well. The majority of these studies are quantitative and include college student and adolescent samples (Bossler & Burruss, 2011; Holt et al., 2010; Holt & Kilger, 2008; Morris, 2011; Rogers et al., 2005; Skinner and Fream, 1997). Still other researchers have taken a qualitative approach to understand attitudes toward hacking and the norms and values of this subculture based on small samples of active or incarcerated hackers (Holt, 2007; Meyer, 1989; Thomas, 2002; Turgeman-Goldschmidt, 2008).

While the majority of the research literature has focused on college student and adolescent samples, a dearth of research exists at national or international levels. The National Institute of Justice sponsored a research study of law enforcement officials. The study was geared to provide an understanding of their experiences with computer crime that included hackers (Stambaugh et al., 2001). Stambaugh et al. (2001) report that hacking offenders were highly knowledgeable about all aspects of computer crime, and they differed from property criminals and violent criminals in having higher than average intelligence levels. Overall, the hacking offender's profile was closer to that of a white-collar criminal, but the majority of offenders in the NIJ study were male college students between the ages of 15 and 25.

Understanding the hacker is important to also gain some perspective about the hacking victim. Hacking victimization does occur. Van Wilsem (2013) examined data from more than 5,000 individuals from the Netherlands. This research revealed that 3.1% of the individuals in the sample had been victims of hacking. Further, van Wilsem (2013) reported that hacking victimization overlapped with other forms of cybervictimization. This indicates that some individuals do report being a victim of hacking.

Some researchers' assessments have come from the digital privacy protection perspective. The digital privacy protection perspective is where an individual uses various techniques (e.g., minimizing information stored electronically or using different forms of antivirus software and spyware for protection). Some researchers have shown that a substantial amount of anxiety comes from being a victim of hacking and anticipating future hacking events. Chai, Bagchi-Sen, Morrell, Rao, and Upadhyaya (2009) examined 285 adolescents to understand their anxiety about being a victim of hacking. Chai et al. (2009) found anxiety to be related to possible future hackings. Elhai and Hall (2016) found anxiety to be high concerning future data hacking.

Data hacking occurs not only at the individual level but also at the macro (i.e., organizational or environmental) level. Organizations are particular targets because of the large amounts of data that they store, and the potential complexity of their computer systems may present a challenge to a hacker. Anecdotally, many organizations have been subjected to hacking. Some have lost billions of dollars due to hacking, and others have lost a substantial amount of data in these situations (Marcum et al., 2014).

Identity Theft

Since the 1950s, criminologists have had an interest in embezzlement and check forgery (Cressey, 1953; Lemert, 1958). This interest started the study and development of knowledge in white-collar crimes. White-collar crimes tend to involve some form of fraud. In the 21st century, with the development of computers along with the Internet, computer-assisted thefts have also become an interest, as have the victims of identity theft.

Identity theft has a number of definitions. Generally, identity theft includes crimes in which a person's identifying information (e.g., driver's license, credit card, or Social Security number) is stolen (Navarro & Higgins, 2017). Some define identity theft as the use of someone else's identity to engage in criminal behavior (Navarro & Higgins, 2017). It should be noted that identity theft to engage in criminal behavior might also be defined as identity fraud. However, whether the use of someone else's identity to carry out criminal behavior is identity theft or fraud, a number of behaviors may result from the theft of someone else's identity. One common behavior is the purchase of goods using someone else's credit card information.

Identity theft may be considered a hybrid crime because it includes both "old" and "new" offenses. "New" criminal activities are made possible by technological advances (i.e., networked computers). In addition, these new technological advances sometimes include large amounts of identifying data stored in public or private databases. For instance, public and private databases include online banking, credit information, and e-business records. The numerous technological advances have unintentionally created an environment for identity theft through hacking or cracking into public and private databases.

"Older" criminal activities may also be classified as identity theft due also to technological advances. These advances provide new avenues for a perpetrator to commit check fraud, financial crimes, counterfeiting, forgery, automobile theft using false

Web Activity 4.1: Hacking Anxiety

Check out the following website www.psychologytoday.com/articles/201409/hacking-fear.

What types of training are available to reduce anxiety about hacking?

Do you think that these trainings will prevent crime? Why or why not?

documentation, human trafficking, and terrorism. It is important to note that these forms of behavior existed as crimes before the concept of identity theft was developed and legally defined (Cole & Pontell, 2006). These activities have an impact on not only organizations but also on individuals.

No one will deny that identity theft is on the rise. The Federal Trade Commission (FTC) indicates that identity theft has influenced more than 30 million people's lives. Pontell and Brown (2011) report that the FTC conducted a survey showing that 7.88% of respondents report being victims of identity theft. The FTC survey also shows that certain minorities appear to consistently be victims of identity theft. For instance, Hispanics and African-Americans are more likely than Asians and Caucasians to be victims of serious types of fraud. In addition to racial minority differences in identity theft victimization, differences in age are present. Specifically, middle-aged individuals are more likely to be victims than any other age group. According to the FTC (2005), victims of identity theft lost substantial amounts of money. These large amounts of money include more than $40 billion in losses, and individuals lose more than $5 billion dollars total (FTC, 2005).

Many perpetrators and victims have things in common. The FTC (2005) survey shows the most common perpetrators are family members. Further, more than half of the victims had prior knowledge of their victims. Most of the time, children are victimized, and, disturbingly, the children do not have any idea that their identities have been stolen and used until they attempt to establish their own credit as young adults. The FTC (2005) survey indicates most victims provide important information about their identities being stolen. Many report their purse or wallet has been stolen or drastic changes have been discovered on statements for financial accounts (e.g., checking or credit card accounts). Unfortunately, identifying information has been found to be used for more than six months before the discovery of the identity theft/identity fraud.

The National Crime Victimization survey also includes national level information concerning identity theft. For instance, more than 3% of the survey respondents indicated that households in the United States have at least one member who had been a victim of identity theft in the previous six months (Baum, 2006). These results are show consistently that identity theft occurs at the individual level. Anderson (2006) analyzed the FTC (2003) survey data to show that age, gender, and income were individual-level predictors of identity theft, but ultimately, the conclusion was that younger adult women and the more affluent were highly likely to become victims.

Web Activity 4.2: Federal Trade Commission

Check out the Federal Trade Commission website at www.consumer.ftc.gov/features/feature-0014-identity-theft. Follow the appropriate links if necessary to answer the following questions.

In what ways should a person protect their privacy?

Do you think that this can help prevent victimization? Explain.

The Federal Trade Commission (FTC) (2015) reports that the number one complaint is identity theft. Further, Harrell and Langton (2013) show that 17.6 million individuals have been victims of identity theft, and they have had a total estimated loss of over $15 billion. Harrell (2015) shows that households with incomes more than $75,000 are more likely to have a victim of identity theft.

Higgins, Hughes, Ricketts, and Wolfe (2008) examined state-level correlates of identity theft. Their study made use of FTC reports and census data. The results indicated that identity theft complaints were higher in states with lower male population, but a higher population of African-Americans, greater residential mobility, more residents receiving public assistance, and many recreation and entertainment venues.

Identity theft does not end with the discovery of the act. Victims of identity theft spend hundreds of hours to reclaim their identities. Many victims will spend nearly 200 hours working with different financial institutions. This amount of time may cause a victim to lose time at work and with family, creating an additional sense of victimization and psychological trauma.

Thus far, identity theft has been presented as an act that occurs only in the United States. Because of the potential technological component of identity theft, the behavior can occur internationally. Researchers have shown that identity theft in the United Kingdom accounts for more than one-tenth of all fraud, and it also occurs in Australia where more than 3% of those over 15 years old were victims of identity theft (Roberts, Indermaur, & Spiranovic, 2013). Importantly, identity theft is not confined to one country. For instance, it is possible for identity theft to begin in one country and influence organizations or individuals in another country.

Malware Victimization

As development and use of technology increases, so does the risk of using digitized information and computer networks. The central culprit creating this risk is malicious software, better known as malware (Symantec Corporation, 2012; Wall, 2007). Criminals use these programs to assist them in their crimes. Malware is a digital "workforce" that automates various functions, among them cyberattacks such as data theft or installation of spyware (Chu, Holt, & Ahn, 2010).

Examples of malware are abundant. Keylogging is one example. Keylogging allows a criminal to track the keystrokes on a computer. These programs can capture sensitive information (e.g., usernames and passwords) without the owner's or operator's knowledge (Holt & Turner, 2012). Other forms of malware are viruses and worms. Viruses and worms have the ability to be disruptive as well as malicious (i.e., deleting and corrupting files, hardware, and software) (Chuet al., 2010). Another example of malware is called botnet. Botnet malware allows the criminal to remotely control someone else's computer. While in control of someone else's computer, the criminal can commit a number of crimes (Cooke, Jahanian, & McPherson, 2005).

Case Study 4.2: Keylogging

Jim explained he saw a TV ad for an online shopping site, shoppingrus.net, while watching the news recently. When Jim went to the site, he lost control of his computer. Jim really likes to shop, but he is not always as careful as he should be. Jim said, "When you see it advertised on TV during the news you figure it's safe."

How would you suggest Jim proceed?

In many countries, the use of malware is illegal. This means that invading, compromising, and stealing information is illegal, even using software. These activities do not come without a price. The Pew Internet and American Life (2005) survey indicated that these types of malware created high costs for removal. The removal has high tangible and intangible costs for individuals and corporations. For instance, individuals and corporations will lose a substantial amount of time and potential credibility due to the malware infections. Another example is that a serious enough malware infection will force the individual or corporation to purchase or rebuild an entire system. A Computer Security Institute (2009) survey estimated that the cost of malware ranged from $40,000 to $400,000.

Media Byte 4.1: Companies Hacked

Check out the following website: www.cnn.com/videos/business/2014/12/01/qmb-hackers-jason-steer-intv.cnn.
What was the impact of the hacking?
What is your opinion of this case?

Individuals and corporations also bear a substantial amount of cost to prevent malware infections. Antivirus software and spyware are two types of malware prevention software, which has the ability to reduce the risk of infections. The problem with these types of software is that they only reduce risk; they do not have the ability to completely eliminate the risk of victimization. PandaLabs (2007) showed that 25% of personal computers had some form of malware, and over one-third of personal computers did not have any form of malware prevention software. Bossler and Holt (2009) reported that this occurs because victims do not know when their systems have been compromised. In other words, systems may be infected and malicious acts taking place without the victim's knowledge. Successful malware infection demands that the action be concealed and work around malware prevention software (Symantec Corporation, 2012). Malware infections tend to show themselves in the form of system errors (Pew Internet and American Life, 2005). Unfortunately, victims usually do not recognize the system errors as malware infections; rather, they see it as a general computer problem. This makes them particularly vulnerable and likely to incur additional problems.

A dearth of empirical research exists in this area. Holt and Bossler (2013) show that college students, faculty, and staff routinely do many things that put them at risk for malware victimization. Ngo and Paternoster (2011) use data from college students to show that deficits in an individual's level of self-control make them susceptible to malware victimization. Bossler and Holt (2009) use data from college students to show that individual characteristics are linked to malware victimization. Besides the Ngo and Paternoster (2011) study, the rest indicate that daily activities on the Internet create an environment where malware victimization is possible.

Child Pornography Victimization

Child pornography (CP) is an important form of criminal behavior, and it involves predation, exploitation, and victimization of youth. CP involves different forms of voyeurism and exhibitionism. When these forms of voyeurism and exhibitionism occur using the Internet, they are known as cybervoyeurism and cyberexhibitionism. Cybervoyeurism involves using a child's webcam to view them when they are undressed or when they are engaging in sexual activity (Bourke & Hernandez, 2009). Cyberexhibitionism refers to a child displaying their genitals via the Internet (Bourke & Hernandez, 2009).

Technology has aided in the development, distribution, and possession of CP. Technology also helps offenders perform these behaviors and avoid detection by law enforcement. Specifically, software has been developed that allows offenders to erase electronic fingerprints, access different networks to obtain, distribute, and possess CP, and locate special areas to store CP. Some software has been used to help offenders work around hard drives to hide their activities.

CP has been on the increase for a number of years. Because of the elusiveness of the behavior, few national or international statistics are available about the offenders or victims of CP. Some data, however, do exist in multiple areas. For instance, the United States Federal Bureau of Investigation (FBI) has developed a specialized unit— the Innocent Images Initiative—to handle these types of cases. Between 1996 and 2005, there was a substantial increase in these cases—over 2,000%. This is because of the increased law enforcement presence on the Internet. For instance, a multi-jurisdictional task force—Internet Crimes Against Children (ICAC)—has provided better education and training for officers and members of the judiciary. With these types of law enforcement agencies, a number of pieces of legislation have been enacted to assist with the prosecution of offenders.

While these efforts are important, they are not enough to completely stop CP. Some report that CP is a multi-billion-dollar industry (Bourke & Hernandez, 2009). The multi-billion-dollar industry has been fueled by the Internet. While this indicates that there is a substantial issue, little is known about the victims of CP.

Discussion Questions

1. What form of malware infection comes to mind the most? How would you guard against this form of malware infection?

2. Do you believe that there is a way to end cybervictimization?
3. Have you ever experienced or seen sexting behavior? Was it handled properly?
4. Describe the different methods you have used to protect your identity.

References

Anderson, K. B. (2006). Who are the victims of identity theft? The effect of demographics. *Journal of Public Policy and Marketing, 25*, 160–171.

Bates, S. (2017). Revenge porn and mental health: A qualitative analysis of the mental health effects of revenge porn on female survivors. *Feminist Criminology, 12*, 22–42.

Baum, K. (2006). Identity theft, 2004: First estimates from the National Crime Victimization Survey. *Bureau of Justice Statistics Bulletin*. Retrieved June 12, 2017, from www.ojp.gov/bjs/pub/pdf/it04.pdf

Baumgartner, S. E., Sumter, S. R., Peter, J., Valkenburg, P. M., & Livingstone, S. (2014). Does country context matter? Investigating the predictors of teen sexting across Europe. *Computers in Human Behavior, 334*, 157–164.

Bossler, A. M., & Burruss, G. W. (2011). The general theory of crime and computer hacking: Low self-control hackers? In T. J. Holt & B. H. Schell (Eds.), *Corporate hacking and technology-driven crime: Social dynamics and implications* (pp. 38–67). Hershey, PA: IGI Global.

Bossler, A. M., & Holt, T. J. (2009). On-line activities, guardianship, and malware infection: An examination of routine activities theory. *The International Journal of Cyber Criminology, 3*, 400–420.

Bourke, M. L., & Hernandez, A. E. (2009). The "Butner Study" Redux: A report of the incidence of hands-on child victimization by child pornography offenders. *Journal of Family Violence, 24*, 183–191.

Chai, S., Bagchi-Sen, S., Morrell, C., Rao, H. R., & Upadhyaya, S. J. (2009). Internet and online information privacy: An exploratory study of preteens and early teens. *IEEE Transactions on Professional Communication, 52*(2), 167–182.

Chu, B., Holt, T. J., & Ahn, G. J. (2010). *Examining the creation, distribution, and function of malware on-line* (NIJ Grant No. 2007-IJ-CX-0018). Washington, DC: National Institute of Justice.

Cole, S. A., & Pontell, H. N. (2006). Don't be low hanging fruit: Identity theft as moral panic. In T. Monahan (Ed.), *Surveillance and security*. London: Routledge.

Computer Security Institute. (2009). *Computer crime and security survey*. Retrieved from http://gocsi.com/sites/default/files/uploads/CSIsurvey2008.pdf

Cooke, E., Jahanian, F., & McPherson, D. (2005). The zombie roundup: Understanding, detecting, and disrupting botnets. In *SRUTI '05 Workshop Proceedings* (pp. 35–44). Berkeley, CA: USENIX Association.

Cressey, D. (1953). *Other people's money: A study of the social psychology of embezzlement.* Glencoe, IL: Free Press.

Dake, J. A., Price, J. H., Maziarz, L., & Ward, B. (2012). Prevalence and correlates of sexting behavior in adolescents. *American Journal of Sexuality Education, 7,* 1–15.

Durkin, K., & Patterson, D. (2011). Cyberbullying, cyberharassing, and cyberstalking. In C. Bryant (Ed.), *Routledge handbook of deviant behavior* (pp. 450–455). New York: Taylor and Francis.

Elhai, J. D., & Hall, B. J. (2016). Anxiety about internet hacking: Results from a community sample. *Computers in Human Behavior, 54,* 180–185.

Federal Trade Commission (FTC). (2003, January). *Identity fraud survey, report presented at the Identity Theft Research Group.* Washington, DC: National Institute of Justice.

Federal Trade Commission (FTC). (2005, January 27). *Identity fraud survey, report presented at the Identity Theft Research Group.* Washington, DC: National Institute of Justice.

Federal Trade Commission. (2015). *Consumer Sentinel Network Data Book for January — December 2014.* Retrieved from www.ftc.gov/system/files/documents/reports/consumer-sentinel-network-databook-january-december-2014/sentinel-cy2014-1.pdf

Gottfredson, M. R., & Hirschi, T. (1990). *A general theory of crime.* Stanford, CA: Stanford University Press.

Harrell, E. (2015). *Victims of identity theft, 2014* (NCJ 248991). Retrieved from www.bjs.gov/content/pub/pdf/vit14.pdf

Harrell, E., & Langton, L. (2013). *Victims of identity theft, 2012* (NCJ 243779). Retrieved from www.bjs.gov/content/pub/pdf/vit12.pdf

Higgins, G. E., Hughes, T., Ricketts, M. L., & Wolfe, S. E. (2008). Identity theft complaints: Exploring state-level correlates. *Journal of Financial Crime, 15,* 295–307.

Holt, T. J. (2007). Subcultural evolution? Examining the influence of on- and off-line experiences on deviant subcultures. *Deviant Behavior, 28,* 171–198.

Holt, T. J., & Bossler, A. M. (2009). Examining the applicability of lifestyle-routine activities theory for cybercrime victimization. *Deviant Behavior, 30,* 1–25.

Holt, T. J., & Bossler, A. M. (2013). Examining the relationship between routine activities and malware infection indicators. *Journal of Contemporary Criminal Justice, 29,* 420–436.

Holt, T. J., Burruss, G. W., & Bossler, A. M. (2010). Social learning and cyber deviance: Examining the importance of a full social learning model in the virtual world. *Journal of Crime and Justice, 33,* 15–30.

Holt, T. J., & Kilger, M. (2008). Techcrafters and makecrafters: A comparison of two populations of hackers. *WOMBAT Workshop on Information Security Threats, Data Collection and Sharing,* 67–78.

Holt, T. J., & Turner, M. G. (2012). Examining risks and protective factors of on line identity theft. *Deviant Behavior, 33,* 308–323.

Jonsson, L. S., Priebe, G., Bladh, M., & Svedin, C. G. (2014). Voluntary sexual exposure online among Swedish youth—social background, internet behavior and psychosocial health. *Computers in Human Behavior, 30,* 181–190.

Jordan, T., & Taylor, P. (1998). A sociology of hackers. *Sociological Review, 46,* 757–780.

Lemert, E. M. (1958). The behavior of the systematic check forger. *Social Problems*, *6*, 141–149.

Lenhart, A. (2009, December 15). Teens and sexting: How and why minor teens are sending sexually suggestive nude or nearly nude images via text messaging. *Pew Internet and American Life Project Research*, 1–6. www.pewinternet.org/Reports/2009/Teens-and-Sexting.aspx

Lippman, J. R., & Campbell, S. W. (2014). Damned if you do, damned if you don't . . . if you're a girl: Relational and normative contexts of adolescent sexting in the United States. *Journal of Children and Media*, *8*, 371–386.

Livingstone, S., & Smith, P. K. (2014). Annual Research Review: Harms experienced by child users of online and mobile technologies: the nature, prevalence and management of sexual and aggressive risks in the digital age. *Journal of Child Psychology and Psychiatry*, *55*, 635–654.

Loper, K. (2000). *The criminology of computer hackers: A qualitative and quantitative analysis*. Ph.D. Dissertation, Michigan State University.

Marcum, C., Higgins, G. E., Ricketts, M. L., & Wolfe, S. E. (2014). Hacking in high school: Cyber-crime perpetration by juveniles. *Deviant Behavior*, *35*, 581–591.

McDowell, M. (2009). *National cyber alert system. Cyber security tip ST04–014. Avoiding social engineering and phishing attacks*. Retrieved April 30, 2013, from www.us-cert.gov/cas/tips/ST04-014.html

Meyer, G. (1989). "The social organization of the computer underground." Master's thesis, Northern Illinois University.

Mitchell, K. J., Finkelhor, D., Jones, L. M., & Wolak, J. (2012). Prevalence and characteristics of youth sexting: A national study. *Pediatrics*, *129*, 13–20.

Morris, R. G. (2011). Computer hacking and the techniques of neutralization: An empirical assessment. In *Corporate hacking and technology-driven crime: Social dynamics and implications* (pp. 1–17), edited by T. J. Holt and B. Schell. Hershey, PA: IGI-Global Press.

Navarro, J. C., & Higgins, G. E. (2017). Familial identity theft. *American Journal of Criminal Justice*, *42*, 218–230.

Navarro, J. N., Marcum, C. D., Higgins, G. E., & Ricketts, M. L. (2016). Addicted to the thrill of the virtual hunt: Examining the effects of Internet addiction on cyberstalking behaviors of juveniles. *Deviant Behavior*, *37*, 893–903.

Ngo, F. T., & Paternoster, R. (2011). Cybercrime victimization: An examination of individual and situational-level factors. *International Journal of Cyber Criminology*, *5*, 773–793.

PandaLabs. (2007). *Malware infections in protected systems*. Retrieved from http://research.pandasecurity.com/blogs/images/wp_pb_malware_infections_in_p rotected_systems.pdf

Pastrikos, C. (2004). Identity theft statutes: Which will protect Americans the most? *Albany Law Review*, *67*, 1137–1157.

Pew Internet and American Life Project. (2005). Spyware: The threat of unwanted software programs is changing the way people use the Internet. *Pew Internet and American Life Project*. Retrieved from www.pewinternet.org/files/old-media/Files/Reports/2005/PIP_Spyware_Report_July_05.pdf.pdf

Pontell, H. N., & Brown, G. C. (2011). Identity theft. In C. Bryant (Ed.), *Routledge handbook of deviant behavior* (pp. 427–433). New York: Taylor and Francis.

Renfrow, D. G., & Rollo, E. A. (2014). Sexting on campus: Minimizing perceived risks and neutralizing behaviors. *Deviant Behavior, 35*, 903–920.

Reyns, B. W., Henson, B., & Fisher, B. S. (2012). Stalking in the twilight zone: Extent of cyberstalking victimization and offending among college students. *Deviant Behavior, 33*, 1–25.

Reyns, B. W., Henson, B., & Fisher, B. (2014). Digital deviance: Low self-control and opportunity as explanations of sexting among college students. *Sociological Spectrum, 34*, 273–292.

Ricketts, M. L., Maloney, C., Marcum, C. D., & Higgins, G. E. (2014). The effect of internet related problems on the sexting behaviors of juveniles. *American Journal of Criminal Justice, 40*, 270. doi:10.1007/s12103-014-9247-5.

Ringrose, J., Harvey, L., Gill, R., & Livingstone, S. (2013). Teen girls, sexual double standards and sexting: Gendered value in digital image exchange. *Feminist Theory, 14*, 305–323.

Roberts, L. D., Indermaur, D., & Spiranovic, C. (2013). Fear of cyber-identity theft and related fraudulent activity. *Psychiatry, Psychology, and Law, 20*, 315–328.

Rogers, M., Smoak, N., & Liu, J. (2005). Self-reported deviant computer behavior: A Big-5, moral choice, and manipulative exploitive behavior analysis. *Deviant Behavior, 27*, 245–268.

Skinner, W., & Fream, A. (1997). A social learning theory analysis of computer crime among college students. *Journal of Research in Crime and Delinquency, 34*, 495–518.

Stambaugh, H., Beaupre, D. S., Icove, D. J., Baker, R., Cassady, W., & Williams, W. P. (2001). *Electronic Crime Needs Assessment for State and Local Law Enforcement*, NCJ 186276, National Institute of Justice, Washington, DC.

Strassberg, D. S., McKinnon, R. K., Sustaita, M. A., & Rullo, J. (2013). Sexting by high school students: An exploratory and descriptive study. *Archives of Sexual Behavior, 42*, 15–21.

Symantec Corporation. (2012). *Symantec Internet security threat report* (Vol. 17). Retrieved from www.symantec.com/threatreport/

Taylor, R. W., Fritsch, E. J., Liederbach, J., & Holt, T. J. (2010). *Digital crime and digital terrorism* (2nd ed.). Upper Saddle River, NJ: Pearson Prentice Hall.

Thomas, D. (2002). *Hacker culture*. Minneapolis, MN: University of Minnesota Press.

Turgeman-Goldschmidt, O. (2008). Meanings that hackers assign to their being a hacker. *International Journal of Cyber Criminology, 2*, 382–396.

van Wilsem, J. (2013). Hacking and harassment: Do they have something in common? Comparing risk factors for online victimization. *Journal of Contemporary Criminal Justice, 29*, 437–453.

Wade, H., Hylender, D., & Valentine, A. (2008). *Verizon business 2008 data breach investigation report*. Retrieved September 26, 2013, www.verizonbusiness.com/re sources/security/databreachreport.pdfS

Walgrave, M., Heirman, W., & Hallman, L. (2013). Under pressure to sext? Applying theory of planned behavior to adolescent sexting. *Behavior and Information Technology, 33*, 86–98.

Wall, D. S. (2007). *Cybercrime: The transformation of crime in the information age*. Cambridge, UK: Polity Press.

Wolak, J., & Finkelhor, D. (2011, March). Sexting: A typology. Durham, NH: Crimes Against Children Research Centre, University of New Hampshire.

Chapter 5

Personal and Property Victimization

Introduction

Personal and property crimes are crimes committed against an individual in which the person often suffers physical injury, as well as emotional and psychological trauma. These include homicide, assault, and robbery, as well kidnapping and rape, which will be covered in Chapter 6.

Murder

According to the FBI's Uniform Crime Report (UCR) (2017), murder and nonnegligent manslaughter is the willful and nonnegligent killing of one person by another. The UCR does not include those who were killed by accident, negligence, suicide, accident, or justifiable homicides, which is the killing of a person in the line of duty when a person is legally permitted to kill someone else (a cop killing a violent suspect or a military person killing an enemy during wartime). In 2015, there were 15,696 murders in the United States, a 10.8% increase from 2014. However, the murder rate still remains relatively low. In terms of location, 45.9% occurred in the South, 21.5% in the Midwest, 20.2% in the West, and 12.4% in the Northeast (FBI, 2015).

As reported by the FBI (2015), circumstances of murder include that 45.6% of all murders involved a single victim and offender. Of the victims, 89% were male. When the victim's race was known (unknown for 196 victims), 53.1% were black or African-American, 44.2% were white, and 2.8% were of other races. The weapon used was a firearm in 71.5% of homicides. Most victims knew their offender, with 29.2% of homicide victims killed by someone they knew who was not a family member: friends, boyfriend/girlfriend, neighbor, acquaintance, and the like. This is followed by victims murdered by family at 12.8% and 10.2% killed by strangers. The context of murder, when it was known (in 60.1% of cases) involved arguments about romantic triangles at 39.9 %, followed by 24.9% of murders that occurred in conjunction with committing another felony crime (rape, robbery, burglary). There were 770 justifiable homicides in 2014. Law enforcement justifiably killed 442 individuals and private citizens killed 328 (FBI, 2015).

Impact on Victims

Murder affects those who cared about the victim. The death of a loved one as a result of murder can have a devastating effect as it is often very sudden, unexpected, and difficult to understand. This leaves the loved ones of a victim dealing with the victimization for a long time. Initially hearing the news that their loved one has been murdered can cause shock, confusion, and disbelief. While notification is never easy, the way that the bereaved is informed can make hearing the news more traumatic. Getting the news on the phone, hearing incomplete or inaccurate information, or finding out through the media can cause additional pain (Parents of Murdered Children, 2017). After finding out the news, there are often time-sensitive and unwanted tasks that loved ones must perform that can cause stress, anxiety, and trauma. This includes identifying the body of the victim, claiming their personal possessions, talking with criminal justice personnel, notifying other family and friends, paying medical bills or ambulance costs, and making funeral arrangements. They also may have to deal with the media if the case has become high profile. There is also additional anguish for loved ones of victims whose murderer is never found as there is no one on whom to focus their anger. Instead, families may direct it at law enforcement for the failure to find the person responsible (Lord, 1987). Even when an offender has been identified, the criminal justice process can often be hard for the loved ones to endure. They may experience frustration, feeling that the accused has more rights than they do. They may feel isolated and removed from the process. Family members might not be notified of court proceedings in the case or if a plea bargain has been offered and accepted. They also may believe that the pain they feel at the loss will be alleviated when the murderer has been punished, but find that is often not the case and they feel no different (Schlosser, 1997).

After a loved one finds out about the crime, the way that they return to functioning in everyday life can vary. Kubler-Ross (1969) outlined the normal grieving process, identifying five stages that a person must go through when they have experienced a loss: denial, anger, bargaining, depression, and acceptance. However, when a person loses a loved one as a result of murder, the reactions that a person experiences are often more severe and complicated than when a person dies in a different way. The circumstances that surround the murder may alter the grieving process. The normal anger that one would experience in losing someone is often directed at the offender or the criminal justice system for failing to find the offender (Doka, 1996). The bereaved also may become fixated on the crime and the horror and suffering that their loved one experienced (Sprang, McNeil & Wright, 1989), causing feelings of extreme depression and guilt. The grieving process and the ability to accept what happened is often prolonged for murder victims' loved ones as a result of the way in which that person died. The fact the person they loved met a violent end and suffered at the hands of another human being is often difficult for people to deal with. As a result, loved ones also may experience posttraumatic stress disorder, nightmares, insomnia, feelings of alienation, hypervigilance, depression, and anxiety (Schlosser, 1997). Religious loved ones of murder victims may lose their faith, which can inhibit the coping process. They also may lose their ability to trust people: the murder victim's family may be ostracized in their community since people do not want to be reminded of death, murder, and crime and being around the victim's loved ones reminds them (Magee, 1983; Fowlkes, 1990; Ressler, Burgess, & Douglas, 1988; Spungen, 1998).

The murder of a loved one also may mean a change in daily life for the bereaved that can increase stress and anxiety. If a spouse is murdered and the couple have children, this means a change in child care and parenting. If a child is murdered, the siblings often try to make up for the loss of the missing child. In addition to the financial stress of funeral expenses, the family may experience the loss of the victim's income if she/he was employed prior to their death. Children of homicide victims suffer in different ways than adults due to their age and development. If they witnessed the murder, they may be called on to testify at trial. Both witnessing a murder and being called upon to relive it can cause posttraumatic stress disorder and other emotional and psychological issues that could affect that child for years (Pynoos & Eth, 1984). If one of a child's parents murdered the other, the child may feel revulsion, betrayal, and anger, along with confusion. The child also may suffer with issues of abandonment and fear relating to their altered living situation.

Media Byte 5.1: Parents of Murdered Children

Check out the website for the organization Parents of Murdered Children: www.pomc.com/index.html

What is your opinion of this website? Do you find it informative?

Do you think that it would be helpful to parents whose child has been murdered? Why or why not?

Provide an example of something that you found on this website that you feel would be beneficial to parents dealing with the loss of a child.

Assault

Simple Assault

Simple assault is the attack or attempted attack of an individual without the use of a weapon that results in no injury or minor injury. Some examples of minor injuries include black eyes, bruises, cuts, scrapes, scratches, swelling, or an injury that requires less than two days in the hospital (Bureau of Justice Statistics, 2017). There were an estimated 3,179,440 simple assaults in 2015. Most victims know their attackers. The attacker is usually a friend, acquaintance, relative, or intimate partner (Bureau of Justice Statistics, 2017).

Aggravated Assault

Aggravated assault is an attack or attempted attack with a weapon that involves any injury or an attack without the use of a weapon that results in serious physical injuries. Serious injuries can include loss of consciousness, internal injuries, an injury that requires two or more days hospitalization, broken bones, or missing teeth (Bureau of Justice Statistics, 2017).The Bureau of Justice Statistics estimates that there were 816,760 reported aggravated assaults in 2015. Most victims know their attackers, who may be a friend, acquaintance, relative, or intimate partner (Bureau of Justice Statistics, 2017). Research on aggravated assault has found that verbal arguments precede the assault, most assaults happen on the weekend, at night, and during the summer months, and that most assaults involve one offender and one victim (Lauritsen & White, 2014).

Impact on Victims

Victims react to the assault differently. Some individuals have an immediate reaction, while others have a more delayed response. For some, a reaction may be triggered after an event or encounter. Victims may feel humiliated, embarrassed, or ashamed about what happened, thinking that they could have prevented the assault or that it was their fault. Individuals may feel rejected or isolated from friends and family afterwards. They also may experience rage associated with the offender. They may feel anger and/or frustration at the criminal justice system for lack of action or punishment of the perpetrator of the assault. Victims also may be in a state of panic, with fear and/or anxiety that they will be attacked again. Victims can develop posttraumatic stress disorder in which they suffer from disrupted sleeping, endure flashbacks to the victimization, and avoid places that remind them of the attack. They also may suffer from depression and anxiety, as well as being easily alarmed or surprised by noises or quick actions (Office of Justice Programs, 2017).

Activity 5.1: Assault

Read the following article about two individuals who assaulted a bus driver and were charged with aggravated assault: www.nj.com/essex/index.ssf/2017/01/woman_accused_of_throwing_hot_coffee_at_bus_driver.html

Do you think that the circumstances of the perpetrator throwing coffee warrants the charge of aggravated assault? Why or why not?

Do you believe that physically shoving someone, as in the situation with the second perpetrator, deserves an aggravated assault charge? Why or why not?

Based upon the information you have read about simple and aggravated assault, do you think that either of these individuals should have been charged with simple assault and not aggravated assault? Explain your answer.

Robbery

Robbery is the attempted or completed act of taking property or cash directly from another individual with the use of force or the threat of force. It can occur with or without a weapon (Bureau of Justice Statistics, 2017). According to the FBI's *Crime in the United States* (2015), there were 327,374 robberies in 2015. The average dollar value of property that was stolen in a robbery was $1,190 and $390 million in total losses. Banks suffered the most losses with $3,884 of loss per offense. In terms of weapons used during a robbery, the FBI (2015) reports that strong-arm tactics were used 42.2% of the time, followed by firearms in 40.8% cases, "other" dangerous weapons 9.1%, and knives/cutting instruments 7.9% of the time. In terms of location, robberies most often occur on a street or highway (39.88%) and are least likely to occur in a bank (1.7%) (FBI, 2015).

Impact on Victims

Individuals who have been robbery victims can suffer physical and emotional consequences to different degrees over a varying period of time as a result of the trauma experienced (Elklit, 2002). They may feel vulnerable and that they have lost control over their life and their decisions. Victims also may be in a state of hypervigilance, being alert to potential dangers or threats. They may feel that they did something to contribute to their victimization or that they are responsible for being a victim. They also may feel upset over the possessions that were stolen during the robbery. Victims may be scared that the person who robbed them will return to harm them or rob them again and take other possessions. They may experience flashbacks and be triggered by certain things. Individuals may feel anger at the robber and experience feelings of wanting revenge or retribution. They also may experience instances of depression, acute stress disorder (ASD; Elklit, 2002; Hansen & Elklit, 2011) or posttraumatic stress disorder (PTSD) (Fichera et al., 2014). The reaction that a victim has to this sort of trauma is affected by their access to social support systems and their overall emotional strength and resilience (Brewin, Andrews & Valentine, 2000; Yap & Devilly, 2004).

Experiencing robbery in the workplace can affect a person's reaction and ability to cope in the aftermath. They may experience flashbacks to the victimization at work, develop PTSD, require increased health care visits, and incur trauma-related absences (Belleville et al., 2012). For those who experience robbery at work, it can be very challenging to return to the scene of the victimization every day. This can cause additional trauma and influence attendance at work as individuals may want to evade a reminder of the incident of robbery (Belleville et al., 2012). Robbery victims also may experience psychological stress that impairs their interactions with customers as well as co-workers (Jones, 2002).

PROPERTY CRIMES

The term *property* refers to items, land, buildings, money, and/or cars—physical things that you can see and touch. Property crime refers to the illegal taking, damaging, or destruction of a person's property. Common forms of property crime include burglary, larceny (theft), motor vehicle theft, and arson. While the definition of property crime often does not include the use or threat of force, this does not mean that force is not used, nor that these are victimless crimes or minor offenses. Property crimes involve property but are committed against people. People who are victims of property crimes suffer in ways similar to victims of other crimes. They may experience physical injury, emotional distress, posttraumatic stress disorder (PTSD), fear, and anxiety issues after the victimization as well as dealing with replacing their property.

According the Office for Victims of Crime (2017) property crime makes up about 75% of all crime in the United States. The most common property crime is burglary, and it occurs most frequently in rented property. Annually, the loss due to property crime is over $10 billion, with more than $4 billion being spent on locks and safes, $1.4 billion on surveillance cameras, and $49 million on guard dogs.

Burglary

Burglary occurs when a person or persons enter or attempt to enter a residence unlawfully. This often involves theft, but not always. The unlawful entrance may involve force such as breaking a window, slashing a screen, or forcing open a door. The unlawful entrance can also occur without force, as when an individual enters through an unlocked door or window. Burglary can occur in buildings that are not a home, such as a garage or shed. In addition, if an individual unlawfully enters a vacation home or hotel, it is considered a burglary even if there was no one staying there at the time (Bureau of Justice Statistics, 2017). According to the FBI's Uniform Crime Report (2015) there were an estimated 1,579,527 burglaries in the United States. In 2015, burglary accounted for 19.8% of all property crime and victims suffered an estimated $3.6 billion in property losses. The average loss per burglary offense was $2,316. Burglary of residential properties was the most common, making up 71.6% of all burglaries for 2015 (FBI, 2015).

Impact on Victims

When a person's home is invaded with a burglary, they may experience a variety of emotions and reactions. While the burglary is not an event in which actual injury or death are threatened, research suggests that it is an event that can elicit similar responses. Victims experience feelings of helplessness, horror, intense fear, and a PTSD-like response (Brown & Harris, 1989; Caballero, Ramos, & Saltijeral, 2000; Maguire, 1980; Mawby & Walklate, 1997; Ostrihanska & Wojcik, 1993). These feelings can persist, occurring months after the victimization (Wohlfarth, Van den Brink, Winkel, & Ter Smitten, 2003). Individuals often may feel shock and disbelief, as well as being frustrated and confused as to how this could have happened to them. They may feel violated and upset. Victims may experience feelings of uneasiness and have trouble relaxing at home. It may take them a while to feel comfortable again in their own home.

Victims also may become more fearful of being in their home after a burglary since someone was in their home unexpectedly. As a result, victims may feel that they need to take extra security precautions in order to feel safe, reduce anxiety, and/or prevent further victimization. This may involve installing security systems in the home and evaluating doors, windows, and lighting. Victims also may feel the need to purchase a firearm or have some other sort of weapon in their home, near them, or on their person to make them feel safe in case someone breaks in again. In order to deal with these feelings, victims of burglary may benefit from talking to and gaining support from friends, family, and/or a counselor or therapist. The reaction of victims to having their home burglarized is often based upon the perceived quality of the police response. Burglary is a unique crime in comparison to many others as most cases are reported to the police. If victims feel satisfied with the response of the police, they often have a better reaction than if they receive a negative response from police (Kilpatrick & Otto, 1987; Orth, 2009; Parsons & Bergin, 2010; Sales, Baum, & Shore, 1984).

Individuals may also experience anger and sadness for the loss of valuable, sentimental, or irreplaceable items. This can be especially hard for children who lose items that are dear to them and may not understand why and/or how their items have been taken. Victims who file a claim with their insurance company may experience additional stress and anxiety. Most insurance companies have systems in place for the procedure and the amount that victims of burglaries are paid for their lost items. Victims may not receive sufficient reimbursement to replace stolen items. For example, a victim has an older television that has depreciated over time. The victim will be reimbursed for the value of the older television, but buying a new television will likely cost more than the reimbursement. In addition, most victims who file a burglary claim pay a deductible, an out-of-pocket cost that can range from $100 to $1,000 depending upon the insurance plan. Victims may thus feel frustrated by their insurance company, feeling that their lost items were not reimbursed sufficiently. There are also those victims of burglary who do not have insurance and must replace the items that they lost without any financial assistance from an insurance company (Office of Victims of Crime, 2017).

Case Study 5.1: Burglars Who Have Themselves a Snack

The Office of the Chief Medical Examiner in New York City, which operates the city DNA laboratory, has spoken about unexpected things that have been found at the scenes of burglaries in the city. A spokeswoman for the office said that these things have included a partially eaten apple, sunflower seed shells, pizza crust, chewed gum, fruit pits, chicken wings, and a partially eaten chocolate cake. While this may seem strange, Detective Anthony Barbee in Brooklyn has indicated that this is not uncommon in New York City. He said that one of the questions that they routinely ask burglary victims is whether there is something missing or newly opened in their refrigerator. Detective Barbee said that many burglars make themselves at home, eating food or taking it with them along with other items they steal from the house. A positive outcome of this is that partially eaten food can be processed for potential DNA testing.

www.nytimes.com/2017/03/20/nyregion/burglars-eat-crime-scene.html?_r=0

Media Byte 5.2: Real-life Hamburglar

In the preceding case study, you learned about burglars who broke into people's homes and ate food in addition to stealing other items. Watch this video clip from CNN of a Washington, DC, man who broke into a Five Guys Burgers and Fries shop and made himself a burger but did not steal anything (www.cnn.com/2016/04/11/us/five-guys-dc-burglary).

Based on what you have learned about burglary, did this man commit burglary? Why or why not?

What do you think that his punishment should be?

Do you think that this was a victimless crime? Please explain.

Motor Vehicle Theft

Motor vehicle theft is the attempted or actual theft of a motor vehicle. This includes motor scooters, snowmobiles, motorcycles, all-terrain vehicles, sport utility vehicles, trucks, and buses. Motor vehicle theft does not include airplanes, farm equipment, bulldozers and other construction equipment, motorboats, sailboats, houseboats, or personal watercraft (FBI, 2017). There were an estimated 707,758 motor vehicle thefts in the United States in 2015, with $4.9 billion lost as a result. The average amount lost for a stolen vehicle was $7,001 (FBI, 2015). Of all stolen motor vehicles, 74.7% were automobiles.

Recently, there have been some developments in the ways that offenders commit motor vehicle theft and victimize individuals because of technology. The development of transponder-equipped or "smart key" has limited would-be thieves' ability to hot-wire a motor vehicle. One of the growing means of motor vehicle theft is through an offender stealing keys from a valet parking area. They also may act as the legitimate car owner who wants a replacement key made by a dealership or locksmith. Offenders also have returned rental cars with a good working key in the ignition and a blank key alongside it. They then return to the lot later with the other working key and steal the car. Offenders also have placed GPS trackers in or on the car and when the car is rented again, they follow it and steal it. Offenders also may create fake identities or use stolen identities to finance a car illegally at a car dealership. Automobiles that are stolen, whether from an individual or a business, often are given a different vehicle identification number (VIN) to hide the fact they are stolen so they can be sold to naive customers (National Insurance Crime Bureau, 2017).

Impact on Victims

While motor vehicle theft is often thought of as an economic crime, it can have an impact on the victims. As with burglary, victims may experience stress and anxiety when dealing with the insurance company and potentially not receiving the full value for their stolen item. They also may miss work if they do not have other means of transportation. The psychological impact on victims is often lesser than seen with burglary, as the car is not imbued with the same privacy and sanctity as a home.

Arson

Arson is the intentional and malicious burning or attempt to burn a house, public building, motor vehicle, aircraft, or personal property of another person. It can also include the intent to defraud (FBI, 2017). The Uniform Crime Report does not include estimates for the crime of arson as the reporting varies. However, the FBI has compiled some data to provide an overview of arson. Law enforcement agencies in 2015 that provided arson data indicated that there were 41,376 reported incidents. Of those, 45.7% involved residential, storage, or public structures, followed by property such as crops, timber, and fences at 29.8% and mobile property at 24.4%. The average loss per arson incident was $14,182 (FBI, 2015). According to the National Fire Protection Association (NFPA) (2017), intentionally set home structure fires are most likely to be set between 3 p.m. and midnight, and the bedroom is the leading area of origin for home fires, with bathrooms being the leading area of origin for public property arsons.

Impact on Victims

Arson victims suffer in the same way as victims of person crimes and property crimes—they suffer physical, psychological, and property damage. The major impacts that arson has on victims include death (civilians and firefighters), physical injury, and property damage. Victims of arson are most commonly harmed through structure fires (involving structural components of a building). Although structure fires comprise only 18% of all fires intentionally set, they make up 92% of deaths, 84% of injuries and 86% of direct property damage and loss. Most structure fires (63%) occur in residential properties, and 80% of these were in use at the time of the arson (Campbell, 2014). There is no typical arson victim; it is a crime that can affect anyone. There is also the potential for third-party victims, such as those who live next door to a building or apartment on fire (NFPA, 2017).

In addition to the physical losses, there are emotional losses as well. Similar to what victims of burglary, robbery and motor vehicle theft experience, victims of arson have lost something that means a great deal to them—sometimes their entire home. Some arson victims who lose their home and cannot find another in the area may be forced to move to an unfamiliar community, which can cause feelings of depression and displacement. Victims also may fear for their safety after finding out that their home was intentionally set on fire (NFPA, 2017).Victims of arson may also worry about their home being looted (when individuals come and take what items have not been damaged by the fire). If the residents of the home were injured in the fire, they may not be able to remove the items before they are stolen, adding another crime to the victimization that they experience. As with burglary victims, victims of arson also will have to deal with the insurance company, and they go through a long and wearisome process of accounting for possessions that were damaged or destroyed, perhaps only to receive inadequate compensation. There are also many victims who do not have insurance, such as those who rent. Victims who apply to a state crime victim compensation program often find that they are able to get only reimbursement and coverage for physical injuries and medical expenses and not the loss of income due to physical injuries or property (FEMA, 1997).

Activity 5.2: Write Your Own Victim Impact Statement

Select one of the following scenarios and write a victim impact statement. You need to pretend that this crime actually happened to you and include details about the crime, the feelings you experienced, and the harm you suffered. It must be a complete statement about how this crime affected your life.

In this statement, you should include:

1. The crime that was committed against you or your loved one. Feel free to create details about the crime not included in the scenario.
2. How that crime affected you and others (emotionally, physically, and financially).
3. What type of sentence you would like the offender to receive (rehabilitation, prison, the death penalty, etc.) and whether or not you are seeking restitution from the offender. After you have written your statement, share it with a peer or the class.

Scenario 1:
You are a family member of a person who was shot and killed. The suspect has been tried and found guilty for murder.

Scenario 2:
You were the victim of an armed robbery. You were robbed at gunpoint while walking on the sidewalk after work. The offender stole your wallet, jewelry, and watch. He has been found guilty of robbery.

Scenario 3:
Your home has been burglarized. The windows have been smashed and many items have been taken from your home. The individual who committed this crime has been found guilty of burglary.

> **Scenario 4:**
> Your home has been intentionally burned down by an arsonist. You have lost your entire home and most of your belongings. The person who did this has been convicted of arson.

Larceny-theft

Larceny-theft is the unlawful taking, leading, carrying, or riding away with the property or possession of another (FBI, 2017). The FBI Uniform Crime Report shows that in 2014 there were 1,238,190 estimated arrests for larceny-theft. The average value of property taken is $929 per offense and the average total loss nationally is estimated to be $5.3 billion (FBI, 2015).

Impact on Victims

Many victims of larceny-theft do not have their property returned to them. This can lead victims to question the goodness of others as well as making them angry that they have lost something that they valued. They may also feel fear of having items stolen again and experience feelings of general insecurity. If the stolen property is irreplaceable, the victim may find the crime especially hard to deal with. Also, if the victim files an insurance claim, the issues of dealing with the insurance company mentioned previously also apply.

"Victimless" Crimes

A victimless crime is an illegal act in which a consenting adult participates and in which there is a no complaining individual (i.e., victim) (Schur, 1965). In these types of crimes, there is either no harm done to a victim, or if there was harm, it is often not viewed as such because the person harmed (the victim) was a willing participant who consented to be involved in the crime (Stitt, 1988). The topic of victimless crimes is often controversial in academia and the community as there are two main viewpoints associated with these crimes. The first is that these acts should not be considered crimes as no one is harmed except the person participating in the act freely. The second is that these acts should be illegal because laws must uphold society's moral standards and there are negative consequences even though they may not be immediately apparent.

Prostitution, drug use, and illegal sports betting are often thought of as victimless since the only people they harm are those who are participating of their own free will. However, in the following overview of these crimes, both sides will be covered, including ways in which these "victimless" crimes do indeed have real and tangible victims.

Prostitution

Prostitution is the illegal exchange of sexual acts for money. Some people believe that prostitution is a victimless crime and that it should be legalized and regulated in the same way as other for-profit businesses. The core of the argument is that the business of sex for sale—acts performed by consenting adults—will never disappear, so we as a society should make it safer and better for those involved. Many believe that sex workers who exchange their services for money should have legitimate employment arrangements just like any other individual in the service industry, and they believe that these changes would protect both the prostitute and the "john" (person who is purchasing sexual services) (Kempadoo, 2005; Klinger, 2003; Kuo, 2003; Weitzer, 2007, 2010).

However, some people believe that the crime of prostitution is harmful and not victimless, and that legalization and/or regulation will not reduce harms. Research has shown that those in the sex trade often start as minors (Estes and Weiner, 2002) and are frequently coerced or forced to engage in such acts against their will or simply to survive (Chapkis, 2003; Flowers, 2001). Prostitutes are often victims of violence at the hands of their pimps, traffickers, or those purchasing the sexual services (Flowers, 2001; Miller, 1993). The life of a prostitute is not glamorous as has been portrayed in such films as *Pretty Woman*, Those who purchase sex from prostitutes, the "johns," are at risk for contracting sexually transmitted diseases, which puts them and their other partners and/or family at risk. Businesses in or near areas where prostitution is visible can be harmed if the area becomes known as a crime-ridden neighborhood (Ayala & White, 2008). Some people believe that prostitution can tear apart marriages and families.

Drug Use

Illegal drug use is often considered a victimless crime: many people argue that the only person who is harmed as a result is the person using the drugs, who is doing so by choice. According to the FBI, drug abuse violations are typically defined as state and/or local offenses while federal, state, and local agencies share enforcement of the drug laws. Criminal charges for drugs often are related to unlawful possession of the drug, but sale, use, growing, or manufacturing of drugs can also be charges. The most common types of drugs illegally consumed by individuals include opium or cocaine and their derivatives, marijuana, synthetic narcotics, and nonnarcotic drugs such as barbiturates (Bureau of Justice Statistics, 2017). According to the FBI's Uniform Crime Report's *Crime in the United States* (2014), the highest number of arrests for any crime in 2014 were drug abuse violations, numbering 1,561,231.

While many consider drug use a victimless crime, others argue the contrary. The person who uses the drugs may become addicted and commit additional crimes, such as theft, in order to feed their addiction, thereby harming others and creating additional victims. They also may suffer negative physical consequences or even death as a result of drug use, and this can be very difficult for their loved ones. The family can experience anxiety, depression, and physical issues if their own self-care falters due to focusing only on taking care of their drug-addicted loved one. The family and friends of drug users often feel hurt, angry, and resentful. These feelings often intensify if the drug abuser lies or steals from them (Powers, 2016).

Illegal Gambling

Gambling is the betting or wagering on outcome, usually on a game or something that is at least partially based on chance. Illegal gambling occurs when individuals participate in gambling that is prohibited by law. This includes gambling in cyberspace. The Professional and Amateur Sports Protection Act (PASPA) was passed by Congress in 1992. It outlawed sports betting in most of the United States. Today, Nevada is the only state where betting on college and professional sports through a licensed bookmaker is legal. According to the American Gaming Association (2017), Americans bet $4.2 billion on Super Bowl 50 and 97% of those bets were illegal. In addition, $90 billion in illegal bets were wagered on National Football League and college football games last season and $2 billion was bet legally.

Many would argue that illegal gambling is a victimless crime as all involved are consenting and no one gets hurt. Proponents such as the American Gaming Association (2017) say that the federal laws regarding illegal gambling have failed to reduce gambling. It is estimated that in 2016, Americans placed $155 billion in illegal sports bets. Supporters claim this means gambling should be legalized. However, many assert that it is not a victimless crime, as there are dangers associated with gambling that might be exacerbated if gambling was legal and thus more accessible. One such danger is gambling disorder (GD), in which individuals gamble compulsively and are unable to stop no matter what the consequences may be. GD has been added to the fifth edition of the Diagnostic and Statistical Manual of Mental Disorders (American Psychiatric Association, 2013) and it is included in the chapter on addictive disorders. Gambling activates the brain's rewards systems in a way similar to substance abuse. A person who suffers from GD can also commit other types of criminal behaviors. These additional crimes are often about obtaining more money to bet, such as fraud and theft (Folino and Abait, 2009). This provides the potential for individuals to be victimized and suffer. Whether or not legalized gambling increases crime is uncertain. There is evidence to suggest that implementation of a casino in a community does increase crime significantly, as well as evidence that it does not. The relationship is not entirely understood (Stitt, Nichols and Giacopassi, 2003). In order to completely understand the impact of legalized gambling, more research is needed. However, it is important to note that whether gambling is illegal or legal, if someone suffers from a gambling addiction, the loved ones of the individual suffer too. They may suffer financially as the gambling addict uses money needed for support of the household to gamble, putting the family in jeopardy of losing their shelter or transportation. They also may put their family at risk if they are illegally betting with "bookies," who may use force to try to coerce or ensure payment of a debt.

Dog Fighting

Dog fighting (like cockfighting) is often a focus of illegal gambling and is considered a victimless crime by some people who view the animals as property and the means to an end, not as "victims." Horse racing is often a part of illegal gambling as well, but the institution of horse racing is legal and the horses do not face the brutal treatment or extreme abuse that fighting dogs do. In dog fighting, the injuries that a dog sustains can be fatal and many fights are to the death. The most common injuries that fighting dogs suffer include severe bruising, deep puncture wounds, and broken bones. If a dog does not die during the fight, they often die as a result of the effects of the fight, such as blood loss, dehydration, shock, exhaustion, or infection. The dogs also are raised in an environment of abuse and severe mistreatment from birth so that they are mean, angry, and ready to fight other dogs on command. The fights themselves last one to two hours until one of the dogs cannot continue because of injury or death. Spectators bet on which dog will win (Humane Society of the United States, 2017).

Although some argue that dogs are seen as property in our society and therefore there is no real victim in dog fighting, dogs are sentient beings capable of experiencing pain and suffering. The "sport" of dog fighting does have victims: the dogs. They suffer from immeasurable acts of cruelty and are not able to change their circumstances as domestic animals rely upon the mercy of humans. This idea is reflected in the law, as dog fighting is a felony in all 50 states. On the federal level, the Animal Welfare Act prohibits it, as well as the transportation of animals for fighting (American Society for the Prevention of Cruelty to Animals, 2017).

Case Study 5.2: Michael Vick and the Bad Newz Kennels

In 2001, Michael Vick was 21 and starting his rookie years as a professional player in the National Football League (NFL). With three associates—Purnell Peace, Quanis Phillips, and Tony Taylor—Vick began a dogfighting operation known as "Bad Newz Kennels." The operation was housed on property Vick had purchased in Surry County, Virginia. They purchased dogs in Virginia and other states and brought them to the kennel. Vick became a registered dog breeder, but the dogs were being used predominantly for fights. In addition to holding brutal dogfights, Vick and his associates tortured, beat, electrocuted, and hung dogs. In 2004 Vick had a 10-year, $130 million contract, and by 2006 he was the highest-paid player in the NFL.

In 2007, when Vick's cousin Davon Boddie was arrested for drug charges, he gave Vick's property as his address. Authorities searching the property found probable cause for animal cruelty and dog fighting. The police discovered 54 dogs (mostly pit bulls) with scars and injuries, and the majority were found to be underfed. They also located a blood-stained fighting area and a stick used to pry dogs apart during fights, as well as treadmills used to condition dogs for fights. The police discovered paperwork that documented the dogfights and performance-enhancing drugs that allowed injured dogs to fight longer and to perform better. Also discovered on the property were mass graves filled with dead dogs that had been used in fighting. Initially, Vick claimed no knowledge of the operation and said that his family members who lived on the property were responsible. When the news of the investigation broke, many people spoke in defense of dogfighting, claiming it wasn't a crime, including other NFL players, such as Clinton Portis, at the time an Atlanta Falcons quarterback.

Five months after the investigation began, Vick and his three associates were indicted by a federal grand jury on two charges. The first was for violating the law which makes it a felony to promote dogfighting for amusement, sport, or financial gain and to transport, sell, own, or train a dog for animal fighting. (The principals were accused of transporting dogs across state lines as well as staging fights with participants from other states at the Bad Newz Kennels.) The second charge was for torture, ill treatment, beating, maiming, mutilation, and killing of animals. Michael Vick was suspended from the NFL.

Vick and his three associates pleaded guilty. They all admitted that dogfighting and illegal gambling had taken place at Bad Newz Kennels. Vick also admitted to knowing about the dogs his associates killed and admitted that he agreed to hanging and drowning six to eight dogs that "underperformed" in 2007. In addition, Vick admitted that he was the financial source of the operation and gambling. The sentencing guidelines for this crime indicate that most first-time offenders would not be incarcerated, but the U.S. attorney, Chuck Rosenberg, who tried the case, said that since the case involved such cruel and heinous treatment of animals the defendants should be incarcerated and the sentence should be harsher than the guidelines recommended. Vick was sentenced to 23 months in prison and three years' supervised probation, during which time he was prohibited from buying, selling, or owning dogs, and was fined $5,000. Vick was also ordered to pay restitution for the dogs that were seized from his property in the amount of $928,073. His associates, Purnell Peace and Quanis Phillips, were sentenced to 18 months in prison and 21 months in prison respectively. Tony Taylor was the first to plead guilty and provide details to the investigation, and he was given a reduced sentence of two months in jail. Michael Vick was released from prison on May 20, 2009, after serving 18 months. He served the remainder of his sentence in his home on house arrest with an ankle electronic monitoring system. Shortly after that, in July of 2009, Vick was reinstated into the NFL and was hired to play for the Philadelphia Eagles. He continued to play in the NFL until February 2017, when he officially announced his retirement.

> After being evaluated, the dogs that were seized from the Bad Newz Kennels were adopted by families, trained as police dogs or service dogs, or were placed in animal sanctuaries. Only one had to be euthanized.

Repeat and Multiple Victimization

Research has shown that victimizations often are not random and seem to be concentrated to affect a small portion of the population (Farrell, Tseloni, & Pease, 2005; Gottfredson, 1984). Farrell and Pease (1993) estimate that 4% of the population suffers 44% of the victimizations. Prior victimization can be an indicator of future victimization (Lauritsen & Davis-Quinet, 1995; Osborn, Ellingworth, Hope, & Trickett, 1996; Osborn & Tseloni, 1998; Pease, 1998). When a person is victimized, they are not taken out of the pool for victimization again, meaning that just because they were already victimized does not mean they cannot be victimized again. Research has shown a relationship between previous victimization and risk for future victimization (Gottfredson, 1984; Hindelang, Gottfredson, & Garafalo, 1978; Ousey, Wilcox, & Brummel, 2008; Tseloni & Pease, 2003). For example, a household can be at risk for a repeat burglary. This tends to happen within six weeks of the first burglary (Polvi et al., 1990). Having already burglarized the house once, the burglars now know more about the location and thus choose to burglarize it again (Hearnden & Magill, 2004). This can be very frustrating and upsetting for victims as they may be trying to cope with their previous victimization only to be victimized again, thus making their recovery process longer and more difficult.

Discussion Questions

1. What do you think would help the family and loved ones of murder victims to cope?
2. Which type of property crime do you think has the most long-term impact on a victim? Why?
3. Do you believe that there is such a thing as a victimless crime? Why or why not?
4. Do you think that the crimes discussed in this chapter are victimless? Explain your answer.

References

American Gaming Association. (2017). Retrieved from www.americangaming.org/

American Psychiatric Association. (2013). *Diagnostic and statistical manual of mental disorders* (5th ed.). Arlington, VA: American Psychiatric Publishing.

American Society for the Prevention of Cruelty to Animals (ASPCA). (2017). *Dog fighting*. Retrieved from www.aspca.org/animal-cruelty/dog-fighting

Ayala, J., & White, J. (2008). *Operation spotlight*. Arlington, TX: Arlington Police Department. Retrieved from www.popcenter.org/library/awards/goldstein/2008/08- 01(F).pdf

Belleville, G., Marchand, A., St-Hilaire, M. H., Martin, M., & Silva, C. (2012). PTSD and depression following armed robbery: Patterns of appearance and impact on absenteeism and use of health care services. *Journal of Traumatic Stress*, *25*(4), 465–468.

Brewin, C. R., Andrews, B., & Valentine, J. D. (2000). Meta-analysis of risk factors for posttraumatic stress disorder in trauma-exposed adults. *Journal of Consulting and Clinical Psychology*, *68*(5), 748–766.

Brown, B. B., & Harris, P. B. (1989). Residential burglary victimization: Reactions to the invasion of a primary territory. *Journal of Environmental Psychology*, 9, 119–132.

Bureau of Justice Statistics. (2017). *Drugs and crime facts*. Retrieved from www.bjs.gov/content/dcf/enforce.cfm

Caballero, M. A., Ramos, L., & Saltijeral, M. T. (2000). Posttraumatic stress dysfunction and other reactions of the victims of house burglary. *Salud Mental*, *23*, 8–17.

Campbell, R. (2014). Intentional fires report. *National Fire Protection Association*. Retrieved from www.nfpa.org/news-and-research/fire-statistics-and-reports/fire- statistics/fire- causes/arson-and-juvenile-firesetting/intentional-fires

Chapkis, W. (2003). Trafficking, migration, and the law: Protecting innocents, punishing Immigrants. *Gender & Society*, *17*(6), 923–937.

Doka, K. J. (Ed.). (1996). *Living with grief after sudden loss*. Washington, DC: Hospice Foundation of America.

Elklit, A. (2002). Acute stress disorder in victims of robbery and victims of assault. *Journal of Interpersonal Violence*, *17*(8), 872–887.

Estes, R. J., & Weiner, N. A. (2002). *The commercial sexual exploitation of children in the U. S. Canada and Mexico: Full Report (of the U.S. National Study)*. University of Pennsylvania School of Social Work Center for the Study of Youth Policy. Retrieved from www.thenightministry.org/070_facts_figures/030_research_links/060_homeless_youth/CommercialSexualExploitationofChildren.pdf

Farrell, G., & Pease, K. (1993). *Once bitten, twice bitten: Repeat victimization and its implications for crime prevention* (Crime Prevention Unit Paper No. 46). London, UK: Home Office.

Farrell, G., Tseloni, A., & Pease, K. (2005). Repeat victimization in the ICVS and the NCVS. *Crime Prevention and Community Safety: An International Journal*, *7*(3), 7–18.

Federal Bureau of Investigation (FBI). (2015). *Crime in the United Sates*. Retrieved from https://ucr.fbi.gov/crime-in-the-u.s/2015/crime-in-the-u.s.-2015

Federal Bureau of Investigation (FBI). (2017). *Offense definitions*. Retrieved from www.ucrdata-tool.gov/offenses.cfm

Federal Emergency Management Agency (FEMA). (1997) *Arson victims: Suggestions for a system response*. Washington, DC. Retrieved from www.iapsonline.com/sites/default/files/Arson%20Victims_0.pdf

Fichera, G. P., Fattori, A., Neri, L., Musti, M., Coggiola, M., & Costa, G. (2014). Post-traumatic stress disorder among bank employee victims of robbery. *Occupational Medicine, 65*(4), 283–289.

Flowers, R. B. (2001). *Runaway kids and teenage prostitution: America's lost, abandoned and sexually exploited children*. Westport, CT: Praeger Publishing.

Folino, J. O., & Abait, P. E. (2009). Pathological gambling and criminality. *Current Opinions in Psychiatry, 22*(5), 477–481.

Fowlkes, M. R. (1990). The social regulation of grief. *Sociological Forum, 5*, 635–652.

Gottfredson, M. R. (1984). *Victims of crime: The dimension of risk* (Home Office Research Study 81). London: Home Office.

Hansen, M., & Elklit, A. (2011). Predictors of acute stress disorder in response to bank robbery. *European Journal of Psychotraumatology, 2*(supp).

Hearnden, I., & Magill, C. (2004). *Decision-making by house burglars: Offender's perspectives* (pp. 1–6). Research, Development, and Statistics Directorate Findings 249, London: Home Office.

Hindelang, M., Gottfredson, M., & Garafalo, J. (1978). *Victims of personal crime*. Cambridge, MA: Ballinger.

The Humane Society of the United States. (2017). *Dog fighting fact sheet*. Retrieved from www.humanesociety.org/issues/dogfighting/facts/dogfighting_fact_shee t.html

Jones, C. A. (2002). Victim perspective of bank robbery trauma and recovery. *Traumatology, 8*(4), 191–204.

Kempadoo, K. (2005). *Trafficking and prostitution reconsidered: New perspectives on migration, sex work, and human rights*. St. Paul: Paradigm Publishers.

Kilpatrick, D. G., & Otto, R. K. (1987). Constitutionally guaranteed participation in criminal proceedings for victims: Potential effects on psychological functioning. *Wayne Law Review, 34*, 7–28.

Klinger, K. (2003, January/February). Prostitution humanism and a woman's choice. *Humanist, 63*(1), 16–21.

Kubler-Ross, E. (1969). *On death and dying*. New York, NY: Palgrave Macmillan.

Kuo, L. (2003). *Prostitution policy: Revolutionizing practice through a gendered perspective*. New York, NY: NYU Press.

Lauritsen, J. L., & Davis-Quinet, K. F. (1995). Repeat victimization among adolescents and young adults. *Journal of Quantitative Criminology, 11*(2), 143–166.

Lauritsen, J. L., & White, N. (2014). *Seasonal patterns in criminal victimization trends. Special Report*. Washington, DC: U.S. Department of Justice, Office of Justice Programs, Bureau of Justice Statistics. NCJ 245959.

Lord, J. H. (1987). *No time for goodbyes*. Berkeley, CA: Pathfinder.

Magee, D. (1983). *What murder leaves behind: The victim's family*. New York: Dodd, Mead.

Maguire, M. (1980). The impact of burglary upon victims. *British Journal of Criminology*, *3*, 261–275.

Mawby, R. I., & Walklate, S. (1997). The impact of burglary: A tale of two cities. *International Review of Victimology*, *4*, 267–295.

Miller, J. (1993). Your life is on the line every night you're on the streets: Victimization and the resistance among prostitutes. *Humanity and Society*, *17*(4), 422–446.

National Crime Information Center (NCIC). (2017). https://archives.fbi.gov/archives/about-us/cjis/ncic/ncic-missing-person-and- unidentified-person-statistics-for-2013

National Fire Protection Association. (2017). Retrieved from www.nfpa.org/

National Insurance Crime Bureau. (2017). Retrieved from www.nicb.org/

Office for Victims of Crime. (2017). Retrieved from www.ovc.gov/

Orth, U. (2009). The effects of legal involvement on crime victims' psychological adjustment. In M. E. Oswald, S. Bieneck, & J. Hupfeld-Heinemann (Eds.), *Social psychology of punishment of crime* (pp. 427–442). Chichester, UK: Wiley- Blackwell.

Osborn, D. R., Ellingworth, D., Hope, T., & Trickett, A. (1996). Are repeatedly victimized households different? *Journal of Quantitative Criminology*, *12*, 223–245.

Osborn, D. R., & Tseloni, A. (1998). The distribution of household property crimes. *Journal of Quantitative Criminology*, *14*(3), 307–330.

Ostrihanska, Z., & Dobrochna, W. (1993). Burglaries as seen by the victims. *International Review of Victimology*, *2*, 217–225.

Ousey, G. C., Wilcox, P., & Brummel, S. (2008). Déjà vu all over again: Investigating temporal continuity of adolescent victimization. *Journal of Quantitative Criminology*, *24*, 307–336.

Parents of Murdered Children. (2017). *Survivors of homicide victims*. Retrieved from www.pomc.com/survivors.html

Parsons, J., & Bergin, T. (2010). The impact of criminal justice involvement on victims' mental health. *Journal of Traumatic Stress*, *23*, 182–188.

Pease, K. (1998). *Repeat victimization: Taking stock* (Crime Detection and Prevention Series No. 90). London: Home Office.

Polvi, N., Looman, T., Humphries, C., & Pease, K. (1990). Repeat break and enter victimization: Time course and crime prevention opportunity. *Journal of Police Science and Administration*, *17*, 8–11.

Powers, T. (2016, January 4). The effects addiction has on family members. *The Jennifer Act*. http://thejenniferact.com/2016/01/04/the-effects-addiction-has-on-family- members/

Pynoos, I. L. S., & Eth, S. (1984). The child as witness to homicide. *Journal of Social Issues 40*(2), 87–108.

Ressler, R. K., Burgess, A. W., & Douglas, J. E. (1988). *Sexual homicide: Patterns and motives*. New York: Free Press.

Sales, E., Baum, M., & Shore, B. (1984). Victim readjustment following assault. *Journal of Social Issues*, *40*, 117–136.

Schlosser, E. (1997, September). A grief like no other. *Atlantic Monthly*, 37–76.

Schur, E. (1965). *Crimes without victims: Deviant behavior and public policy*. Englewood Cliffs, NJ: Prentice-Hall.

Sprang, M. V., McNeil, I. S., & Wright, R., Jr. (1989). Psychological changes after the murder of a significant other. *Social Casework*, *70*(3), 159–164.

Spungen, D. (1998). *Homicide: The hidden victims. A guide for professionals*. Thousand Oaks, CA: Sage.

Stitt, B. G. (1988). Victimless crime: A definitional issue. *Journal of Crime and Justice*, *11*(2), 87–102.

Stitt, B. G., Nichols, M., & Giacopassi, D. (2003). Does the presence of casinos increase crime? An examination of casino and control communities. *Crime and Delinquency*, *49*(2), 253–284.

Tseloni, A., & Pease, K. (2003). Repeat personal victimization: Boost or flags? *British Journal of Criminology*, *43*, 196–212.

Weitzer, R. (2007). The social construction of sex trafficking: Ideology and institutionalization of a moral crusade. *Politics and Society*, *35*(3), 447–475.

Weitzer, R. (2010). The mythology of prostitution: Advocacy research and public policy. *Sexuality Research and Social Policy*, *7*(1), 15–29.

Wohlfarth, T. D., Van den Brink, W., Winkel, F. W., & Ter Smitten, M. (2003). Screening for posttraumatic stress disorder: An evaluation of two self-report scales among crime victims. *Psychological Assessment*, *15*, 101–109.

Yap, M. B. H., & Devilly, G. J. (2004). The role of perceived social support in crime victimization. *Clinical Psychology Review*, *24*(1), 1–14.

Chapter 6

Rape, Sexual Assault, and Kidnapping

Keywords

- Rape
- Sexual assault
- Child sexual abuse
- Secondary survivors
- Campus sexual assault
- Sex trafficking
- Kidnapping
- Stockholm Syndrome

Activity 6.1: What Is the Difference Between Rape and Sexual Assault?

What is the difference between rape and sexual assault?
Why do you think that there are two different categories of offenses?
Do you believe that this is beneficial to victims? Explain.

Defining Rape and Sexual Assault

In 2013 the FBI's Uniform Crime Report, *Crime in the United States*, began collecting data for rape using a new definition. The previous definition read as follows: "the carnal knowledge of a female forcibly and against her will" was changed to "penetration, no matter how slight, of the vagina or anus with any body part or object, or oral penetration by a sex organ of another person, without the consent of the victim" (FBI, 2013). The new definition includes both heterosexual and homosexual rape, as well as attempts and/or the verbal threat of rape. All of these are included in the FBI's rape statistics, but statutory rape and incest are not.

The most current statistics are from the FBI's 2015 report, *Crime in the United States*, which utilizes the new definition of rape. These data show that there were 90,185 rapes. The National Intimate Partner Violence and Sexual Assault Survey (2010) found that 1 in 5 women and 1 in 71 men are raped at some point in their lives (Black et al., 2011). Minors who experience rape are often at greater risk of experiencing it as adults: 35% of women and 28% of men who were raped as adults were also raped as minors (National Intimate Partner and Sexual Violence Survey (NISVS, 2010).

Sexual assault differs from rape as it includes the act, or attempted acts, of any unwanted sexual contact. This can include unwanted grabbing, fondling, kissing, or touching as well as verbal threats, whereas rape includes penetration only (Bureau of Justice Statistics, 2017). It is difficult to know the true extent of sexual assault as it is often grouped together with rape by agencies that compile statistics. However, on average annually, there are 321,500 victims age 12 or older who experience rape and sexual assault (Department of Justice, 2015).

Most rapes and/or sexual assaults occur near or in a victim's home (55%). The next most likely location is an open or public place (15%), then in or near a relative's home (12%), in an enclosed area such as a garage or parking lot (10%), or at school (8%). At the time the crime occurred, most victims were at home (48%), running errands or traveling to work or school (29%), working (12%), attending school (7%), or engaged in some other activity (4%) (RAINN, 2017).

Child Sexual Abuse

Children can also be victims of rape and sexual assault. Childhood sexual abuse includes any sexual activity with a minor, and it does not need to include physical contact between a perpetrator and child. For example, exhibitionism, or exposing oneself to a child, as well as obscene phone calls, speech, text messages, or online and/or digital interaction fall under the category of child sexual abuse.

It is often difficult to know the true extent of child sexual abuse as it often goes unreported. Research estimates that 1 in 4 girls and 1 in 6 boys will experience sexual abuse before the age of 18 (Finkelhor et al., 1990). Annually, 63,000 child sexual abuse cases are substantiated by Child Protective Services and the most common perpetrator is the parent (80%) (U.S. Department of Health and Human Services, 2014). The *National Intimate Partner and Sexual Violence Survey* (NISVS) (2010) reveals that 8.5 million women experienced rape and 1.5 million men were forced to penetrate another before the age of 18. The perpetrators of these offenses are typically family, friends, acquaintances, and/or unrelated people in the lives of the children, such as caregivers, teachers, or coaches.

Impact on Victims as Children

A child who is being victimized sexually may have some warning signs that are physically visible, such as bleeding, bruising, and/or swelling, as well as pain, itching, and/or burning in the genital area. The child may have problems sitting or have frequent and/or reoccurring yeast infections. A child's clothes may be torn or stretched/damaged, and they may have blood in their underwear. A child may exhibit behavioral warning signs if they are being sexually abused. The caretaker of the child may notice a change in the hygiene habits of the child, such as not wanting to bathe or wanting to bathe all the time. The child may have developed inappropriate sexual knowledge or begin exhibiting sexual behaviors. The child may have nightmares, wet the bed, develop phobias and/or fears, and regress to behaviors such as thumb sucking. A sexually abused child can show signs of depression or PTSD, express suicidal thoughts or make suicide attempts, begin self-harming behaviors, engage in substance abuse, and have trouble in school. Running away from home or school is also a strategy that many children employ in order to escape the abuse and/or the abuser. They also may express a dislike of physical contact or touch from others (Merrill et al., 2001).

Impact on Child Sexual Abuse Victims as Adults

Individuals who suffer from child sexual assault often experience mental health problems as adults (Johnson, 2004), and coping is an ongoing process throughout the lifetime (Banyard & Williams, 2007). Individuals who suffered sexual abuse as a child often have many negative emotions as adults, such as rage, fear, guilt, shame, anger, and humiliation, and they may suffer from posttraumatic stress disorder (PTSD; Negrao II, Bonanno, Noll, Putnam, & Trickett, 2005). One way adults attempt to cope with childhood sexual assault is to try to escape their memories, for example through substance abuse. Some victims of child sexual abuse also suffer from dissociative amnesia, in which they have trouble remembering and recalling the abuse and/or parts of it (Dalenberg, 2006; Herman, 1998). This is a coping mechanism to help individuals deal with very traumatic events. It can involve emotional numbness, depersonalization of experiences or events, and/or feelings of being "out-of-body" (Gleavest al., 2001). Individuals who experience dissociative amnesia still may recall elements of the victimization through flashbacks and nightmares (van der Kolk & Fisler, 1995). Coping with child sexual abuse has been correlated to the adult's outlook on life, and those who have hope, optimism, and resilience are more likely to have positive outcomes in therapy, enjoy physical health, and achieve overall psychological adjustment (Snyder, 2002).

Media Byte 6.1: Check Out the Darkness to Light Website

Check out the website for Darkness to Light, an organization dedicated to preventing child sexual abuse: www.d2l.org/get-help/

Do you think that this website is successful in raising awareness about these issues?

Do you think that this site helps with prevention? Why or why not?

What kind of educational opportunities are offered on this website?

Case study 6.1: Child Sexual Abuse and the Catholic Church

The Catholic Church has faced numerous allegations and investigations of child sexual abuse committed by Catholic priests, nuns, and other members of the Roman Catholic Church. Many of these investigations have resulted in trials and convictions. These cases include anal and oral penetration, pornography, and fondling and touching. John Jay College of Criminal Justice (2004) conducted extensive research on cases of sexual abuse committed against children by Catholic priests from 1950 to 2002. The research revealed that the number of priests who had allegations against them from 1950 to 2002 was 4,392 out of a total of 109,694 priests who served during that time period. Most priests who abused children were assigned to be pastor or associate pastor of a church, positions that gave them a wide range of access to children. The ages of the priests ranged from mid-20s to 90 at the time they first committed the crime, with the majority (40%) being between the ages of 30 and 39. Most priests had one victim (56%). However, 3.5% of priests were responsible for the sexual abuse of 26% of children who had come forward to report the abuse by 2002. Most of the victims sexually abused by priests were male.

Many of the cases of abuse span several decades and were brought forward years after the abuse occurred. Most victims did not disclose their victimization at the time, and the signs of the abuse were not detected by friends or family. The silence of the victims lasted from the 1950s and continued through the 1990s, when victims began to come forward, and was a factor in why the abuse continued. Cases have also been brought against members of the church who did not report sex abuse allegations to law enforcement. Instead of removing accused priests from their positions, the Catholic Church moved them to other parishes where the abuse often continued against other children. The Holy See, the governing body of the Catholic Church, has been reviewing child sexual abuse allegations concerning 3,000 priests and spanning the past 50 years. As of this writing, they have settled with more than 500 victims and their families, paying out more than $740 million in monetary damages, an amount so vast that the church has had to sell property and take out loans to be able to pay the victims.

Read the full John Jay report here: www.usccb.org/issues-and-action/child-and-youth-protection/upload/The-Nature-and-Scope-of-Sexual-Abuse-of-Minors-by-Catholic-Priests-and-Deacons-in-the-United-States-1950–2002.pdf

Activity 6.2: Catholic Church Settles With Victims

Read the following article and watch the corresponding video, *L.A. Archdiocese Settles Final Priest Abuse Case for $13 Million*: www.latimes.com/local/la-me-archdiocese-settlement-20140219-story.html

Answer the following questions:

1. How much money did each victim receive in a settlement from the Los Angeles Archdiocese?
2. What is your opinion about this case?
3. Do you think that the money helped the victims to cope and recover from their victimization? Why or why not?

Disclosure Among Victims

Disclosing that you have been a victim of rape or sexual assault can be very hard for individuals, whether a child or adult. Only about 16% of rapes are reported to law enforcement (Kilpatrick et al., 2007), and victims rarely use services that are available to assist them. There are many reasons that a victim may not report these crimes or seek out help, such as fear, embarrassment, shame, and lack of awareness or information about available services (Fisher et al., 2000; Fisher et al., 2003). Victims may feel that sex activity is a private matter, and whether it is consensual or not, they may feel that it is not something to be discussed with strangers or outsiders. Child victims may be unaware that what is occurring is wrong or abusive. They also may be afraid to tell due to what they believe would happen as a result. They may fear reprisal from their abuser or, if it is a family member, they may be afraid of what disclosing would do the family and/or their home life.

Cost to and Impact on Victims

Rape and sexual assault has a devastating physical, psychological, and monetary impact on victims, as victims are more likely to suffer from physical injuries and mental health issues. Victims often experience depression, posttraumatic stress disorder, and anxiety, and may become suicidal (Black et al., 2011). As a result, each rape costs $151,423 on average, and each year, rape (excluding the costs of child sexual abuse) costs the United States $127 billion, which is more than other crime (Delisi et al., 2010). Sexual assault victims often have reduced income. Half of victims who experienced sexual violence had to leave their jobs, either quitting or being forced to leave, due to the severity of the reactions they had to their victimization (Ellis, Atkeson & Calhoun, 1981). Individuals who suffered sexual abuse as children often enter adulthood with a lower level of education and lesser earnings (MacMillan, 2000), as well as poorer overall job performance (Anda et al., 2004), with an estimate total lifetime income loss of $241,600 (MacMillan, 2000). Violence and abuse constitutes 37.5% of health care costs, or about $750 billion annually (Dolezal, McCollum, & Callahan, 2009). For women who were sexually abused as children, their health care cost is 16% higher than those not abused as children (National Coalition to Prevent Child Abuse and Exploitation, 2012).

Females who are raped may become pregnant as a result. Research has shown that 5% of women who are within the age of reproduction (12–45)—an estimated 32,101 women—become pregnant from rape each year. Of these women, 32.4% did not discover that they were pregnant until after entering the second trimester, 50% had an abortion, and 32.2% kept the child; 11.8% spontaneously abort and 5.9% put the child up for adoption (Holmes, Resnick, Kilpatrick, & Best, 1996).

Case Study 6.2: Bill Cosby Sexual Assault Case

Bill Cosby, popular comedian and star of the 1980s sitcom *The Cosby Show*, was charged with three felony counts of aggravated indecent assault for allegedly drugging and subsequently sexually assaulting Andrea Constand in his home in 2004. A mistrial was declared in June 2017, after the jury deliberated for 52 hours without a verdict. The prosecution said that they plan to retry the case. The lack of physical evidence in the case was cited as an issue. Cosby had testified to giving pills to Constand, but asserted that the pills were over-the-counter Benadryl. Cosby also admitted to having sexual contact with Constand, but contended that it was consensual. Constand said that she would never have consented to sexual contact, as she is gay. Sixty women have publicly accused Cosby of rape, sexual assault, and sexual harassment occurring in the 1960s through the 2000s. The statute of limitations for most of these cases has expired, which is why charges were not brought in many cases. The prosecution for the Constand case wanted to have other women who accused Cosby testify in the Constand trial to establish a pattern of Cosby's abuse against women, but Judge Steven T. O'Neill ruled against this, and only one other woman was allowed to testify.

Cosby was tried in Norristown, Montgomery County, Pennsylvania, which is outside Philadelphia. However, the jury was selected from Pittsburgh, about 300 miles west of Norristown, due to the large amount of publicity the case had received. The jury was sequestered after testimony, but a mistrial was declared. The prosecution plans to retry Cosby, but will still face the challenges of finding jurors unfamiliar with Cosby or the case.

Media Byte 6.2: Releasing Names of Jurors in the Cosby Trial

Read the following article and watch the corresponding video:

http://abcnews.go.com/Entertainment/jurors-names-bill-cosby-trial-released/story?id=48137224

Do you think that the names of the jurors in this case should be released? Why or why not?

Do you think that the names of the jurors should be released in all cases? Explain.

Campus Sexual Assault

Emerging research indicates male sexual assault on college campuses is a cause for concern: 1 in 5 women and 1 in 16 men are sexually assaulted while in college (Krebs et al., 2007). Women ages 18–24 have higher rates of sexual victimization than any other age group, and the victimization often is not reported to police (Sinozich & Langton, 2014). The Bureau of Justice Statistics (2015) recently found that male college students were 78% more likely to be sexually assaulted than non-students. Similarly, findings from a recent National Crime and Victimization Survey (NCVS) (Department of Justice, 2014), covering the timespan from 1995 to 2013, indicated that 17% of college sexual victimizations were perpetrated against men.

Sexual assaults on college campuses often involve similar circumstances. Victims usually know their assailants (Fisher et al., 1999; Sinozich & Langton, 2014) and there is often a connection between victim alcohol consumption or ingestion of drugs and sexual assault (Combs-Lane & Smith, 2002; Siegel & Williams, 2003). Not only is a drunk individual more easily victimized, but the perpetrators may use drugs to incapacitate victims and then commit a sexual victimization while the victim is unconscious and/or unable to give consent (Krebs, Linquist, Warner, Martin, Fisher & Martin, 2007).

College students who experience sexual assault are more likely to confide in a friend (Fisher et al., 2003) and not report incidents to the police (Sloan, Fisher & Cullen, 1997; Fisher, Daigle, Cullen, & Tuner, 2003; Kilpatrick, Resnick, Ruggiero, Conoscenti, & McCauley, 2007; Sinozich & Langton, 2014). One reason is that many victimized college students may not identify their unwanted sexual experiences as sexual victimization (Bondurant, 2001; Fisher, Daigle, Cullen & Tuner, 2003). Individuals sexually victimized once in college often experience reoccurring victimizations (Fisher, Daigle, & Cullen, 2010; Gidycz, Coble, Latham, & Layman, 1995).

Impact on Victims

Sexual victimization of a college student can impact their life in many ways. A student who has been victimized may no longer feel safe on campus, in public areas, or even where they live (Culbertson, Vik, & Kooiman, 2001). As a result, victims are at an increased risk of withdrawing from the institution (Harned, 2001). Students who have experienced sexual victimization are also more likely to suffer from mental health issues. This can include posttraumatic stress disorder, depression, and anxiety, as well as thoughts of harming themselves and suicide attempts or completion (Aosved, Long, & Voller, 2011; Bryan, McNaughten-Cassill, Osman & Hernandez, 2013). Victims may also try to self-medicate with alcohol (Littleton et al., 2013), illegal drugs (Brener et al., 1999), and/or prescription drug abuse (McCauley et al., 2011).

Secondary Victims of Sexual Assault

Sexual assault affects not only the victim but also those close to the victim, such as spouses/romantic partners, family, and friends, who are often referred to as secondary victims or secondary survivors. Looking at the number of individuals who were victimized, we can assume that there is at least one person (often more) who loves and cares for the victim. When victimization occurs, it sends out a ripple effect, affecting those who care about the victim. When a sexual assault occurs, it is as if there is a doubling (or tripling or quadrupling) of victims for each sexual assault in terms of suffering and coping as the primary victims have people who care about them and suffer right alongside them.

A common initial response of anger by romantic partners, usually male partners, is that they want to harm the perpetrator (Holstrom and Burgess, 1979). Emotional and sexual intimacy with couples who have had one partner experience sexual assault can be an issue, with problems establishing and maintaining sexual relationships (Bacon and Lein, 1996; Finkelhor, Hotaling, Lewis and Smith, 1989; Gill and Tutty, 1999; Jacob and Veach, 2005; Nelson and Wampler, 2002). Partners of sexual assault victims often report that they have experienced significant stress and anxiety themselves as a result of their partner's victimization (Nelson and Wampler, 2002), unhappiness and discontent in general, as well feelings of guilt and shame (Chauncy, 1994). If a couple has children, sexual victimization can influence parenting as well. It can lead to disagreements about parenting, poor communication patterns and a decrease in the cohesion of the family in general (Nelson and Wampler, 2002). The degree to which the relationship is influenced is contingent upon many factors, such as the type and extent of sexual victimization that occurred, as well the support that the partner provided for the victim after the incident and/or the disclosure.

In addition to partners of sexual assault victims, parents are affected. The initial reactions of parents are similar to that of partners as the parents may wish to harm the person who abused their child. But one parent may also have displaced anger at a family member, blaming them for the child's victimization and believing they played a role in the child's harm even if the other parent was not the offender. The parents also may blame themselves, especially if a family member or friend was the offender (Clevenger, 2016). Parents also report feeling helpless, vulnerable, and panic-stricken. The sexual abuse of a child also can exacerbate marital problems of the parents (Burgess et al., 1990), especially when women take on the main role of helping the child to cope with their victimization. It can cause resentment and anger in one partner (Clevenger, 2016). The parent-child relationship as well may become strained (Burgess, Hartman & McCormack, 1987; Regehr, 1990).

The fact that mothers suffer more than fathers when a child has been sexually victimized has been attributed to child-rearing roles. Mothers represented the main support figure to the child while the child is attempting to deal with the recovery from their victimization (Burge, 1983; Clevenger, 2016). Mothers, in particular, often feel that they have failed in their role as caretaker or protector if their child experiences sexual violence (Clevenger, 2016).

Friends are often a main source of support for victims and experience suffering along with the victim. Adolescents who are sexually assaulted will confide in and look to friends for support.. They also typically disclose to friends before anyone else as they feel closer to and trust their friends. Adults who have been victimized also turn to their friends for support. There is not much research detailing the experience of friends of victims, but one study (Ahrens & Campbell, 2000) surveyed 60 friends of adult female rape victims and found that the most common emotions that friends experience was anger at the perpetrator and a desire to get even, as well as shock that this happened to their friend. Friends of the victim also experienced nightmares, were fearful of what others would think about the victimization of their friend, and felt isolated in coping with the sexual violence committed against their friend.

Media Byte 6.3: Mothers of Sexually Abused Children

Check out the Mothers of Sexually Abused Children (MOSAC) website: www. mosac.net/

Do you think that this site is helpful to mothers of sexual assault victims?

What types of services and information does this website provide?

What do you think would be the most helpful?

Sex Trafficking

Sex trafficking occurs when a person is made to perform a sexual act as a result of the use of force or threat of force and/or coercion by another. It can occur with juveniles or adults. Sex trafficking can be referred to as prostitution as well. However, under U.S. federal law any individual under the age of 18 who is involved in commercial sex against their will is considered a victim of sex trafficking (Polaris Project, 2017). The United States is the second largest destination for sex trafficked women and children, after Germany (Mizus, Moody, Privado & Douglas, 2003). It is hard to know the exact numbers of those who are trafficked each year, but the U.S. government estimates that 600,000–800,000 people are trafficked annually, of which 80% are female and 50% are minors. Of this total number (600,000–800,000), 70% are sex trafficked, while others are trafficked for other reasons (U.S. Department of State, 2016).

An individual becomes involved in sex trafficking in various ways. Sex trafficking can involve debt bondage, in which an individual is forced to perform sexual acts for money in order to pay off an illegal debt that was incurred from transportation or the sale of that individual or a family member into modern-day forms of slavery. This is often involves immigrants or children who are forced to work in commercial sex until the debt is paid off. However, often included in this debt are the living expenses the victim is purported to accrue each year, making the debt ever-increasing and near impossible to pay off. Vulnerable populations are frequently targeted by traffickers, such as runaway youth, homeless victims of domestic and/or sexual violence, people suffering various forms of social discrimination, or those with addiction problems.

Individuals also become victims of sex trafficking through a romantic relationship with someone who forces, coerces, and/or manipulates them into commercial sex. Individuals also may enter sex trafficking when duped by a perpetrator who offers a legitimate job such as modeling, acting, or dancing, but instead forces or coerces the victim into the commercial sex industry (Polaris Project, 2017).

Sex trafficking can occur in different locations. Victims of sex trafficking can be forced to work the streets or truck stops. They also may work in fake massage businesses or operate out of a strip club. There may be brothels where the victims live permanently or temporarily and the paying customers come to them, such as a house, apartment, or motel room. The Internet has made it very easy for traffickers to market sex online. This is often done with online ads, escort services, or by using the online marketplaces Craigslist or Backpage.com. Although an investigation conducted by a Senate subcommittee that lasted over 21 months revealed that the "adult" section on Backpage.com was knowingly facilitating child and adult sex trafficking and the adult section shut down, there is arguably still sex trafficking of both adults and juveniles occurring on the site under the section "dating." There are posts that solicit commercial sex by saying things like "blow jobs and hand jobs," "Take my virginity," and "Summer Special," with sexually explicit and suggestive photos and contact information. In an effort to curb sex trafficking, before entering Backpage's dating section, users must agree that they understand and the site is not to be used for sex trafficking.

Activity 6.3: Stopping Sex Trafficking in Hotels

Read the following article: http://time.com/3525640/sex-trafficking-victim-prostitution-hotel/

Then answer the following questions:

1. What are some ways that sex trafficking can be identified at check-in?
2. Explain how housekeeping can help identify possible incidents of sex trafficking.
3. What are some signs that you as a traveler or guest at a hotel can look for to identify sex trafficking?

Media Byte 6.4: Protecting Children From Sex Trafficking in the Travel and Tourism Industry

Check out the website for the Code: www.thecode.org/
> What is the Code?
> What are some steps that are being taken to protect children?
> Do you think that this works to prevent victimization?

Impact on Victims

Victims of sex trafficking suffer physically and psychologically. Physically they may suffer injuries such as broken bones, bruises, burns, and brain trauma. This can be from transport or as a result of violence that the traffickers use to control, dominate, or punish. They may also suffer from starvation and infectious diseases. Victims experience rape and sexual assault and as a result, they may suffer physical injury to their genitals and the rest of the body, gynecological issues, and STDs, including AIDS. They may also experience pregnancy, miscarriages, and/or forced abortions (World Health Organization, 2017).

The psychological harm suffered by victims of sex trafficking can include posttraumatic stress disorder (PTSD), depression, anxiety, suicidal thoughts/attempts, Stockholm syndrome (see section below on this topic), and substance abuse (World Health Organization, 2017).

Media Byte 6.5: FBI's Kidnapped and Missing Persons

Check out the website for the FBI's Kidnapped and Missing Persons:
www.fbi.gov/wanted/kidnap

Do you think that this website and the information contained on it are successful in finding these individuals? Why or why not?

Do you think that there is a better strategy to find missing persons? Explain.

Kidnapping

Kidnapping is the unlawful seizure or carrying away of an individual by force or fraud, or seizing and detaining a person against their will with the intention to carry away that person at a later date. The laws regarding kidnapping differ by jurisdiction, and most state and federal laws that define the offense do so broadly. This crime is not included in the Uniform Crime Report (UCR) or National Crime Victimization Survey (NCVS). However, the FBI did create the National Crime Information Center (NCIC) and the Missing Person File in 1975 to assist with finding kidnapped or missing persons. The file remains open until the person is found or the record cancelled by the agency. As of January 1, 2014 (the most recent data available), there were 84,136 active missing persons (adults and children) entries and 1,810,409 total files for missing persons (NCIC, 2017). The most recent year available for the NCIC is 2013, and that year there were 454,214 reported missing persons, of which 440,625 were juveniles and 4,589 were adults. Close to 90% of children who are classified as "missing" often have gotten lost or run away, misinterpreted directions, or did not clearly communicate their plans to their caregivers. In terms of kidnapped children,

99.8 % who go missing do come home. A family member in a custody battle kidnaps 9% of children. A majority of kidnapped children are taken by an acquaintance (57%) or a family member (26%), and 3% of children are kidnapped by non-family-members, typically during the commission of another crime such as sexual assault, but this is still usually someone that the child knows. Only about 100 children each year, or a fraction of 1%, are kidnapped by a stranger in the stereotypical kidnapping scenario that is reported in the news and the topic of many "stranger danger" kidnapping prevention talks. About half of these 100 children are found and come home (NCIC, 2017).

Case Study 6.3: Jaycee Dugard

On June 10, 1991, Jaycee Dugard was abducted as she walked alone to the school bus stop. She was 11 years old. Her abductors were Phillip and Nancy Garrido. At the time Phillip Garrido, a sex offender who was convicted in 1976 for the rape and kidnapping of another young girl, Katie Calloway, was on parole. A pinecone was the last thing Jaycee held onto before being tased and dragged into the car. Jaycee was taken to the Garridos' residence in Antioch, California, where she was held against her will for 18 years. The Garridos kept her locked up initially in what they referred to as "the studio," a structure that was separate from the house. Jaycee ate and drank only what Philip and Nancy provided. There was no bathroom in the studio, so Jaycee had to use a bucket and relied upon Philip or Nancy to empty it for her. Philip took Jaycee on what he called "runs," sessions in which he drugged and brutally raped her for hours. He forced her to wear sexy outfits and positioned her in many different ways that he had seen in pornography. Jaycee said that she was able to endure these awful experiences by going "somewhere else" in her mind and making up stories to distract herself from what was actually going on.

Philip threatened Jaycee and told her that he would hurt her and her mom if she misbehaved and/or tried to leave. Philip never used a condom when raping Jaycee, and inevitably Jaycee became pregnant. She gave birth to her first daughter on August 18, 1994, when she was 14, and her second daughter on November 12, 1997, when she was 17.

After the birth of her second child, Philip and Nancy let Jaycee leave the studio and go into the backyard after Philip built a fence. Nancy was jealous of the children that Jaycee had, and made the children call her "mom" and told them that Jaycee was their sister. Jaycee and her daughters now lived in a tent in the Garridos' backyard. As the girls got older, they did not go to school, because Philip thought that there were too many bad influences in school, such as drugs. Jaycee worked to teach her children at home. Jaycee and the girls did get to go out in public with Nancy and Philip on some occasions. However, it was not until Garrido was on the University of California, Berkeley campus seeking an event permit that a police officer and special events manager grew suspicious. The officer did a background check on Garrido and found he was a sex offender. She contacted his parole officer expressing concern over Garrido and his daughters and found that the parole officer too was concerned as Garrido had no daughters. Philip was requested to meet with his parole officer. He brought Nancy, Jaycee, and the two girls in for the meeting. He admitted to kidnapping Jaycee and told the authorities that the girls were his. Jaycee was then able to call her mom and Philip and Nancy were arrested.

They both pleaded guilty to kidnapping and rape. Philip received a sentence of 431 years to life and Nancy was sentenced to 36 years to life. At their sentencing, Jaycee's mom read a victim impact statement as Jaycee did not want to attend. Because Philip was a registered sex offender on parole, during the 18 years of Jaycee's captivity, parole officers visited the Garrido residence over 60 times! They never reported anything suspicious. The state of California granted Jaycee a $20 million settlement due to the mistakes made by the officers. Jaycee used this money to create the JAYC Foundation to help individuals and their families who have experienced familial or non-familial abduction.

Media Byte 6.6: Interview with Jaycee Dugard

This is a clip from a 2011 interview conducted with Jaycee Dugard by Diane Sawyer. http://abcnews.go.com/US/jaycee_dugard/jaycee-dugard-interview-diane-sawyer-future-surviving-philip/story?id=14040269

After reading the case study and watching the video clip, what are your thoughts about this interview and Jaycee's perspective?

Activity 6.4: The JAYC Foundation

For this assignment, explore the JAYC Foundation website at http://thejaycfoundation.org/ and answer the questions below.

1. Describe the reunification services.
2. What do the LEO workshops do?
3. What happens in the school-based workshops?
4. Which of the programs offered by the foundation do you think is the most likely to effect change and why?
5. What is your reaction to Jaycee Dugard using her money to help others?
6. Do you think this foundation helps prevent victimization? Why or why not?

Stockholm Syndrome

The term *Stockholm syndrome* originated in 1973. Two men entered a bank in Stockholm, Sweden, to rob it. The robbers kept people as hostages at gunpoint, some strapped with explosives, locked in the bank vault for six days. When police tried to rescue the hostages, the hostages fought the police, defending their captors. When the hostages were freed, they set up a fund to assist in paying for their captors' legal defense. After this incident, this phenomenon, which has been seen and recognized before in other studies of prisoner and abusive situations, was given the official name

Stockholm syndrome. Stockholm syndrome occurs when people come to identify with and even care for their captors in a desperate, usually unconscious act of self-preservation. This happens in psychologically traumatic events, often in individuals who are hostages or who have been kidnapped. It has also been seen in battered spouse cases, abused children, prisoners of war, concentration camp prisoners, prostitutes with their pimps, hijack victims, and in members of destructive cults. The effect upon the individual may not end when the crisis ends. In the classic cases, victims continue to defend and care about their captors even after they escape.

In order for Stockholm syndrome to occur, there must be an uneven power relationship between the captor and the captive, who may be suffering abuse. There must be a threat of injury or death at the hands of the captor as well as a self-preservation instinct on the part of the victim. There must also be a form of isolation, whether it is physical or emotional/psychological isolation. Victims of crimes in which Stockholm syndrome occurs do not consciously chose to feel supportive of their captor or abuser; it is a coping strategy that the mind employs to get through traumatic situations. Victims often develop positive feelings toward their abusers or captors and may begin to identify with the cause of their captors and support their actions. A victim may begin to have negative feelings toward his or her abuser or captor, but may still resist release or detachment (De Fabrique et al., 2007).

Discussion Questions

1. Do you think it is helpful to have two definitions for sexual crime, sexual assault and rape? Why or why not?
2. What do you think is the hardest part of coping with sexual victimization? Please explain.
3. Do you think that secondary victims of sexual assault should have more involvement in the criminal justice system process? Why or why not?
4. What is your opinion of Stockholm syndrome?

References

Ahrens, C. E., & Campbell, R. (2000). Assisting rape victims as they recover from rape: The impact on friends. *Journal of Interpersonal Violence*, *15*(9), 959–986.

Anda, R. F., Fleisher, V. I., Felitti, V. J., Edwards, V. J., Whitfield, C. L., Dube, S. R., & Williamson, D. F. (2004). Childhood abuse, household dysfunction, and indicators of impaired worker performance in adulthood. *The Permanente Journal*, *8*(1), 30–38. Retrieved from http://xnet.kp.org/permanentejournal/winter04/childhood.pdf

Aosved, A. C., Long, P. J., & Voller, E. K. (2011). Sexual revictimization and adjustment in college men. *Psychology of Men & Masculinity*, *12*(3), 285–296.

Bacon, B., & Lein, L. (1996). Living with a female sexual abuse survivor: Male partner's perspectives. *Journal of Child Sexual Abuse*, *5*, 1–16.

Banyard, V. L., & Williams, L. M. (2007). Women's voices on recovery: A multimethod study of the complexity of recovery from child sexual abuse. *Child Abuse & Neglect*, *31*, 275–290.

Black, M. C., Basile, K. C., Breiding, M. J., Smith, S. G., Walters, M. L., Merrick, M. T., & Stevens, M. R. (2011). *The National Intimate Partner and Sexual Violence Survey: 2010 summary report*. Retrieved from the Centers for Disease Control and Prevention, National Center for Injury Prevention and Control: www.cdc.gov/ViolencePrevention/pdf/NISVS_Report2010-a.pdf

Bondurant, B. (2001). University women's acknowledgment of rape: Individual, situational and social factors. *Violence Against Women*, *7*, 294–314.

Brener, N. D., McMahon, P. M., Warren, C. W., & Douglas, K. A. (1999). Forced sexual intercourse and associate health-risk behavior among female college students in the United States. *Journal of Consulting and Clinical Psychology*, *67*(2), 252–259.

Bryan, C. J., McNaughten-Cassill, M., Osman, A., & Hernandez, A.M. (2013). The associations of physical and sexual assault with suicide risk in nonclinical military and undergraduate samples. *Suicide and Life-threatening behavior*, *43*(2), 223–243.

Bureau of Justice Statistics. (2015). *Rape and sexual assault*. Retrieved from www.bjs.gov/index.cfm?ty=tp&tid=317

Bureau of Justice Statistics. (2017). *Rape and sexual assault definitions*. Retrieved from www.bjs.gov/index.cfm?ty=tp&tid=317

Burge, S. K. (1983). *Rape: Individual and family reactions*. In C. R. Figley & H. I. McCubbin (Eds.), *Stress and the family: Coping with catastrophe* (Vol. 2, pp. 103–119). New York: Bruner/Mazel.

Burgess, A., Hartman, C., Kelley, S., Grant, C., & Gray, E. (1990). Parental response to child sexual abuse trials involving day care settings. *Journal of Traumatic Stress*, *3*, 395–405.

Burgess, A., Hartman, C., & McCormack, A. (1987). Abused to abuser: Antecedents of social deviant behaviors. *American Journal of Psychiatry*, *144*, 1431–1436.

Chauncy, S. (1994). Emotional concerns and treatment of male partners of female sexual abuse survivors. *Social work*, *39*, 669–676.

Clevenger, S. L. (2016). Mothers of sexual assault victims; How women 'do mother' after their child has been sexually assaulted. *Feminist Criminology*, *11*(3), 227–252. doi:10.1177/1557085115586024.

Combs-Lane, A. M., & Smith, D. W. (2002). Risk of sexual victimization in college women: The role of behavioral intentions and risk-taking behaviors. *Journal of Interpersonal Violence*, *17*(2), 165–183. doi:10.1177/0886260502017002004.

Culbertson, K. A., Vik, P. W., & Kooiman, B. J. (2001). The impact of sexual assault, sexual assault perpetrator type, and location of sexual assault on ratings of perceived safety. *Violence Against Women*, *7*(8), 858–875.

Dalenberg, C. (2006). Recovered memory and the Daubert criteria: Recovered memory as professionally tested, peer reviewed, and accepted in the relevant scientific community. *Trauma, Violence, & Abuse*, *7*(4), 274–310.

De Fabrique, N., Romano, M. A., Vecchi, G. M., & Van Hasselt, V. (2007). Understanding Stockholm syndrome. *FBI Law Enforcement Bulletin*, *76*(7), 10–15.

Delisi, M., Kosloski, A., Sween, M., Hachmeister, E., Moore, M., & Drury, A. (2010). Murder by numbers: Monetary costs imposed by a sample of homicide offenders. *The Journal of Forensic Psychiatry & Psychology*, *21*, 501–513. doi:10.1080/14789940903564388

Department of Justice, Office of Justice Programs, Bureau of Justice Statistics, National Crime Victimization Survey, 2010–2014. (2015). Retrieved from www.bjs.gov/index.cfm?ty=dcdetail&iid=245

Dolezal, T., McCollum, D., & Callahan, M. (2009). Hidden costs in health care: The economic impact of violence and abuse. *Academy on Violence & Abuse*. Retrieved from www.ccasa.org/wp-content/uploads/2014/01/economic-cost-of-vaw.pdf

Ellis, E. M., Atkeson, B. M., & Calhoun, K. S. (1981). An assessment of long-term reaction to rape. *Journal of Abnormal Psychology*, *90*, 263–266.

Federal Bureau of Investigation. (2013). *Crime in the United States. Rape*. Retrieved from https://ucr.fbi.gov/crime-in-the-u.s/2013/crime-in-the-u.s.-2013/violent- crime/rape

Finkelhor, D., Hotaling, G. T., Lewis, I. A., & Smith, C. (1990, December). Sexual abuse and its relationship to later sexual satisfaction, marital status, religion, and attitudes. *Journal of Interpersonal Violence*, *4*(4), 379–399. http://dx.doi.org/10.1177/088626089004004001

Fisher, B., Cullen, F., & Turner, M. (2000). *The sexual victimization of college women* (NCJ 182369). Retrieved from the National Criminal Justice Reference Service: www.ncjrs.gov/pdffiles1/nij/182369.pdf

Fisher, B. S., Cullen, F. T., & Turner, M. G. (1999). *Extent and nature of the sexual victimization of college women: A national-level analysis* (Final report and instrument). Retrieved from www.ncjrs.gov/pdffiles1/nij/grants/179977.pdf

Fisher, B. S., Daigle, L. E., & Cullen, F. T. (2010). *Unsafe in the Ivory Tower: The sexual victimization of college women*. Thousand Oaks, CA: Sage.

Fisher, B. S., Daigle, L. E., Cullen, F. T., & Tuner, M. G. (2003). Acknowledging sexual victimization as rape: Results from a national-level study of college women. *Criminal Justice and Behavior*, *30*, 6–38.

Gidycz, C. A., Hanson, K., & Layman, J. L. (1995). A prospective analysis of the relationships among sexual assault experiences: An extension of previous findings. *Psychology of Women Quarterly*, *19*, 5–29.

Gill, M., & Tutty, L. (1999). Male survivors of childhood sexual abuse: A qualitative study and issues of clinical consideration. *Journal of Child Sexual Abuse*, *7*, 19–33.

Gleaves, D. H., May, M. C., & Cardena, E. (2001). An examination of the diagnostic validity of dissociative identity disorder. *Clinical Psychology Review*, *21*, 577–608.

Harned, M. S. (2001). Abused women or abused men? An examination of the context and outcomes of dating violence. *Violence and Victims, 16* (3), 269–285.

Herman, J. L. (1998). *Trauma and recovery*. London: Pandora.

Holmes, M.N., Resnick, H. S., Kilpatrick, D. G., & Best, C. L. (1996). Rape-related pregnancy: estimates and descriptive characteristics from a national sample of women. *American Journal of Obstetrics and Gynecology, 175* (2), 320–4.

Jacob, C., & Veach, P. (2005). Intrapersonal and familial effects of child sexual abuse on female partners of male survivors. *Journal of Counseling Psychology, 52*, 284–97.

John Jay College of Criminal Justice. (2004). *The Nature and scope of sexual abuse of minors by Catholic priests and deacons in the United States 1950–2002*. Washington, DC: The United States Conference of Catholic Bishops. Retrieved from www.usccb.org/issues-and-action/child-and-youth-protection/upload/The-Nature-and-Scope-of-Sexual-Abuse-of-Minors-by-Catholic-Priests-and-Deacons-in-the-United-States-1950–2002.pdf

Johnson, C. F. (2004). Child sexual abuse. *The Lancet, 364*, 462–470.

Kilpatrick, D. G., Resnick, H. S., Ruggiero, K. J., Conoscenti, L. M., & McCauley, J. (2007, July). Drug-facilitated, incapacitated, and forcible rape: A national study. Retrieved from www.ncjrs.gov/pdffiles1/nij/grants/219181.pdf

Krebs, C. P., Lindquist, C., Warner, T., Fisher, B., & Martin, S. (2007). *The campus sexual assault (CSA) study: Final report*. Retrieved from the National Criminal Justice Reference Service: www.ncjrs.gov/pdffiles1/nij/grants/221153.pdf

Littleton, H. L., Grills-Taquechel, A. E., Buck, K. S., Rosman, L., & Dodd, J. C. (2013). Health risk behavior and sexual assault among ethnically diverse women. *Psychology of Women Quarterly, 37*(1), 7–21.

MacMillan, R. (2000). Adolescent victimization and income deficits in adulthood: Rethinking the costs of criminal violence from a life-course perspective, *Criminology, 38*, 553–588. doi:10.1111/j.1745–9125.2000.tb00899.x

McCauley, J. L., Amstadter, A. B., MacDonald, A., Danielson, C. K., Ruggiero, K. J., Resnick, H. S., & Kilpatrick, D. G. (2011). Non-medical use of prescription drugs in a national sample of college women. *Addictive Behaviors, 36*(7), 690–695.

Merrill, L. L., Thomsen, C. J., Sinclair, B. B., Gold, S. R., & Milner, J. S. (2001). Predicting the impact of child sexual abuse on women: The role of abuse severity, parental support, and coping strategies. *Journal of Consulting and Clinical Psychology, 69*(6), 992–1006.

Mizus, M., Moody, M., Privado, C., & Douglas, C. A. (2003). Germany, U.S. receive most sex-trafficked women. *Off Our Backs, 33*(7), 4.

National Crime Information Center (NCIC). (2017). *Missing persons and unidentified persons*. Retrieved from https://archives.fbi.gov/archives/about-us/cjis/ncic/ncic-missing-person-and-unidentified-person-statistics-for-2013

National Coalition to Prevent Child Sexual Abuse and Exploitation. (2012). *National plan to prevent the sexual abuse and exploitation of children*. Retrieved from www.preventtogether.org/Resources/Documents/NationalPlan2012FINAL.pdf

National Intimate Partner and Sexual Violence Survey (NISVS). (2010). *NISVS: An overview of 2010 summary report findings*. Centers for Disease Control, National Center for Injury Prevention and Control, Division of Violence Prevention. Retrieved from http://healthandwelfare.idaho.gov/Portals/0/Health/Sexual%20Violence%20Prevention/NISVS_Overview_2010Summary-Report.pdf

Negrao, Il. C., Bonanno, G. A., Noll, J. G., Putnam, F. W., & Trickett, P. K. (2005). Shame, humiliation, and childhood sexual abuse: Distinct contributions and emotional coherence. *Child Maltreatment, 10*(4), 350–363.

Nelson, B., & Wampler, K. (2002). Further understanding the systematic effects of childhood sexual abuse: A comparison of two groups of clinical couples. *Journal of Child Sexual Abuse, 11*, 85–106.

Polaris Project. (2017). Retrieved from https://polarisproject.org/

Rape Abuse and Incest National Network (RAINN). 2017. *Child sexual abuse*. Retrieved from www.rainn.org/articles/child-sexual-abuse

Regehr, C. (1990). Parental responses to extrafamilial child sexual assault. *Child Abuse & Neglect, 14*, 113–120.

Siegel, J. A., & Williams, L. M. (2003). Risk factors for sexual victimization of women: Results from a perspective study. *Violence Against Women, 9*(8), 902–930. doi:10.1177/1077801203255130

Sinozich, S., & Langton, L. (2014). *Rape and sexual assault victimization among college- age females, 1995–2013* (Report NCJ24847). Washington, DC: US Department of Justice Bureau of Justice Statistics. Retrieved from www.bjs.gov/content/pub/pdf/rsavcaf9513.pdf

Sloan, J. J., Fisher, B. S., & Cullen, F. T. (1997). Assessing the student right-to-know and Campus Security Act of 1990: An analysis of the victim reporting practices of college and university students. *Crime & Delinquency, 43*, 148–168.

Snyder, C. R. (2002). Hope theory: Rainbows in the mind. *Psychological Inquiry, 13*(4), 249–275.

United States Department of Health and Human Services, Administration for Children and Families, Administration on Children, Youth and Families, Children's Bureau. (2014). *Child Maltreatment Survey*, 2013. Washington, DC.

United States Department of State. (2016). *Trafficking in persons report*. Washington, DC.: United States Department of State.

van der Kolk, B. A., & Fisler, R. (1995). Dissociation and the fragmentary nature of traumatic memories: Overview and exploratory study. *Journal of Traumatic Stress, 8*(4), 505–525.

World Health Organization. (2017). *Sex trafficking*. Retrieved from http://apps.who.int/iris/bitstream/10665/77394/1/WHO_RHR_12.42_eng.pdf

Intimate Partner Violence

Activity 7.1: What is Intimate Partner Violence? Who is a Victim of Intimate Partner Violence?

Draw a picture of who you think a victim of intimate partner violence is and/or what you think intimate partner violence is. Then share your illustration with a partner or the class, and explain how you interpreted the terms *victim* and *intimate partner violence*. Why did you draw it that way? What influenced that decision?

Defining Intimate Partner Violence (IPV)

Intimate partner violence (IPV), also referred to as intimate partner abuse (IPA), includes behaviors and actions that have the *intent* to *harm* an individual in an intimate relationship. The perpetrator is a current or former intimate partner and can be from any sexuality, including transgender. Intimate partner violence occurs across all racial, ethnic, educational, and socio-economic backgrounds, and it can include physical, sexual, psychological, emotional, financial, and/or reproductive abuse. These forms of abuse can occur simultaneously, separately, or vary.

Physical Abuse

One in four women and 1 in 7 men have suffered from physical violence in an intimate partner relationship. This can include, but is not limited to, being hit with a fist or object, slammed against something, pushed, strangled, and/or kicked. A large amount of female and male IPV victims indicate that they had experienced violence for the first time before the age of 25 (Black et al., 2011), with women between the ages of 18 and 24 being the most commonly abused by intimate partners (National Coalition Against Domestic Violence, 2017). Women are also significantly more likely than men to be injured during an assault from an intimate partner, 39% of women compared to 25% of men (Centers for Disease Control and Prevention, 2017). IPV has resulted in 2 million injuries and 1,300 deaths annually for women in the United States.

Of those injured in an intimate partner violence incident, only 34% receive care for their injuries and 20% of those have medical care sought for them by family, friends, neighbors, or co-workers trying to intervene (National Coalition Against Domestic Violence, 2017).

Impact on Victims

Physical abuse in an intimate partner relationship can have devastating effects on the victim. Conditions may be a direct consequence of the physical abuse, such as broken bones, bruises, cuts, scrapes, stab wounds, pain, headaches, or brain injury. However, physical abuse and the psychological stress that accompanies it can cause long-term chronic health problems and negatively affect the victim's overall quality of life. This can include cardiovascular, gastrointestinal, and endocrine issues as well as a negative impact on the immune system (Black, 2011; Breiding, Black & Ryan, 2008; Crofford, 2007; Leserman & Drossman, 2007). Examples of health issues that are linked to physical IPV include: asthma, bladder and kidney infections, circulatory conditions, cardiovascular disease, fibromyalgia, irritable bowel syndrome, chronic pain syndromes, central nervous system disorders, gastrointestinal disorders, joint diseases, migraines, and ordinary headaches (Centers for Disease Control and Prevention, 2017).

In addition to the physical issues that the primary victim of IPV may face, children may become injured during a domestic violence incident that occurs between their parents (Appel & Holden, 1998; World Health Organization, 2017). IPV is also linked to higher rates of infant and child mortality and morbidity (illness, injury, disease) (World Health Organization, 2017). It is estimated that 15 million children in the United States are exposed to IPV annually, with 7 million being exposed to severe violence in their homes (Graham-Berman & Levendosky, 2011). These estimates make for a large number of potential victims. A child's exposure to physical IPV also can have other consequences. Males who witnessed IPV were more likely to perpetrate acts of violence than females who witnessed it (Hamby, Finkelhor, Turner, & Ormrod, 2011). and this can also affect offenses committed by adult men (Murrell et al., 2005), particularly violent offenses (World Health Organization, 2017). Children who witness IPV can experience mental health effects such as depression, anxiety, posttraumatic stress disorder, and suicide attempts (Kitzmann et al., 2003; Lang and Stover, 2008; Wolfeet al., 2003).

Case study 7.1: Ray Rice

Ray Rice, former running back for the Baltimore Ravens, was captured on video (see Media Byte 8.1) in the Revel Casino in Atlantic City, New Jersey, hitting his then-fiancée, now wife, Janay Palmer, in the head and then dragging her unconscious body from an elevator in February 2014. Initially, the video just showed Rice pulling her unconscious body from the elevator. The NFL gave him a two-game suspension. Then TMZ released the full video of Rice punching Janay in the head, rendering her unconscious. After that, the Ravens released him and the NFL suspended him indefinitely. Rice and Palmer were both initially charged with simple assault due to the fact the couple were physically violent with each other, but at a grand jury hearing on March 27, 2014, his charges were increased to third-degree aggravated assault. The charges against Palmer were dropped. On March 28, 2014, Rice and Palmer were married. Rice rejected a plea deal and in exchange was accepted into a pretrial intervention program. Rice was to complete a 12-month program that included anger management classes, pay a $125 fine and not get into further trouble during that time. If he met these conditions, the case would not appear on his record. This type of program occurs in less than 1% of all domestic violence cases in New Jersey and is usually reserved for crimes that do not involve violence or those that are considered "victimless." The Atlantic City prosecutor, Jim McClain, who handled this case, said he approved this program after evaluating the circumstances and talking with Palmer. Rice appealed his suspension from the NFL and was reinstated. He has publicly pledged to donate his salary to domestic violence charities. However, as of this writing, no team has signed him and he remains a free agent. Rice and Palmer are still married. There have been no public reports of further IPV.

- What is your opinion of the punishment he received? Do you feel the punishment was just or unjust? Why or why not?
- Do you think that his fame was a factor in his sentence? Why or why not?

Media Byte 7.1: Ray Rice

In the preceding case study, you learned about the Ray Rice case. Watch the video found here: www.tmz.com/videos/0_ekaflcqq/

Based on what you have learned about physical IPV in this chapter, do you think that what you see in this video constitutes IPV? Why or why not?

Sexual Abuse

People in intimate relationships can experience sexual abuse or violence. This can include rape, which is completed, attempted, and/or unwanted vaginal, anal, and/or oral penetration with a body part or object. The perpetrator may use force and/or threats to hurt the victim. Sexual abuse also includes incidents when the victim is unable to consent, such as if they were unconscious, drunk, drugged, and/or unable to give consent verbally. The National Intimate Partner and Sexual Violence Survey found that 51% of females who were raped were raped by an intimate partner (Black et al., 2011).

Sexual coercion involves a perpetrator using non-physical means to pressure or coerce their partner to engage in unwanted vaginal, anal, or oral penetration without the use of force, but it is still considered a type of sexual abuse. This can occur when one intimate partner threatens to end the relationship or harm the partner, their loved ones, or family pets if they do not comply with the partner's wish for sexual contact. It can also consist of being lied to by their partner or their partner making insincere promises and/or being worn down by repeated pressure to engage in sexual acts.

In an intimate partner relationship, there can also be unwanted sexual contact between partners that does not involve penetration—for example, unwanted kissing, fondling, stroking, and/or touching. Some forms of sexual abuse do not involve physical contact, such as one partner exposing themselves to the other and/or making the victim show their body. It can also involve forcing the victim to watch the offender masturbate or making the victim masturbate in front of the offender. Coercing the victim to take sexual and/or nude photos or make videos is another example.

Impact on Victims

The effects of sexual abuse in an intimate partner relationship on a victim can include physical issues such as pelvic inflammatory disease, sexual dysfunction, gynecological disorders, sexual dysfunction, and sexually transmitted diseases (STDs). It can also result in an unintended pregnancy as well as an increased likelihood of miscarriage, stillbirths, or induced abortions (Centers for Disease Control and Prevention, 2017). There are also psychological consequences that result from sexual IPV, such as depression, post-traumatic stress disorder, anxiety, disordered eating and sleeping, and suicide attempts. Women also developed drinking problems (World Health Organization, 2017).

Media Byte 7.2: NO MORE

> Check out the website for NO MORE, an organization dedicated to preventing intimate partner violence and sexual violence. Watch the ads featuring NFL players pledging "no more." http://nomore.org/nflplayerspsa/. Do you think that this campaign is successful in raising awareness about these issues? Do you think that this could help with prevention? Why or why not?

Reproductive Abuse and Reproductive Coercion

Reproductive abuse is behavior used to maintain control and/or power over the reproductive health of a person with whom one is in a romantic or sexual relationship. The most common type of reproductive abuse is damaging or sabotaging contraception—for example, interfering with birth control pills by hiding, withholding, or destroying them. It can also involve purposefully damaging a condom or removing it during intercourse to promote pregnancy. The removal of intrauterine devices (IUDs), contraceptive patches, or vaginal rings to promote pregnancy without discussing it with the partner is another example. Partners also can commit reproductive abuse by knowingly exposing their partner to human immunodeficiency virus (HIV), other sexually transmitted diseases (STDs), and/or a sexually transmitted infection (STI) without telling their partners about the risk. In addition to reproductive abuse, there is reproductive coercion. This includes threatening to harm a partner if they do not agree to become pregnant and/or carry the pregnancy to term, or forcing a partner to terminate her pregnancy against her will. It can also involve harming a partner and causing her to have a miscarriage.

The National Crime Victimization Survey reveals that 1 in 5 adolescent girls and young women have experienced pregnancy coercion and 1 in 7 have experienced interference with contraception. Clark et al., (2014) found that 16% of women ages 18–44 experienced reproductive coercion and one-third of women who experienced reproductive coercion also experienced IPV. In a nationwide survey of over 30,000 calls made to the National Domestic Violence Hotline, it was found that 1 in 4 women had experienced pregnancy coercion and birth control sabotage (Family Violence Prevention Fund,

2011). Women in IPV relationships were more likely to be forced into not using a condom and more likely to be pressured to become pregnant as men who perpetrate IPV are more likely to report erratic or no condom use (Miller et al., 2010; Raj et al., 2007).

Impact on Victims

One of the main consequences of reproductive abuse and coercion is pregnancy. Among pregnant women in IPV relationships there are many negative health consequences, among them substance abuse, chronic pain, complicated pregnancies and other gynecological issues, unsafe abortions, miscarriages, stillbirths, neonatal mortality, and low birth rates (World Health Organization, 2017). In addition, pregnant women in IPV situations are at risk for injury or death by their partner. The leading cause of death in pregnant women in the United States is homicide (Cheng & Horon, 2010; Chang, Berg, Saltzman, Herndon, 2005). Women with unintended pregnancies were four times more likely to experience IPV than women who had planned their pregnancy and IPV is nearly three times greater for women seeking an abortion than those maintaining their pregnancy (Bourassa & Berube, 2007). Miller et al. (2015) found that 15% of women who comprised a sample of family planning clinic patients experienced physical violence at the hands of the intimate partner as well as birth control sabotage. Women who experience physical and psychological abuse in their relationships also experienced increased sexually transmitted infections (Coker et al., 2009).

Case Study 7.2: Man Convicted of Rape for Condom Removal

In a landmark case, in January 2017 a man was convicted of rape in Switzerland for the removal of a condom during sex. The man was not named, nor was the victim in the case. It was ruled a rape as the woman consented to have sex with the man only if he was wearing a condom. The lack of condom negated the consent. The man started having sex with the woman wearing one, but removed it during sex. She did not know until after. The Swiss court found the man guilty of rape and gave him a twelve-month suspended sentence.

- What is your opinion of the sentence this man was given? Do you think that it was just or unjust? Explain your answer.
- Do you think that the sentence in this case will influence prosecution of this crime in other places around the world? Why or why not?

Psychological and Emotional Abuse

Half of women and men in the United States have experienced psychological and emotional abuse in an intimate partner relationship (Black et al., 2011). Psychological and emotional abuse can include verbal or nonverbal behaviors. Verbally, abusers can call the victim names or insult, degrade, and/or reject them. But an offender can also do these things through non-verbal hostile actions, using just body language, gestures, and/or facial expressions. Abusers can terrorize victims psychologically by threatening to physically harm them, someone they love, or pets, and/or their favorite objects/possessions. Psychological and emotional abuse can also involve an abuser denying or withholding affection and/or showing no interest or emotion when interacting with the victim, as well as ignoring them. An abuser can commit psychological or emotional abuse against their victim through corruption or exploitation in which they force their partner to engage in behaviors or acts that they do not want to participate in and that may be against their moral or religious beliefs. For example, forced or coerced intercourse with another partner, forced or coerced prostitution, forced or coerced drug use, and/or forced or coerced participation in pornography.

Impact on Victims

Psychological and emotional abuse are similar to other types of IPV in that victims can experience anxiety, depression, posttraumatic stress disorder, sleep disturbance and disorders, and suicidal behaviors. Victims of this type of abuse can also suffer from low self-esteem, feelings of low self-worth, and emotional detachment. Victims may feel like they are not worthy of being treated better and that they deserve the treatment that they get.

Financial Abuse

Abusers can use financial means to hurt, coerce, and control their victims. This can limit the victim's ability to leave, seek assistance, or maintain independence, as controlling the finances of the victim allows the abuser to control and have power over the victim. In abusive relationships, 98% of victims experience financial abuse. This can be one of the main factors why a victim stays in an abusive relationship or returns to one (National Network to End Domestic Violence, 2017).

An abuser can commit financial abuse in a variety of ways. They can forbid the victim to work using threats and coercion as to what will happen if they do work. The abuser also could sabotage the victim's opportunities for employment or jeopardize their current job. For example, the abuser could harass the victim at work, lie about the victim's past or current lifestyle, and/or physically or sexually batter the victim, preventing them from going to work or an interview, or hinder job advancement opportunities. An abuser could force the victim to work in a family restaurant without pay. There is also the other end of the spectrum for financial abuse, in which the abuser refuses to work or contribute anything financially to the household income, forcing the victim to work (often multiple jobs), take loans, or incur credit card debt.

Abusers can control all of the money and assets and not let the victim have access to any of the accounts. The abuser may also hide financial assets, not making the victim aware of their existence. They may withhold money and give the victim an allowance or only allow the victim enough money to buy necessities for themselves or their children such as food or medicine. An abuser may also take all the money from a victim's inheritance and can force the victim to turn over public benefits. They also can commit identity theft in which they take out loans, credit cards, or mortgages in the name of the victim and fail or refuse to pay them to ruin the credit of the victim, thus making them rely upon the abuser financially. An abuser also may file false insurance claims in the name of the victim.

Impact on Victims

Financial abuse can be life-shattering for a victim. It can prevent the victim from leaving to seek safety from the abuser and make it impossible for the victim to be independent financially. If a victim has no assets, no money, and ruined credit or lack of credit history, it can be difficult to find housing. It can also be difficult to establish a bank account or get a job that may require a credit check. There also may be legal issues that victims face in regard to unpaid taxes or mortgages. As a result, victims can suffer psychological issues such as depression, anxiety, and fear. The lack of options for victims as a result of financial abuse are why many choose to stay with their abusers and sometimes even return if they do leave.

Cycle of Violence

IPV often follows a similar pattern over time. Lenore E. Walker (1979) created a theory, the "cycle of violence," that illustrates how IPV occurs. First is the *tension building* stage. During this stage, the victim can feel tension and heaviness in the relationship between them and their partner, yet the victim has tried to keep things calm by heeding the abuser's wishes, doing nice things, and trying not to upset the abuser. The second stage is the *acute abuse incident*, in which a major, violently abusive action has occurred. It is often labeled as an "explosion" of physical, sexual, psychological/emotional, financial, or reproductive abuse. The final stage is the *honeymoon* phase. In this phase, the abuser apologizes and begs for forgiveness, often promising it will never happen again and that they will change. The abuser often changes their behavior and is very kind and may shower the victim with gifts and attention, as well making promises for the future. At the end of the honeymoon stage, the whole process repeats itself. It is often easier for victims to believe the promises and temporary change in behavior that is seen during the honeymoon phase, but as time goes on, the honeymoon phase may get shorter or even non-existent as the abuser will blame the victim for their actions and no longer feels the need to apologize or make up for their actions.

Battered Woman Syndrome/Battered Spouse Syndrome

IPV is generally understood as part of gender violence as many more women are victimized than men. This is why Lenore Walker coined the term *battered woman syndrome*. Later, as more was learned about IPV against men, battered man syndrome or battered spouse syndrome were created to include this population as well. Battered spouse syndrome is a subcategory of posttraumatic stress disorder. While not all battered spouses who suffer from this meet the criteria for PTSD, many do. Battered woman syndrome/

battered spouse syndrome is based upon the idea of learned helplessness. This means that the victim feels that there is nothing that can be done to change the situation she is in and she must accept the circumstances and live through it. There are four characteristics that individuals experience and that must be met if this is going to be used as a defense at trial. First, the victim must believe that the IPV was her fault. Second, no one else is responsible for the IPV, except her. She must think she is solely responsible. Third, the victim must be in constant fear for the safety of herself and her children. Finally, the victim must believe the abuser is always present or around, watching or knowing what is happening, even if they are not physically there (Gosselin, 2005).

Costs of IPV

IPV is a huge financial cost to the victims, employers, and society. For victims, there are often health care and mental health costs, as well as lost wages. The cost of health care for *each* IPV incident is $948 for female victims and $387 for male victims. Women utilized more emergency room visits, inpatient hospitalizations, and physician services than males. Mental health services for victims cost $257 for women and $224 for men (Centers for Disease Control, 2003). Annual health care costs are significantly higher for victims of IPV, particularly women, with costs averaging $5,000 or more per year (Ulrich, Cain, Sugg, Rivara, Rubanowice & Thompson, 2003). These increased annual health care costs can continue for as long as 15 years after the abuse stops (Centers for Disease Control and Prevention, 2003). Employers also lose money each year as employees are not able to work due to IPV injuries or incidents. $727.8 million dollars in lost productivity and 7.9 million paid workdays are lost to IPV annually, as well 5.6 million days of household productivity. IPV affects not only productivity at work, but also at home.

Society also suffers financial losses as a result of IPV. Costs of IPV exceed $8.3 billion annually, which includes the medical care and mental health services for victims, as well as time away from work. This includes $460 million for rape, $6.2 billion for physical abuse, $461 million for stalking, and $1.2 billion in the value of lost lives (Max, Rice, Finkelstein, Bardwell, Leadbetter, 2004). Women who experience IPV who may not be able to work, or are forbidden to work by their abusive partners, are more likely to be unemployed, have chronic health issues and/or receiving public assistance, which also factors into the societal cost of IPV (Lloyd & Taluc, 1999). Victims of IPV also may be receiving state crime victim compensation benefits.

IPV in LGBTQ Populations

While national statistics can estimate the amount of IPV that is occurring in hetero-sexual relationships, that is not always the case for same-sex IPV. Most national-level statistics only reflect heterosexual IPV. Early research did not include lesbian, gay, bisex-ual, transgender, or queer (LGBTQ) individuals. A homophobic culture in the United States marginalizes these communities and the heterosexist viewpoint on IPV reflects in the statistics (Merrill & Wolfe, 1996). While research has suggested that same-sex IPV rates are comparable to heterosexual couples' (Bograd,1999; McClennen, 2003; 2005), there is also research to indicate that the rates may actually be higher. According to the Centers for Disease Control National Intimate Partner Violence Sur-vey (NIPVS), bisexual women have a greater number of lifetime IPV incidents than het-erosexual women (Walters et al., 2013). One research study found that 26.9% of gay men experienced IPV within their lifetime and 12.1% of the sample had experienced it in the past year (Goldberg & Meyer, 2013).

The National Coalition of Anti-Violence Programs (NCAVP) examined 1,976 survivors of IPV across 14 states and released a report titled *Lesbian, Gay, Bisexual, Transgender, Queer and HIV-Affected Intimate Partner Violence in 2015*. This research showed that 77% of IPV homicides and 54% of the total population sampled were people of color. LGBTQ individuals with disabilities were four times more likely to experience financial abuse and transgender women were three times more likely to experience sexual and financial abuse than heterosexual individuals. Other research has estimated that 25–43% of transgender people have reported experiencing IPV (Lombardi et al, 2001; Xavier, 2000).

LGBTQ individuals who experience IPV have different barriers than heterosexual victims do when seeking help or treatment, and this is often due to homophobia (Erbaugh, 2007). It can play a role in whether they choose to come forward about the abuse. Research has shown that because of fear of the reaction and the potential for homophobia, LGBTQ individuals are reluctant to report (Bornstein, Fawcett, Sullivan, Senturia, & Shiu-Thornton, 2006; Erbaugh, 2007; Girshick, 2002; Merrill & Wolfe, 2000; McLaughlin & Rozee, 2001; Renzetti, 1992; Ristock, 2002). When LGBTQ indi-viduals do come forward, they may face different obstacles than heterosexual victims. Reporting to police is often strained and negative experiences can influence reporting (Guadalupe-Diaz & Yglesias, 2013; McClennen, 2005). Police may be indifferent to the needs of LGBTQ or openly hostile. LGBTQ individuals often experience misarrest, where both the victim and the perpetrator are arrested or no arrest is made (NCAVP,

2016). Individuals may opt not to come forward for fear of "revictimization" by police (Balsam, 2001; Herek, Cogan, & Gillis, 2002). When LGBTQ individuals do come forward, they also face issues in the courtroom with the prosecution of the case relating to homophobia, discrimination, and victim blaming (Lundy & Leventhal, 1999).

There is also the issue that many services are geared specifically for females, or females leaving a heterosexual relationship. The NCAVP (2016) research revealed that 44% of individuals trying to access emergency shelters were denied access, with 71% claiming they were denied because of their gender identity. Domestic violence shelters are usually for women. This can be a problem for gay men and transgendered individuals trying to escape an abusive partner. However, it can also be an issue for lesbians. Past research has shown that lesbians do not feel welcome in domestic violence shelters as they perceive them to serve heterosexual IPV victims (McLaughlin & Rozee, 2001; Renzetti, 1992; Ristock, 2002; West, 2002).

Why Do People Stay in Abusive Relationships?

When it comes to intimate partner violence situations, the most common question is "Why doesn't she/he just leave?!" There are many reasons that an individual would continue to stay in an abusive relationship. The victim may have low self-esteem and believe that they are to blame for the abuse. They may think that this type of behavior is normal in a relationship and may have grown up in a household where this occurred. The victim could also believe that the offender will change and they do not mean what they do. They could make excuses for the offender, rationalizing the abuse as something that only occurs when that person is drunk and/or had a bad day at work. They may feel embarrassed about what is happening and not want to tell anyone. They may still have feelings of love and attachment for their abuser, even though the abuser hurts them.

Fear can prevent the victim from leaving the offender. They may be scared that the offender will harm them, their family, and/or their pet if they try to leave, or escalate the abuse in retribution for attempting to leave. The abuser might threaten to take the victim's children away. If the victim does have children, they also may worry about how taking their children out of their home will affect them. The victim also may want their children to grow up with two parents. In addition, they could have religious or moral beliefs about marriage that would prevent them from wanting to leave.

Financially, the victim may be dependent upon the abuser. The abuser may control the money and assets and the victim may not want to leave out of fear for survival. The victim also may have nowhere to go, especially if the abuser has isolated them from friends and family.

The "Why Doesn't She Just Leave?!" Project

One common theme in victim blaming for intimate partner abuse is that the victim deserves the abuse that they receive because they stay with the person who is harming them.

For this assignment, you are to assume the role of either a heterosexual woman OR a woman in a same-sex relationship (pick one) with a high school education. The only work experience you have is two years in retail working as a full-time cashier making minimum wage ($5.50 at the time) at the supermarket from 2003 to 2005. You have three children, ages seven, four, and six months. You also have a 25-pound dog that you do not want to leave behind as your spouse physically abuses the dog. You have been a stay-at-home mother and wife for the past seven years. You have no money of your own. Your name is not on the bank account or the credit cards. Your spouse gives you an "allowance" every month of $50 to buy things for yourself. Your spouse handles the rest of the money and pays for everything. The car is also in your spouse's name only, as is the cellular phone, the house, and all bills.

For this assignment, you are to research how much it would cost for a woman in this situation to:

1) Initially be able to leave her abuser
2) Function on her own on a monthly basis, without the assistance of friends or family (as he has isolated her from them) and without the help of social service agencies.

You should select a name for this fictional character and refer to her as such in your assignment. You can select names for the children and dog too if you wish. You must be specific and include details for each of the items in the Costs section below. You also must provide a grand total of how much it would cost to live each month and how much the woman makes.

Part 1: Costs

Cite the source and the day you found this information. Also, you must estimate the monthly cost and also the initial cost to move out of the abusive situation. Be specific for each estimate! This is to be for your local area. See examples below.

Specifically you must identify:

1. Monthly rent for at least a two-bedroom apartment that allows pets. Include the security and pet deposit, if applicable, and what utilities are included in the rent. Example: $650 a month found on Jan. 8 on Craigslist. $650 security deposit and $500 pet deposit. Sewage and garbage included. Monthly cost: $650. Move in cost: $1150.
2. Estimate for one month's utilities in apartment (whatever the rent does not include, such as gas, water, garbage, or electricity).
   Example: Gas estimate $83/month for a two-bedroom apartment.
3. Cost to obtain a cellular phone (startup fee, price of phone, price per month). Include carrier, type of phone, and type of plan you are selecting.
4. Price of a used car, including an insurance estimate for monthly coverage and monthly gas expenditure OR one month's bus fare in Bloomington-Normal.
5. Cost of day care for three children. (either by month or day)
   Example: Debbie's Day Care
   Estimate given 1/9. 1 child under 2 = $46 a day, 1 child age 3 and over = $32, 1 child school age, $16 (after school) = $94 a day
   Assuming that the mom works only Monday through Friday, the total cost for day care each month would be: $94 a day x 5 days a week = $470 a week. $470 x 4 weeks= $1880 a month in day care costs.
6. Employment that she would be qualified for with her background.
   Example: Craigslist 1/8: Mafelite: Call Center Representatives: $10/hour. Requirements: high school diploma. $10 x 40 hours a week= 400 (a week before taxes, $800 every two weeks before taxes). $1600 a month income.
7. Estimate for groceries each month to feed her and the three children, and also the dog. Formula and diapers must be included in the estimate.
8. Estimate for replacing *necessary* items that she could not take with her when she left her abuser (furniture, lamps, beds, clothes, toothbrush, toothpaste, etc.). This should be an initial cost *only*. You must list items and prices.

9. Estimate her average health care costs per month.
10. Estimate the costs for doing laundry at a Laundromat, including laundry detergent for one month.

Part 2: Assistance

For this part of the assignment, please find five organizations in the community that could potentially help the victim leave and/or live each month. The first part of your assignment dealt with how much it would cost to leave the abuser and live on your own without assistance from any organizations. Now you must find groups you could turn to for help.

You must provide:

1. The name of the organization
2. Its contact information
3. Brief description of how it can help you

Part 3: Reflection

Finally, provide a written response reflecting upon the experience of this assignment and the information you uncovered.

Things to consider in your response:

- The amount of money you need to leave your abuser and live each month and the money that the fictional victim could earn
- How finances can affect a person's decision to stay in an abusive relationship and how that can affect a person emotionally
- How help from a social services organization could be beneficial to the victim based on your research
- Why a woman in this position might not want to seek help from an organization
- How a woman and her children might feel in this position
- How having a dog could influence your decision
- The background story of this woman (education, work experience) and how it affects her opportunities or ability to leave

- How her abuser forced her to isolate from family and friends and how that might affect her decision
- The way that this assignment has influenced (if at all) the way you think about IPV
- *If you selected the woman in a same-sex relationship, you must address how her experience of this process could be different than the heterosexual woman's*

Moving Forward

In order to address IPV, the priority must be preventing violence, not responding to violence. To prevent IPV, education and awareness are key. Focusing on healthy relationships and communication throughout a person's life is essential, especially educating children about what constitutes a healthy relationship and behavior in a relationship. Youth-focused and parent-focused programs, as well as projects that focus on adolescent dating violence, can help. For example, the Centers for Disease Control (CDC) Dating Matters Project has been developed for youth in high-risk urban areas. It promotes healthy relationship behaviors and prevention strategies for IPV for teens, parents, and educators (Centers for Disease Control and Prevention, 2017). This program could be expanded and revised to other areas and different populations to spread education and awareness regarding IPV.

A Coordinated Community Response Team (CCRT) is another innovative way to address IPV moving forward. First developed by the Domestic Abuse Intervention Project (DAIP) in Duluth, Minnesota, it is often referred to as the Duluth model. A CCRT is made up of criminal justice agencies, social service agencies, human service agencies, advocates, local businesses, media, clergy, and health care professionals all working together to assist and protect IPV victims and hold perpetrators accountable. All of these entities work to create a network of support for victims, being able to direct and/or refer victims to a person or agency that can help them. This can be an effective model to use to combat IPV locally, if the community is committed to working together.

Discussion Questions

1. Do you think that all types of IPV (physical, sexual, reproductive, psychological, and financial) should be punished the same way, or should there be different punishments for different types? Explain your answer.

2. Which type of IPV do you think has the most lasting impact on a victim? Why?
3. Can you understand the reasons that a person would stay in a relationship where IPV was occurring? Why or why not?
4. What do you think would be the most successful strategy in reducing and/or preventing IPV? Please explain.

References

Appel, A. E., & Holden, G. W. (1998). The co-occurrence of spouse and physical child abuse: A review and appraisal. *Journal of Family Psychology, 12*, 578–599.

Balsam, K. F. (2001). Nowhere to hide: Lesbian battering, homophobia, and minority stress. *Women & Therapy, 23*(3), 25–37.

Black, M. C. (2011). Intimate partner violence and adverse health consequences: Implications for clinicians. *American Journal of Lifestyle Medicine, 5*(5), 428–439.

Black, M. C., Basile, K. C., Briedling, M. J., Smith, S. G., Walters, M. L., Merrick, M. T., Chen, J., & Stevens, R. (2011). *The National Intimate Partner and Sexual Violence Survey (NISVIS): 2010 summary report*. Atlanta, GA: National Center for Injury Prevention and Control, Centers for Disease Control and Prevention.

Bograd, M. (1999). Strengthening domestic violence theories: Intersections of race, class, sexual orientation, and gender. *Journal of Marital and Family Therapy, 25*(3), 275–289.

Bornstein, D. R., Fawcett, J., Sullivan, M., Senturia, K. D., & Shiu-Thornton, S. (2006). Understanding the experiences of lesbian, bisexual and trans survivors of domestic violence: A qualitative study. *Journal of Homosexuality, 51*(1), 159–181.

Bourassa, D., & Berube, J. (2007). The prevalence of intimate partner violence among women and teenagers seeking abortion compared with those continuing pregnancy. *Journal of Obstetrics & Gynaecology, 29*, 415–423.

Breiding, M. J., Black, M. C., & Ryan, G. W. (2008). Chronic disease and health risk behaviors associated with intimate partner violence—18 U.S. states/territories, 2005. *Annals of Epidemiology, 18*, 538–544.

Centers for Disease Control and Prevention. (2003). *Costs of intimate partner violence against women in the United States*. Atlanta, GA: CDC, National Center for Injury Prevention and Control.

Centers for Disease Control and Prevention. (2017). *Dating matters*. Retrieved from www.cdc.gov/violenceprevention/datingmatters/

Centers for Disease Control and Prevention. (2017). *Intimate partner violence*. Retrieved from www.cdc.gov/violenceprevention/intimatepartnerviolence/

Chang, J., Berg, C. J., Saltzman, L. E., & Herndon, J. (2005). Homicide: A leading cause of injury deaths among pregnant and postpartum women in the United States, 1991–1999. *American Journal of Public Health, 95*, 471–477.

Cheng, D., & Horon, I. L. (2010). Intimate-partner homicide among pregnant and postpartum women. *Obstetrics & Gynecology, 115*, 1181–1186.

Clark, L. E., Allen, R. H., Goyal, V., Raker, C., & Gottlieb, A. S. (2014). Reproductive coercion and co-occurring intimate partner violence in obstetrics and gynecology patients. *American Journal of Obstetrics and Gynecology, 210*(42), 1–8. doi: http://dx.doi.org/10.1016/j.ajog.2013.09.019

Coker, A. L., Smith, P. H., Bethea, L., King, M. R., & McKeown, R. E. (2009). Physical health consequences of physical and psychological intimate partner violence. *Archives of Family Medicine, 9*, 451–457.

Crofford, L. J. (2007). Violence, stress, and somatic syndromes. *Trauma Violence Abuse, 8*, 299–313.

Erbaugh, E. (2007). Queering approaches to intimate partner violence. In *Gender Violence: An Interdisciplinary Perspective* (Ch 32, pp. 451–459). New York, NY: New York University Press.

Family Violence Prevention Fund. (2011). *National Domestic Violence Hotline Survey results*. Retrieved from www.thehotline.org/2011/02/1-in-4-callers-surveyed-at-the-hotline- report-birth-control-sabotage-and-pregnancy-coercion/

Gazmararia, J. A., Adams, M. M., Saltzman, L. E., Johnson, C. H., Bruce, F. C., & Marks, J. S. (1995). The relationship between pregnancy intendedness and physical violence in mothers of newborns. The PRAMS Working Group. *Obstetrics & Gynecology, 85*, 1031–1038.

Girshick, L. B. (2002). No sugar, no spice reflections on research on woman-to- woman sexual violence. *Violence Against Women, 8*(12), 1500–1520.

Goldberg, N., & Meyer, I. (2013). Sexual orientation disparities in history of intimate partner violence: Results from the California Health Interview Survey. *Journal of Interpersonal Violence, 28*(5), 1109–1118.

Gosselin, D. K. (2005). *Heavy Hands: An Introduction to the Crimes of Family Violence.* Upper Saddle River, NJ: Prentice Hall.

Graham-Berman, S. A., & Levendosky, A. A. (2011). *How intimate partner violence affects children: Developmental research, case studies, and evidence-based intervention.* Arlington, VA: American Psychological Association.

Guadalupe-Diaz, X. L., & Yglesias, J. (2013). "Who's Protected?" Exploring perceptions of domestic violence law by lesbians, gays, and bisexuals. *Journal of Gay & Lesbian Social Services, 25*(4), 465–485.

Hamby, S., Finkelhor, D., Turner, H., & Ormrod, R. (2011). *Children's exposure to intimate partner violence and other family violence.* U.S. Department of Justice. Office of Justice Programs. Washington, DC: Office of Juvenile Justice and Delinquency Prevention.

Herek, G. M., Cogan, J. C., & Gillis, J. R. (2002). Victim experiences in hate crimes based on sexual orientation. *Journal of Social Issues, 58*(2), 319–339.

Kitzmann, K. M., Gaylord, N., Holt, A., & Kenny, E. (2003). Child witnesses to domestic violence: A meta-analytic review. *Journal of Consulting and Clinical Psychology, 71*(2), 339–352.

Lang, J. M., & Stover, C. S. (2008). Symptom patterns of youth exposed to intimate partner violence. *Journal of Family Violence, 23*, 619–629.

Leserman, J., & Drossman, D. A. (2007). Relationship of abuse history to functional gastrointes-tinal disorders and symptoms. *Trauma Violence Abuse, 8*, 331–343.

Lloyd, S., & Taluc, N. (1999). The effects of male violence on female employment. *Violence Against Women, 5*, 370–392.

Lombardi, E. (2001). Enhancing transgender health care. *American Journal of Public Health, 91*(6), 869–872.

Lundy, S., & Leventhal, B. (Eds.). (1999). *Same-sex domestic violence: Strategies for change*. Thousand Oaks, CA: Sage Publications.

Max, W., Rice, D. P., Finkelstein, E., Bardwell, R. A., & Leadbetter, S. (2004). The economic toll of intimate partner violence against women in the United States. *Violence and Victims, 19*(3), 259–72.

McClennen, J. C. (2003). Researching gay and lesbian domestic violence: The journey of a non LGBT researcher. *Journal of Gay & Lesbian Social Services, 15*(1–2), 31–45.

McClennen, J. C. (2005). Domestic violence between same-gender partners recent findings and future research. *Journal of Interpersonal Violence, 20*(2), 149–154.

McLaughlin, E. M., & Rozee, P. D. (2001). Knowledge about heterosexual versus lesbian batter-ing among lesbians. *Women & Therapy, 23*(3), 39–58.

Merrill, G. S., & Wolfe, V. A. (2000). Battered gay men: An exploration of abuse, help seeking, and why they stay. *Journal of Homosexuality, 39*(2), 1–30.

Miller, E., Decker, M. R., McCauley, H. L., Tancredi, D. J., Levenson, R. R., & Waldman, J. (2010). Pregnancy coercion, intimate partner violence and unintended pregnancy. *Contraception, 81*, 316–322.

Murrell, A. R., Merwin., R. M., Christoff, K. A., & Henning, K. R. (2005). When parents model violence: The relationship between witnessing weapon use as a child and later use as an adult. *Behavior and Social Issues, 14*, 128–133.

National Coalition of Anti-Violence Programs (NCAVP). (2016). *2015 report on intimate partner violence in lesbian, gay, bisexual, transgender, queer and HIV-affected communities in the U.S.* New York, NY: NCAVP.

National Coalition Against Domestic Violence. (2017). Retrieved from www.ncadv.org/

National Network to End Domestic Violence. (2017). Retrieved from http://nnedv.org/

Raj, A., Reed, E., Miller, E., Decker, M. R., Rothman, E. F., & Silverman, J.,G. (2007). Contexts of condom use and non-condom use among young adolescent male perpetrators of dating violence. *AIDS Care, 19*, 970–973.

Renzetti, C. M. (1992). *Violent betrayal: Partner abuse in lesbian relationships*. Thousand Oaks, CA: Sage Publications.

Ristock, J. L. (2002). *No more secrets: Violence in lesbian relationships*. London: Psychology Press.

Ulrich, Y. C., Cain, K. C., Sugg, N. K., Rivara, F. P., Rubanowice, D. M., & Thompson, R. S. (2003). Medical care utilization patterns in women with diagnosed domestic violence. *American Journal of Preventive Medicine, 24*(1), 9–15.

Walker, L. E. (1979). *The battered woman*. New York: Harper & Row.

Walters, M. L., Chen, J., & Breiding, M. J. (2013). *The National Intimate Partner and Sexual Violence Survey (NISVS): 2010 findings on victimization by sexual orientation*. Atlanta, GA: National Center for Injury Prevention and Control, Centers for Disease Control and Prevention.

West, C. M. (2002). Lesbian intimate partner violence: Prevalence and dynamics. *Journal of Lesbian Studies*, *6*(1), 121–127.

Wolfe, D. A., Crooks, C. V., Lee, V., McIntyre Smith, A., & Jaffe, P. G. (2003). The effects of children's exposure to domestic violence: A meta-analysis and critique. *Clinical Child and Family Psychology Review*, *6*(3), 171–187.

World Health Organization. (2017). *Intimate partner violence*. Retrieved from www.who.int/mediacentre/factsheets/fs239/en/

Xavier, J. M. (2000). *The Washington, DC, Transgender Needs Assessment Survey final report for phase two: Tabulation of the survey questionnaires; presentation of findings and analysis of the survey results; and recommendations*. Washington, DC.

Chapter 8

School and Work Victimization

Activity 8.1: How Safe Are You?

Check out the United States Department of Education's website for Campus Safety and Security http://ope.ed.gov/campussafety/#/. Download the data for your school. Are you surprised at the number of crimes occurring on your campus? Do you feel as if you were provided this information openly by the school when you applied and enrolled?

The pictures of the 20 children who lost their lives in December 2012 at Sandy Hook Elementary School in Newtown, Connecticut, will haunt the memories of millions of American citizens forever. Adam Lanza, a socially awkward young man, shot and killed his mother, Nancy, before driving to Sandy Hook Elementary School and gunning down the children and six staff members. He then shot himself in the head before authorities could apprehend him. Lanza's actions marked this shooting as the deadliest mass shooting at an elementary or high school in the United States, and the second deadliest mass shooting behind the events at Virginia Tech in 2007.

Sometimes people automatically think of heinous and extreme acts like Sandy Hook when they consider the definition of school and work victimization. However, there are actually many different ways a person can victimized at school or work. In this chapter, the definition of each form of victimization is explained, as well as the different concepts associated with it. The frequency of each occurrence is explored in depth, as well as the methods currently used to attempt to prevent these types of victimization. Throughout the text, interesting facts, activities, and websites are provided to further your understanding of the phenomenon as it stands today.

Defining School Victimization

We often associate atrocious crimes like mass shootings with school victimization, but lethal violence is actually fairly rare compared to the other forms of victimization. School violence and victimization can include physical and verbal bullying, theft of possessions, and vandalism. Victimization at school occurs between students, but can also involve teachers and staff as victims. For example, students may post mean and untrue comments about teachers on social networking websites or spray-paint vulgarity on a staff member's car in the parking lot of the school (Doerner & Lab, 2014).

It is also important to consider that school victimization does not have to occur in a school building (Doerner & Lab, 2014). It can occur at any school-related event in any geographical area. For instance, bullying can occur on a school bus ride home or to a field trip. Acts of violence can occur on football fields at a home institution or miles away. In summary, victimization does not have to occur in a classroom (Doerner & Lab, 2014).

Elementary and Secondary Education Schools

On February 29, 2016, an eighth-grade student walked into the school cafeteria at Madison High School in Middletown, Ohio, and fired at least six shots with a .380-caliber handgun. Two students were hit, but survived the attack. This is one of the most recent violent victimizations to occur in a secondary educational setting.

When a school shooting occurs, it is often a jarring reminder of one of the most infamous acts of violence, at Columbine High School in Littleton, Colorado. In April 1999, Eric Harris and Dylan Klebold murdered 12 students and one teacher before committing suicide. The two had planned an attack even larger than the Oklahoma City bombing, with additional uses of various explosives. While Columbine was not the first shooting to occur in a high school, the tailspin of media explosion, panic, and legislative changes will always be remembered by those who were old enough to remember the day's events. School security measures, bullying policies, and gun control arguments still contain evidence pointing at preventing another tragedy like Columbine's.

Although these events are the most sensationalized, research has indicated that crimes involving guns are one of the least likely forms of victimizations to occur at schools. The National Center for Education Statistics sponsors the Crime and Safety Surveys program, which collects data on crime and safety measures in elementary and secondary schools in the United States (Robers, Zhang, Morgan, & Misu-Gillette, 2015). Data are compiled from multiple sources to create the most comprehensive picture of victimization in schools: the National Crime Victimization Survey, the School Crime Supplement to the National Crime Victimization Survey, the Youth Risk Behavior Survey, the School Survey on Crime and Safety, the Schools and Staffing Survey, EDFacts, and the Campus Safety and Security Survey. These surveys are completed by principals, teachers, or students (Robers et al., 2015).

During the 2011–2012 academic year, there were 45 fatalities involving students, staff and non-student affiliations, with 26 of those deaths being homicides (Robers et al., 2015). During this same year, 9% of teachers reported being threatened by a student (a higher percentage compared to the 7% rate in academic years 2003–2004 and 2006–2007). Nonfatal victimizations were higher for students at school compared to away from school. Students experienced approximately 1.4 million victimizations on campus (mainly theft and assault) compared to over 770,000 incidences of nonfatal victimizations off campus. On a positive note, the overall victimization rates for students age 12–18 declined between the years 1992 and 2013 and student fear of victimization decreased greatly between 1993 and 2012, from 12% to 3%) (Robers et al., 2015).

A more recent study produced by the National Center for Education Statistics (2016) examined reports of school victimization through 2014. There were a little over 850,000 nonfatal victimizations at school, including 486,400 violent victimizations. Approximately 7% of students had been injured or threatened with a weapon on school grounds. Interestingly, of the students who were victimized, rural students were more likely to be victimized compared to suburban students in 2014 (53 versus 28 victimizations per 1,000 students). However, between 1992 and 2014, school victimization had decreased by an amazing 82%, indicating safety procedures and prevention policies were working.

Bullying

As students embark on their educational voyage, it is not unusual for them to form peer networks or cliques based on common interests (Swartz, Reyns, Wilcox, & Dunham, 2012). They often group by shared interests (sports or music) or by social similarities (race or socioeconomic status), which supports the principle of homogamy (i.e., individuals associate with persons similar to themselves as it is more comfortable for them). Unfortunately, there are always students who become isolated and lonely, and they are sometimes the target of bullying in schools. Bullying has received media attention in various capacities over the past few years prior to this writing, especially the extreme cases that result in suicide and violence as a reaction to the victimization. Smith et al. (2008) accurately defined physical bullying as intentional aggressive acts against a victim who cannot easily defend himself/herself, but this definition can be easily applied to cyberbullying as well.

The School Crime Supplement, a part of the National Crime Victimization Survey, gathered data from 12- to 18-year-old students from 6th to 12th grade and specifically asked questions pertaining to bullying experiences in public schools during the school years 2004–2013. The survey asked questions about the following bullying behaviors: rumor spreading, exclusion from activities, name calling, and property destruction. Results indicated that bullying was the lowest in 2013 (22% victimization rate) compared to all the other years reported in the study. When separating the sexes, rates were still the lowest in 2013 compared to the other years. However, females were more likely (24%) to be victimized at school than male students (20%) in 2013 (United States Department of Education, 2016a).

Cyberbullying, a prevalent form of cybercrime among adolescents, is an intentional, aggressive form of victimization in which adolescents use electronic devices instead of bullying in person (Hinduja & Patchin, 2009; Reekman & Cannard, 2009). Cyberbullying can occur on multiple media in several different ways, such as sending repetitive, often offensive messages, unauthorized sharing of personal information, and posting untrue information about a victim (Beckstrom, 2008; Hinduja & Patchin, 2008; Kowalski, Limber, & Agatston, 2008). Cyberstalking, often used in romantic relationships as an intrusive monitoring device is the use of the Internet and other technological devices to monitor or harass another person in a threatening way (Bocij & McFarlane, 2003; Reyns et al., 2012). The cyberstalker can gather personal information to threaten or intimidate the victim, or send unwanted, repetitious emails or instant messages (Baum et al., 2009). Some perpetrators use sophisticated methods such as computer spyware, listening devices and bugs, and video/digital cameras to stalk online. Lastly, sexting is "sending sexually suggestive nude or nearly nude photos or videos of yourself" (Lenhart, 2009, p. 16). This behavior is increasing in adolescent populations, and may have legal repercussions involving federal charges of possession or distribution of child pornography.

School-based and electronic victimization are both associated with low self-esteem, high stress, anxiety, and symptoms identified with depression (Zins & Elias, 2007). In fact, Menesini, Mondina and Tani (2009) reported that the victims in bullying incidents were more likely than bullies or uninvolved individuals to experience depression-related symptoms. Electronic victimization has also been associated with increased alcohol and drug use (Ybarra, Diener-West, & Leaf, 2007), fear of school attendance (Raskauskas & Stolz, 2007), and higher delinquency rates (Hinduja & Patchin, 2008).

The United States Department of Education (2016) determined that approximately 7% of middle and high school students in 2013 were cyberbullied, with female students having a higher likelihood of victimization. Twenty-seven percent of those cyberbullied report the occurrence at least once or twice a month.

Colleges and Universities

In middle school and high school, Seung-Hui Cho was diagnosed with severe anxiety disorder and received therapeutic and special education services. Due to privacy laws, Virginia Polytechnic and State University (Virginia Tech) was unaware of his previous diagnosis upon his admittance to the school. He was accused of stalking two female students in 2005 and ordered by a special justice to seek mental health treatment. However, this did not prohibit him from purchasing firearms as he was not institutionalized.

Victimization is not unknown to university and college students, but normally occurs in the form of theft or assault rather than extreme violent acts. Date rape, addressed more thoroughly in the sexual victimization chapter, is unfortunately a very under-reported yet prominent crime on university campuses. Approximately 80% of rapes occurring against college and university students are not reported, often for fear of repercussion or belief that it is a personal matter (Bureau of Justice Statistics, 2014). For female students, over half of the assailants were friends, intimate partners, or acquaintances, and less than 20% received any sort of assistance or resources after the assault.

Media Byte 8.1: Rape Kits

Check out the website for CNN's *The Hunting Ground*, a documentary on the underreporting of sexual assault on college campuses. A feature story on the first rape kit is featured on the website at www.cnn.com/2015/11/20/health/rape-kit-history/index.html. How has this affected the higher education community in regard to combating and preventing crime?

The United States Department of Education has a designated sector, Campus Safety and Security, that annually collects and reports data on campus crime (see Table 8.1). Not surprisingly, burglary was the most reported crime on and off campus. Students' money, computers, phones, and other personal items are stolen out of unlocked cars, unmonitored purses or backpacks, or dorm rooms. These crimes are generally based on opportunity and have little planning.

Table 8.1 *Number of Known University Student–Related Crimes, 2014*

	Rape	Robbery	Aggravated Assault	Burglary	Motor Vehicle Theft
On Campus	4454	1259	2235	14004	3127
Residence Halls	3658	168	711	7369	10
Off-Campus	507	206	382	1453	429
Public Property	216	1766	1273	N/A	1493

Source: U.S. Department of Education (2016). Campus Security: Data on Campus Crime. Retrieved December 15, 2016 from http://ope.ed.gov/campussafety/#/

Case Study 8.1: Umpqua Community College

In October 2015 Christopher Harper-Mercer, 26, walked into the classroom of his writing class at Umpqua Community College in Roseburg, Oregon, and fired a warning shot. He then handed a flash drive to a student, demanding he give it to the police, and then opened fire, killing eight students and the assistant professor and wounding nine others. Two of the victims were asked to stand up and state if they were Christian. After they affirmed their religious beliefs, Harper-Mercer shot and killed them. He then leaned out of the classroom to shoot at police, and was wounded. He immediately shot himself in the head and killed himself. After the incident, law enforcement found at the crime scene, as well as at his apartment, multiple firearms that had been legally purchased (Almaguer & Helsel, 2015).

Harper-Mercer had a history of mental health issues before the shooting. He was discharged after five weeks in basic training for the United States Army, allegedly for a suicide attempt. He graduated from a school for teenagers with learning disabilities and emotional issues in 2009, and then attended another community college before enrolling in Umpqua. His mother kept multiple loaded weapons in their apartment and Harper-Mercer was trained in proper shooting techniques. On the day of the shooting, he gave a survivor a flash drive with documents showing he had studied mass shootings, had racist views, and felt extremely isolated.

Was there any way to prevent this atrocity from happening?

Legislation and Prevention

Preventing violence on the primary and secondary school level can be extremely difficult, as these are often spontaneous acts and therefore hard to predict. The infamous shooting at Columbine High School caused many schools to install locks on exterior doors that can be unlocked only by people inside the school. Some schools with a high prevalence of weapons installed metal detectors. And other schools require all teachers and/or students to wear identification badges, use closed-circuit televisions, and/or hire guards and school resource police officers.

Zero-tolerance policies against physical violence and bullying have also become quite popular in primary and secondary schools. Resources for reporting have become more readily available, and there is a reliance on suspension and expulsion punishment for students who break school rules. Other schools have become creative and less punitive with their methods, and allow first and non-violent youth offenders to participate in conflict resolution or management programs.

In regard to extreme forms of violence at schools, such as firearm usage, it is more difficult to plan for prevention. However, the International Association of Police (2000) issued a lengthy list of warning signs that school staff can use to identify youth who may have a high likelihood for violence and hopefully redirect before tragedy occurs. The following are a few of the warning signs that are most notably seen in youth who have participated in violent crimes:

- Violent behavior in the past
- Exhibition of antisocial behaviors from a young age
- Torment of animals or young children
- Victim of continuous bullying
- Sadistic, violent, or prejudiced attitudes

In 1986 Jeanne Clery was raped, beaten, and murdered in her dorm room at Lehigh University in Bethlehem, Pennsylvania. The assailant was another student, Joseph Henry. Clery's parents learned that prior to her death, there were over 150 reports of auto-locking doors being left open by residents (Henry was suspected of getting into the dorm via an unlocked door). Howard and Connie Clery believed that Lehigh University had underreported criminal activity at the school so not to deter individuals from enrolling, and in turn pushed for changes in legislation to hold universities accountable. The Clerys founded the Clery Center for Security on Campus and in 1990, the Jeanne Clery Act was passed (Clery Center for Security on Campus, 2012).

The Clery Act (Clery Center for Security on Campus, 2012) drastically changed the responsibility of universities in regard to reporting crime on campus and mandated repercussions if the schools did not comply. It requires all colleges and universities that receive federal funding to accurately report criminal activity on campus in a publicly accessible annual security report, as well as enumerate the safety measures taken by the school to combat crime. Survivors of sexual assault and domestic violence must be provided opportunities to change living, transportation, and academic situations. as the act also provides specific rights to both parties in disciplinary processes. Lastly, the Clery Act requires schools to outline the specific processes associated with emergency notifications, publishing reports, and options for victims (Clery Center for Security on Campus, 2012).

Additional legislation related to the Clery Act involving student protective practices includes Title IX, which prohibits gender discrimination in any form by institutions of education. The Federal Education Rights and Privacy Act (FERPA) protects the release of student records unless authorized by the student. Lastly, the Violence Against Women Act (VAWA), passed in 1994, improved criminal justice responses to violence against women in multiple forms. In March 2013 President Barack Obama strengthened and reauthorized VAWA by requiring that institutions must address jurisdiction of security personnel, as well as specified reporting of various types of victimization and the safety procedures in place. Additional rights were given to victims of sexual assault, domestic violence, and stalking. In addition, information about hate crimes must also be reported.

For universities and colleges nationwide, September is National Campus Safety Awareness Month. Institutions of higher learning have a month of activities, fairs, and training to educate students and faculty on violence prevention. For instance, many universities will have a candlelight vigil for individuals who have died due to campus violence. Efforts like the Red Flag Campaign focus on bystander training and providing resources to victims.

Web Activity 8.1: Exploring the Clery Act

Check out the Clery Center for Security on Campus website at http://clerycenter.org. In what ways have the Clery Act and the Violence Against Women Act jointly changed the perception of campus violence and treatment of offenders?

Workplace Victimization

On December 2, 2015, Syed Rizwan Farook, 28, and his wife, Tashfeen Malik, 27, burst into the county health department in San Bernardino, California, and fatally gunned down 14 employees attending a party. The couple had been practicing their shooting for weeks at a local gun range. This act of violence in the workplace was not fueled by a perception of bias, discrimination, or unfair workplace treatment, nor did it involve suspects with diagnosable mental illness or disability. Instead, Farook and Malik had been radicalized by ISIS and were carrying out orders from the terrorist organization (McLaughlin, 2015).

Approximately 2 million Americans are victims of workplace violence every year (OSHA, 2002). While workplace violence can occur anywhere at any time, some occupations are at particular higher risk for victimization. For instance, individuals who exchange money with individuals in the public or persons who work late-night shifts (e.g., taxi drivers or convenience store clerks) are at higher risk for victimization. People who work alone or in high-crime areas are also more likely to get victimized.

Lastly, hospital and social service workers are at high risk for workplace violence. These individuals often work with involuntary and/or highly agitated clients who may not be happy with the current life circumstances. Probation and parole officers, nurses, and psychiatrists put themselves in danger on a continuous basis simply because of the people they help.

Defining Workplace Victimization

Workplace violence, sometimes crudely referred to as "going postal," can be defined in different ways. The National Institute of Occupational Safety and Health (NIOSH) defined workplace violence as "violent acts, including physical assaults and threats of assault, directed toward persons at work or on duty." While this definition does not include intimidation, bullying, or verbal aggression, the Workplace Bullying Institute (2015) has made huge improvements in adding the concept of workplace bullying to in the concept of workplace victimization, indicating that not all workplace victimization involves physical altercations.

Workplace bullying is repeated, abusive conduct that can be threatening or intimidating, sabotaging of work, and/or verbal barrage (Workplace Bullying Institute, 2015). Much like all forms of bullying, it is based on the offender's need to control and intimidate the victim. However, workplace bullying can lead to failure on the job, destroyed relationships, and even termination of employment. A 2014 survey indicated that approximately 27% of employees have experienced some form of workplace bullying and the majority of offenders are supervisors/administration (Workplace Bullying Institute, 2015).

In order to properly define workplace violence, it is necessary to define *workplace*. Some places, like a factory, government building, office, or school, can be obviously defined as a workplace. However, some individuals do not have one set workplace and often move around geographically every day. For instance, utility companies (e.g., water, gas, electric) hire men and women to obtain meter readings during the day. Police officers, firefighters, and postal workers can cover large amounts of ground every day performing their jobs. When considering workplace violence, the location (or locations) where the employee is working needs to be considered.

How to define a workplace violence offender also must be considered (Doerner & Lab, 2015). Some policies define a workplace violence offender very strictly, as a current or former employee. However, we feel it is more appropriate to include in the definition clients or vendors at a workplace, or even complete strangers. Essentially, a "workplace violence offender" should be considered as any person in a workplace environment who commits any act of physical, verbal, or psychological aggression or assault. The California Occupational Safety and Health Administration initially introduced a typology of workplace violence in the 20th century that attempted to categorize workplace violence based on the location and type of offender, which was updated by the Centers for Disease Control and NIOSH (2006).

Type I, *Criminal Intent*, is violence purposely committed by someone who has no legitimate relationship with the workplace. These crimes usually include terrorism, robbery, and shoplifting. In fact, 85% of homicides occurring in the workplace are categorized as Type I.

Type II, *Customer/Client*, is violence that occurs while a person is being served at a workplace. Perpetrators can encompass a large group of the population, including inmates, students, patients, or customers. Victims of this form of violence are often patient caregivers in health care, but can also include teachers, police officers, or prison staff. Approximately 3% of workplace homicide falls into this category of violence.

Type III, *Worker-on-Worker*, is when an employee (or former employee) threatens or initiates an attack on another employee (or past employee). These confrontations have resulted in 7% of workplace homicides.

Type IV, *Personal Relationship*, is the final category of workplace violence according to NIOSH (2006). The Type IV offender usually does not have a relationship with the workplace but does have a personal relationship with the victim. Victims and offenders are often a combination of spouses or significant others, siblings, children, friends, and other intimate relationships. This last categorization accounts for 5% of workplace homicides.

Activity 8.2: Gun Violence in the Workplace

Choose one of the following incidences of recent gun violence in a workplace:

1. San Bernardino mass shooting (2015)
2. Planned Parenthood clinic shooting, Colorado Springs (2015)
3. Excel Industries mass shooting, Heston, Kansas (2016)

Explain the timeline of events that led up to the shooting. Based on the typologies discussed, how would you categorize the shooting?

Sexual Harassment

While sexual harassment is not necessarily a violent crime that directly causes homicide, it is most certainly a form of workplace victimization. Berdahl (2007) asserted that this form of harassment entails any behavior that "derogates, demeans or humiliates an individual based on that individual's sex" (p. 644). While sexual harassment can include a plethora of behaviors, below are those most seen in the workplace:

- Anti-female or anti-male jokes
- Comments about women not belonging in the workplace or management
- Unwanted touching
- Pressure for dating
- Bribes or threats to terminate employment if sexual acts are not performed

Sexual harassment is legally defined in two ways. *Quid pro quo* is sexual harassment when compliance with a request for sexual favors positively affects a person's employment. In other words, agreeing to participate in sexual acts in exchange for a raise or promotion is quid pro quo sexual harassment. *Hostile work environment* is sex-related behavior that creates an intimidating work environment, such as displaying posters depicting scantily clad women or dirty jokes directed at a specific person (Sexual Harassment, 29 C.F.R 1604.11 [a][2][3]). Sexual harassment can be offensive, uncomfortable, and cause psychological distress for individuals who are victimized. Women are more likely to be victims of sexual harassment (O'Leary-Kelly, Bowes-Sperry, Bates, & Lean, 2009), often when attempting to break through boundaries and professional fields historically associated with men (Berdahl, 2007). However, men can most definitely be sexually harassed in the workplace as well.

Case Study 8.2: Sexual Harassment

Jonathan is a cashier at a large retail store and Cindy is the shift manager. For the past three weeks, she has been making crude gestures toward him, as well as telling him inappropriate jokes that make him uncomfortable. Jonathan mentioned the occurrences to a co-worker, who laughed at him and told him he should enjoy an attractive woman "hitting on him." After a few more days of the behavior, Jonathan nicely told Cindy he really did not like those jokes and asked her to stop. She grabbed his arm and laughed, telling him to stop being such a baby and it was all a joke. Then she kissed him on the cheek.

Based on the information provided by the Equal Employment Opportunity Commission at www.eeoc.gov/laws/types/sexual_harassment.cfm, is Jonathan a victim of sexual harassment? If so, how would you suggest he proceed?

Frequency of Workplace Violence

Based on what is seen in the media, it is not unreasonable for someone to assume that workplace violence is a normal and increasing occurrence. However, the Bureau of Justice Statistics actually indicates the opposite, as workplace victimization in both the private and public sectors has declined (Harrell, 2013). Between 1994 and 2011, local, state, and federal government (public sector) employee victimizations decreased by 82% and private sector by 72%. However, there was a significant difference between victimization for workers in the private and in the public sector. Below are highlights from the workplace violence study:

- In 2011 government employees were three times more likely than private sector employees to be victimized by workplace violence.
- In 2011, 1 in 5 victims of workplace homicide was a government employee.
- About 56% of government employees who experienced workplace violence were law enforcement or security personnel.
- Serious violence in the workplace accounted for a larger amount of private-sector employees (25%) than government employees (15%).
- Government employees (12%) were less likely to encounter an offender with a weapon than were private sector employees (20%).
- Male government employees (68%) were more likely than female government employees (38%) to face a stranger during a workplace violence incident (Harrell, 2013).

The study, sponsored by the Bureau of Justice Statistics, also revealed that among public-sector (government) employees, white employees were more likely than those of any other race to be victimized by workplace violence (Harrell, 2013). In addition, government employees ages 25 to 34 and those who were divorced or separated were more likely to be victims. Private-sector employees had no noticeable difference in victimization rates based on sex, but American Indian/Alaska Natives had the highest likelihood of victimization in regard to race. And in the private sector, workers age 25–34 had the highest rate of victimization.

While workplace violence rarely results in fatalities, fatalities definitely receive the most media attention due to their severity and tragedy. The Bureau of Labor Statistics (2013) investigated the differences in fatal workplace shootings by industry in 2010. Individuals in the retail trades experienced the highest likelihood of workplace homicide (24%), closely followed by leisure and hospitality (17%). The full distribution can be seen in Figure 8.1.

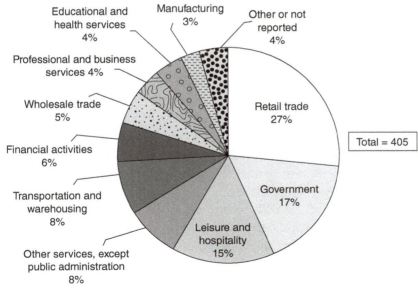

Workplace homicides due to shootings, by industry, 2010

Figure 8.1 Distribution of Fatal Workplace Shootings

Source: www.bls.gov/iif/oshwc/cfoi/osar0016.htm

Fortunately, it appears as if workplace homicide is declining based on more recent research. According to the Bureau of Labor Statistics (2015), fatalities by persons or animals in the workplace had declined slightly in 2014 compared to 2013 (749 versus 773 incidents). Among workplace fatalities involving females as victims, significant others or relatives were most likely to be the assailant (32%). Males, on the other hand, were most likely to be killed by robbers (33%) (Bureau of Labor Statistics, 2015).

Combating Workplace Violence and Victimization

While it is impossible to prevent all forms of workplace violence and victimization, there are different steps that can be taken to decrease the likelihood of violence. OSHA (2002) suggested the best way for an organization to protect employees from workplace victimization: simply to implement a zero-tolerance policy. Employees should be made aware that bullying, harassment, and violence will not be tolerated and punitive action will ensue if offending behaviors occur. In addition, employees should be educated on what constitutes workplace violence, bullying, and sexual harassment.

Specific to sexual harassment, Title VII prohibits employers from discrimination against any employee based on an individual's sex, race, color, or religion. *Barnes v. Costle* (1977) was the first case in federal court that recognized sexual harassment as a Title VII violation, as women had lost employment for refusing a supervisor's sexual demands. U.S. Supreme Court cases such as *Meritor Savings Bank v. Vinson* (1986) and *Harris v. Forklift Systems, Inc.* (1993) recognized that a hostile work environment could constitute sexual harassment. Later court cases addressed specific information, such as what a reasonable person would consider to be hostile and abusive, as well as clarifying that sexual harassment does not have to be a demand for sex but has to be sex-based discrimination in some form.

Morgan (2010) and the United States Department of Justice (2007) have suggested other strategies that can be implemented to prevent workplace victimization. *Environmental design prevention strategies* focus on making the workplace a less attractive target for violence and victimization. For instance, better lighting, bullet-proof glass, and silent alarms help to improve workplace safety. *Organizational and administrative strategies* put responsibility on administrators to reduce workplace victimization with better training with security equipment, recording suspicious behavior, and providing resources to employees who report victimization. Lastly, *behavioral strategies* place responsibility on employees to reduce risk of victimization. Training is provided on conflict resolution, anticipating and reacting to violence, and nonviolent responses (Morgan, 2010; USDOJ, 2013).

NIOSH (2006) has provided more detailed strategies for workplace violence prevention and meeting employee needs. *Type I* prevention strategies address environmental intervention (entry and exit control, cash control), behavioral interventions (training on how to respond to threatening individuals or criminal behaviors), and administrative changes (hours of operation, cooperation with the police). *Type II* addresses customer/client violence via improved staffing measures, communication techniques, and training. *Type III* focuses on worker relationships, such as better screening of employees, reporting behaviors, and orientation. Lastly, *Type IV* strategies pinpoint potential dangers with personal relationships. Training on domestic violence cues and reporting, as well as support networks for victims, are part of these strategies (NIOSH, 2006).

Surprisingly, there is not a national standard specific to prevention of workplace victimization. The Occupational Safety and Health Administration (OSHA) and the United States Department of Labor, as discussed previously in the text, have provided suggestions for prevention and protection of victims. Some states do enforce standards approved by OSHA, while other states employ different policies. However, all workplaces must provide a safe work environment that removes all recognizable hazards with repercussions of civil liability and/or criminal charges in noncompliant situations (Occupational Safety and Health Act of 1970, Pub. L. 91–596).

Activity 8.3: Protecting Our Law Enforcement

Police officers have one of the highest levels of on-the-job homicide compared to all other industries. However, police work is not performed in just one location and requires constant geographical movement. During the past five years, the City of Anytown has had five police officer shootings, three of them fatalities. You are an independent safety consultant hired by the chief of police of Anytown to implement better safety measures and training for police officers to decrease police officer shootings. Name and describe two new training policies for officers and one new safety measure to better increase safety for Anytown law enforcement.

Discussion Questions

1. Which act of school violence resonates the most in your mind? Has it had an effect on the way you consider your safety?
2. Do you believe the current methods of promoting and preventing school safety are effective? Why/why not?
3. Have you ever experienced or seen sexual harassment in the workplace? Was it handled in an appropriate way?
4. The workplace is supposed to be a safe and healthy environment. In what ways have we seen this change for better or worse in the past 10 years?

References

Almaguer, M., & Helsel, P. (2015). Survivor of Umpqua Community College rampage describes shooting. *NBCNews.com*. Retrieved from www.nbcnews.com/storyline/oregon-college-shooting/survivor-umpqua-community-college-shooting-describes-rampage-n442146

Barnes v, Costle, 561 F.2d 983 (D.C. Cir. 1997).

Baum, K., Catalano, S., Rand, M., & Rose, K. (2009). Stalking victimization in the United States. Washington, DC: US Department of Justice. Retrieved from www.victimsofcrime.org/docs/src/baum-k-catalano-s-rand-m-rose-k-2009.pdf?sfvrsn=0

Beckstrom, D. (2008). State legislation mandating school cyberbullying policies and the potential threat to students' free speech rights. *Vermont Law Review, 33*, 283–321.

Berdahl, J. (2007). Harassment based on sex: Protecting social status in the context of gender hierarchy. *Academy of Management Review, 32*(2), 641–658.

Bocij, P., & McFarlane, L. (2003). Cyberstalking: The technology of hate. *The Police Journal, 76*, 204–221.

Bureau of Justice Statistics. (2014). *Rape and sexual assault higher among college-age non-student females than female college students 1995–2013*. Retrieved from www.bjs.gov/content/pub/press/rsavcaf9513pr.cfm

Bureau of Labor Statistics. (2013). *Workplace homicides from shootings*. Washington, DC: U.S. Department of Labor. Retrieved from http://www/bls/gov/iif/oshwc/cfoi/osar0016.htm

Bureau of Labor Statistics. (2015). *Census of fatal occupational injuries summary, 2014*. Retrieved from www.bls.gov/news.release/cfoi.nr0.htm

Doerner, W. & Lab, S. (2014). *Victimology* (7th Ed). Routledge.

Fredstrom, B., Adams, R., & Rich, G. (2011). Electronic and school-based victimization: Unique contexts for adjustment difficulties during adolescence. *Journal of Youth and Adolescence, 40(4)*, 405-415.

Harrell, E. (2013). *Workplace violence against government employees, 1994–2011*. United States Department of Justice, Office of Justice Programs, Bureau of Justice Statistics. NCJ 241349.

Harris v. Forklift Sys (1993). 114 S. Ct. 367.

Hinduja, S., & Patchin, J. W. (2008). Cyberbullying: An exploratory analysis of factors related to offending and victimization. *Deviant Behavior 29(2)*: 1–29.

Hinduja, S. & Patchin, J. W. (2009). *Bullying beyond the schoolyard: Preventing and responding to cyberbullying*. Thousand Oaks, CA: Sage.

Kowalski, R. M., Limber, S. P., & Agatston, P. W. (2008). *Cyber bullying: Bullying in the digital age*. Malden, MA: Blackwell.

Lenhart, A. (2009). *Teens and sexting: how and why minor teens are sending sexually suggestive nude or nearly nude images via text messaging*. Washington, DC: Pew Internet & American Life Project.

McLaughlin, E. (2015). Many factors make San Bernardino rate among mass shootings. *CNN. com*. Retrieved from www.cnn.com/2015/12/03/us/san-bernardino-shootings-four-things-unusual/index.html

Menesini, E., Modena, M., & Tani, F. (2009). Bullying and victimization in adolescence: Concurrent and stable roles and psychological health symptoms. *Journal of Genetic Psychology, 170*(2), 115–133.

Meritor Savings Bank v. Vinson, 477 U.S. 57 (1986).

Morgan, P. (2010). Workplace violence training and education. In B. S. Fisher & S. P. Lab (Eds.), *Encyclopedia of victimology and crime prevention* (Vol. 2, pp. 1076–1078). Thousand Oaks, CA: Sage.

NIOSH. (2006). *Workplace violence prevention strategies and research needs* (NIOSH Publication No. 2006–144). Cincinnati: NIOSH. Retrieved from www.cdc.gov/niosh/docs/2006-144/pdfs/2006-144.pdf

Occupational Safety and Health Act of 1970, Pub. L. 91–596.

O'Leary-Kelly, A., Bowes-Sperry, L., Bates, C., & Lean, E. (2009). Sexual harassment at work: A decade (plus) of progress. *Journal of Management, 35*(3), 503–536.

OSHA. (2002). *OSHA fact sheet: Workplace violence*. Retrieved from www.osha.gov/OshDoc/data_General_Facts/factsheet-workplace-violence.pdf

Raskauskas, J., & Stoltz, A. D. (2007). Involvement in traditional and electronic bullying among adolescents. *Developmental Psychology, 43*, 564–575.

Reekman, B. & Cannard, L. (2009). Cyberbullying: a TAFE perspective. *Youth Studies Australia, 28*, 41–49.

Reyns, B. W., Henson, B., & Fisher, B. S. (2012). Staking in the twilight zone: Extent of cyberstalking victimization and offending among college students. *Deviant Behavior, 33*, 1–25.

Robers, S., Zhang, A., Morgan, R., & Misu-Gillette, L. (2015). *Indicators of school crime and safety: 2014* (NCES 2015–072, NCJ 248036). National Center for Education Statistics, U.S. Department of Education, U.S. Department of Justice Office of Justice Programs.

Smith, P. K., Mahdavi, J., Carvalho, M., Fisher, S., Russell, S., & Tippett, N. (2008). Cyberbullying: Its nature and impact in secondary school pupils. *Journal of Child Psychology and Psychiatry, 49*, 376–385.

Swartz, K., Reyns B. W., Wilcox, P., Dunham, J. R. (2012). Patterns of victimization between and within peer clusters in a high school social network. *Violence and Victims, 27*, 710–729.

United States Department of Education. (2016a). *Campus security and safety, 2014*. Retrieved from http://ope.ed.gov/campussafety/#/

United States Department of Education. (2016b). *Trends in bullying at school among students: Ages 12 to 18* (NCES 2016–004). Retrieved from http://nces.ed.gov/pubs2016/2016004.pdf

United States Department of Justice, Office of Justice Programs. (2007). *Bureau of Justice Statistics* (NCJ 241349). Retrieved from www.bjs.gov/content/pub/pdf/wvage9411.pdf

Workplace Bullying Institute. (2015). *2014 W.B.I. U.S. Workplace Bullying Survey, February 2014*. Retrieved from www.workplacebullying.org/wbiresearch/wbi-2014-us-survey/

Ybarra, M., Diener-West, M., & Leaf, P. (2008). Examining the overlap in Internet harassment and school bullying: Implications for school bullying. *Journal of Adolescent Health, 41*, 42–50.

Zins, J. E., & Elias, M. J. (2007). Social and emotional learning: Promoting the development of all students. *Journal of Educational & Psychological Consultation, 17*(2), 233–255. doi:10.1080/10474410701413152

Chapter 9

Victimization of Special Populations

Keywords

- Abandonment
- Adam Walsh Child Protection and Safety Act
- Elder Justice Act
- Maltreatment
- Megan's Law
- Neglect
- Physical Abuse
- Prison Rape Elimination Act (PREA)
- Psychological Abuse
- Sexual Abuse

Victims in general are a special population managed in our criminal justice system. However, within that group are subcategories of individuals who have special needs and considerations. They have characteristics that make them attractive targets: vulnerability, inability to understand or report, and a variety of other factors. In fact, some of these victims may also be a victimizer at some point. Each section in this chapter discusses the characteristics that make members of a particular group ideal targets for victimization, as well as responses by the community and government to better protect these special populations.

Persons Who Are Incarcerated

Incarceration does not automatically equate to daily victimization by rape, despite societal stereotypes. Nevertheless, it is ironic that a population consistently supervised and monitored by correctional officers is at risk for victimization. In fact, the Eighth Amendment guarantees protection for inmates from foreseeable attack during incarceration (*Farmer v. Brennan*, 1994). However, due to a multitude of factors, including low staff-to-inmate ratio, gang activity, and simply a subculture of violence (especially in male facilities), individuals who are incarcerated are at high risk for victimization. Victimization likelihood is higher in the first six months of incarceration (Hensley, Castle & Tewksbury, 2003; Hensley, Koscheski, & Tewksbury, 2005), presumably due to the belief that "fresh meat" (new inmates) are easier prey and not familiar with the threats present in a particular facility. Theft is a regular occurrence in corrections facilities, and simple assault, aggravated assault, and sexual assault, while not necessarily daily occurrences, are common as well.

There are multiple contributing factors to victimization of the incarcerated. For instance, male inmates are more likely to be physically aggressive based on biological and sociological factors, and thus often find themselves in physical altercations with other inmates and staff. In other words, males often result to settling disputes with a physical reaction rather than verbal mediation. Violence is often an instinctual reaction, especially for men who have been raised in environments where it is expected for survival. Inmates who are homosexual or small in stature also have an increased likelihood of victimization (Beck & Harrison, 2003; Hensley, Castle, & Tewksbury, 2003).

In addition, racial tension is prevalent in male facilities (Hassine, 2009). Inmates often voluntarily segregate themselves by race. Prison gangs are racially segregated, and non-affiliated inmates may join a gang for protection after entering prison. This increases the likelihood of physical victimization for males.

Activity 9.1: Violence Behind Bars

It is not difficult to find a recent story in media involving inmate violence. Find an example of a recent event of violence against an inmate in the news. What happened to the inmate, and was there an explanation of what incited the event? What underlying factors do you believe caused the event or were missing to prevent it? Based on the subculture of violence permeating the prison, what can the corrections system do to decrease violence in prison?

Past abuse also contributes to increased likelihood of victimization for inmates. Multiple studies have found that victimized female inmates especially have past histories of physical, mental, and sexual abuse (Covington & Bloom, 2006; Gido & Dalley, 2009; Wolff, Shi & Siegal, 2009). A study by Wolff et al. (2009) found that, of the inmates who were victimized in childhood (before age 18), about half of these were later victimized while in prison or jail. Understandably, incarceration can be extremely psychologically traumatizing (Haney, 2003). Abuse victims often cope with the stress through criminal activity rather than positive resources and outlets (which are often not available).

Victimization in prison can occur in various ways. Theft by coercion or deception is prevalent. Money is not an item of value in prison, so clothing, food, and electronics are often stolen or traded for favors. Physical altercations are also very common in prison, as violence is often a first resort to handle disagreements, perceptions of wrongdoing, and words perceived as disrespectful. Wolff, Shi and Siegel (2009) collected data from 12 adult male prisons and one female prison in a single state. Twenty-one percent of male and of female inmates reported inmate-on-inmate physical victimization, but a much larger percentage of males (25%) reported physical victimization by a staff member compared to staff victimization of female inmates (8%).

Sexual victimization is unfortunately also a common event in correctional facilities. Wolff et al. (2009) found that more female inmates (24%) reported sexual victimization than male inmates (10%). In fact, female inmates were more likely to report multiple forms of victimization; in other words, those who reported physical victimization were much more likely to report sexual victimization as well. As a result of a notable increase in sexual victimization in correctional facilities, President George W. Bush signed into legislation the Prison Rape Elimination Act (PREA) in 2003 (Pub. L. 108–79). PREA implemented a zero tolerance policy for sexual assault in prison, including severe punishments for all offenders, whether staff or inmates. PREA also required an annual report provided to the general public on the amount of sexual assaults occurring in prison and jail facilities each year. The purpose of these efforts was to provide more transparency and accountability for the prisons, as well as justice for the victims.

In 2011 over 8,700 allegations of sexual victimization were reported in prisons and jails, with 10% of those allegations substantiated (Bureau of Justice Statistics, 2014). Almost half of those allegations involved staff sexual misconduct. Reports indicated the most common location for inmate-on-inmate sexual victimization was a victim's cell, while staff-on-inmate victimization most often occurred in a common room. Beck and Harrison (2003) found that females were more likely than males to be sexually victimized by other inmates. White inmates were also more likely to be victimized by other inmates. In regard to victimization by staff members, male inmates were more likely to be sexually assaulted by staff compared to female inmates, as well as black inmates were more likely to be victimized compared to white inmates. Lastly, two interesting predictors of sexual victimization were education and age. More educated inmates have a higher likelihood of sexual victimization by both inmates and staff, while inmates under the age of 25 were more likely to be sexually victimized by staff (Beck & Harrison, 2003).

Web Clips 9.1: PREA

The National PREA Resource Center provides a plethora of information on training, events, and other related resources to assist government and private entities with prison sexual assault. Using its website, at www.prearesourcecenter.org, find three surprising statistics about the victims of prison sexual assault. For instance, is there a certain geographical region with more occurrences? Is there a difference based on level of prison security (e.g., minimum, medium, maximum)?

A correctional institution can take different proactive or reactive steps to try to improve the safety of individual inmates. A proactive measure is effective classification (Daigle & Muftic, 2015), which is the process of placing offenders in appropriate security levels and treatment programs based on risk and need. Inmate current offense, past incarceration behaviors, diagnosed mental illness, and other conditions are considered. Classification can occur multiple times during the incarceration of an inmate, but ideally the placement should meet the needs of the inmate and keep him or her safe during the entire incarceration. However, in the event an inmate gets attacked or feels unsafe, there is another option. Protective custody (PC)—secure housing where an inmate is confined for 23 hours a day in isolation—is meant to protect threatened inmates from victimization, or further events of victimization. However, PC is managed in the same way as solitary confinement (used as a punishment) and prevents inmates from participating in programming and other positive activities.

Persons with Disabilities

Individuals with disabilities are a particularly vulnerable group in the criminal justice system, especially as disabilities can occur in different forms. A physical disability challenges a person's ability to physically function, hindering such actions as walking, lifting, or basic hygiene functions (Daigle & Muftic, 2016). Developmental disabilities affect a person's cognitive abilities. According to the Centers for Disease Control and Prevention (2015), developmental disabilities manifest before age 22 and cause impairment in at least three of the following areas: language, learning, independent living, mobility, and self-care. Examples of developmental disabilities include autism, cerebral palsy, and intellectual disability.

Persons with disabilities may possess certain characteristics that make them extremely vulnerable to victimization. They may not be able to recognize risk, such as interacting with untrustworthy people or being in a dangerous location. Many people with disabilities rely on others for assistance, such as a home health care worker or a family member, to manage their finances. Possessions, medications, and money can be stolen from the disabled without their knowledge. Or, based on limitations in communication abilities, they may be unable to express what has occurred or know who to report it to in order to get help. In addition, if they are sexually abused, based on lack of sexual education they may not even be aware it is inappropriate behavior (Daigle & Muftic, 2016; Petersilia, 2001). Lastly, people with disabilities are more likely to live in poverty, which increases the likelihood that they will live in high-crime neighborhoods and be subject to victimization (Petersilia, 2001).

Web Clips 9.2: Hatred in Chicago

In January 2017 four young adults in Chicago streamed a live video on Facebook of the harassment and torture of a special needs teen whom they had kidnapped. In the video the attackers assaulted the teen with a knife and made racial slurs against white people and insults against President-elect Donald Trump. Check out coverage of some of the video and discussion of the contents at www.cnn.com/2017/01/05/us/chicago-facebook-live-beating/index.html. At the time of the CNN clip, the teens were charged with hate crimes against a disabled person.

Do you see evidence of a hate crime based on a disability?

Using data acquired by the National Crime Victimization Survey, Harrell (2015) investigated crimes committed against people with disabilities from 2009 to 2013. Persons with disabilities experienced 1.3 million violent victimizations, which was more than twice the amount experienced by persons without disabilities between 2009 and 2013. In 2013 alone the rate of serious violent victimizations was three times the amount for persons with disabilities and twice the amount when considering simple assaults. However, persons with disabilities were slightly more likely to report violent victimization compared to those without disabilities (48% versus 44%), as well as seek help from victim services agencies (12% versus 8%) (Harrell, 2015).

When examining rates of victimization for specific groups of persons with disabilities, there were differences in some of the groups (Harrell, 2015). There was no statistical significance between males and females. However, whites with disabilities had higher rates of victimization in 2013 (38 per 1,000) than did blacks (31 per 1,000). Persons with cognitive disabilities had the highest rate of victimization of all forms measured compared to other types of disability (Harrell, 2015).

Persons Who Are Elderly

There has been a slow increase in the number of elderly persons in the American population, due mostly to the large number of babies born after the end of World War II. A number of factors, including lower infant mortality rates and longer life expectancy, has resulted in a higher percentage of older persons in the population. According to the Administration on Aging (2012), there were 41.4 million individuals 65 years or older in 2011, an 18% increase since 2000.

Characteristics of this growing population make them attractive targets for victimization. For instance, almost half of women over 75 years old live alone, often without guardianship during the day and night, leaving them fearful of victimization. Ironically, the elderly have one of the lowest rates of victimization compared to other age groups, yet have the highest level of fear of crime based on life circumstances (Doerner & Lab, 2015). The elderly have experienced a multitude of life experiences and hold characteristics not common to younger adults, so there are multiple ways the elderly can be victimized. *Physical elder abuse* is injury, impairment, and/or pain inflicted through physical assault, force-feeding, and drug administration (National Center on Elder Abuse, 2016). As the elderly are often unable to defend themselves due to diminished physical capacity, they are often easy to physically coerce and intimidate. *Psychological abuse* means inflicting emotional distress via verbal assault, harassment, and humiliation, while *sexual abuse* can involve unwanted sexual activity or viewing of pornography. Persons who are responsible for care of an elderly person can be charged with *neglect* or *abandonment* if they fail at meeting those responsibilities. In addition, *financial exploitation*, a common form of victimization by family members and caretakers, is the illegal and improper use of a senior's property and assets.

In the News 9.1: Crime Does Not Pay . . . Or Does It?

Dr. Aria Sabit, a Detroit-area physician, was sentenced to almost 20 years in prison for health care fraud, which involved theft of approximately $11 million from Medicare, Medicaid, and private insurance companies for unnecessary operations or operations that never occurred. The federal court judge hoped to make him an example to deter other physicians from committing fraud.

Do you believe such a severe sentence can deter other health care professionals from committing health care fraud, or will this be considered an unlucky break for Sabit?

According to the Family Caregiver Alliance (2015), over 8 million persons receive care from some form of a long-term care service, including the 1.38 million in nursing homes. Health care providers and institutions are elder abuse offenders based on the vulnerabilities of the seniors in their care. For instance, doctors and hospitals can overbill for procedures not administered, or overmedicate or undermedicate a senior in order to commit fraud (Robinson, de Benedictis, & Segal, 2011). Nursing homes have received particular scrutiny for abuse and neglect, beginning in the 1970s when facilities were not regulated or monitored. In 2014 the National Ombudsmen Reporting System found that 7.6% of the 188,599 complaints reported to ombudsman programs involved abuse, gross neglect, or exploitation of nursing home residents (National Center for Elder Abuse, 2016).

Fortunately, there are multiple resources for the elderly or concerned family and friends. The Elder Justice Act (P.L. 111–148), signed into law in 2010, provided $400 million for adult protective services, support for long-term care ombudsman program, and support for forensic centers relating to elder abuse. States have different forms of legislation to protect elders and provide resources, with the most common being mandatory reporting laws for neglect and abuse and requirement for social services provisions with these reports. There has been criticism of mandatory reporting laws, as they often create confusion on a definition of abuse and the appropriate outlets of where to report. In other words, the reports are made but often do not go any further than the original piece of paper on which the report is written (Payne, 2011).

Web Clips 9.3: Protecting Our Elderly

Our elderly population is often the forgotten generation, and as a result, the federal government is making strides in protecting this group. Check out the United States Department of Justice's Elder Justice Initiative at www.justice.gov/elderjustice. In your opinion, is the federal government doing enough to prevent victimization? What about your home state?

Persons With Mental Illness

Individuals with mental illness are overrepresented in the criminal justice system, and thus have a large percentage of resources designated for their care and treatment. After deinstitutionalization policies in the 1950s shut down many institutions for the mentally ill (Silver, 2002), many individuals were unable to obtain treatment and medicine required to manage their mental illness. As a result, the criminal justice system began to see an increase of appearance of persons with mental illness. Currently, approximately 60% of offenders have some diagnosable form of mental illness, from mild depression to severe schizophrenia. Individuals with a mental illness are also more likely to be victims of crimes (especially violent crimes) (Levin, 2005).

The American Psychiatric Association defines mental illness as a health condition that involves changes in thinking, emotion, or behavior (Parekh, 2015). Symptoms can range from mild to severe, and are associated with distress and problems in life activities. Approximately 20% of American adults experience a form of mental illness, including the 4.1% of adults who have a serious mental illness and 8.5% who have a substance use disorder. Mental illness can affect persons of all ages, races, and sexes (Parekh, 2015).

Mental illness can be indicated by the following behaviors: withdrawal from social situations, illogical thinking, mood changes, decrease in functioning, and unusual behaviors (Parekh, 2015). Many mental illnesses and their symptoms are familiar to the American public, such as depression, bipolar disorder, and Alzheimer's disease. In addition, mental illness can include such behaviors as hoarding disorder, eating disorder, and obsessive-compulsive disorder.

Several factors increase the potential for victimization of persons with mental illness. Many individuals are unable to obtain regular medical care, therapy, and medication, causing increased symptoms of the mental illness. This can make it difficult for mentally ill persons to defend themselves or recognize a risky situation. Some individuals with mental illness are homeless and/or are substance abusers, both of which conditions also increase their susceptibility to victimization (Teasdale, 2009). Lastly, symptoms of certain mental illnesses may involve hallucinations and delusions, which are linked to violent behaviors (Appelbaum, Robbins, & Monahan, 2000; Teasdale, 2009). A person with mental illness exhibiting violent behavior may provoke violence in others, causing victimization.

Controversial Considerations 9.1: Protecting Offenders?

A large percentage of the American inmate population has some form of mental illness, ranging from mild depression to violent schizophrenia. These individuals are often victimized while incarcerated based on their inability to recognize risk factors or their susceptibility to manipulation. In addition, inmates with mental illness who are released from incarceration often return to the criminal justice system with new offenses due to lack of access to treatment and medication. Is it possible to stop this revolving door?

It is difficult to estimate the victimization rates of individuals with mental illness as many of the occurrences go unreported. However, some studies have attempted to uncover the frequency of these occurrences and these generally focus on severe mental illness. For example, using data from the National Crime Victimization Survey (NCVS) and from persons receiving psychiatric services in Chicago, Teplin, McClelland, Abram, and Weiner (2005) specifically examined adults with severe mental illnesses and found that 25% of this group had experienced some form of violent crime victimization (almost 12 times higher the victimization rate of that reported in the NCVS). Females with severe mental illness were more likely to experience sexual assault and theft, and severely mentally ill males were more likely to experience robbery. Almost 30% of the group in Chicago experienced a property crime, which was four times the rate of respondents to the NCVS (Daigle & Muftic, 2015). Supplementing these findings in a more recent study, a 2009 meta-analysis of victimization studies reported that the severely mentally ill were found to be 2.3 to 140.4 times more likely to be victimized, especially those who were abusing drugs and alcohol (Maniglio, 2009).

Activity 9.2: Repairing Wrongs

On January 21, 2017, an editorial in the *Los Angeles Times* asserted that reparations should be made to those who were violated and sterilized in the eugenics movement in the first half of the 20th century. Thirty-two states allowed sterilizations to be performed on the mentally disabled and mentally ill, including people judged sexually promiscuous, at state-run mental institutions. Over 60,000 individuals were sterilized, with 20,000 of those persons in the state of California. Governor Gray Davis issued a formal apology in 2003, but no financial reparations have been made. In a small group, develop a persuasive argument for or against providing further compensation for the victims of the eugenics movement and their families.

Persons Who Are Minors

The protections afforded to a child have been a work in progress for hundreds of years. In the past, abused, delinquent, and orphaned children were often treated as though they were adult offenders. The groundbreaking case, *Kempe et al.* (1962), was the first public admission of parents intentionally abusing their children. This case introduced the term *battered child syndrome*. Since that time, a vast number of child maltreatment laws and regulations have passed.

The federal Child Abuse Prevention and Treatment Act (42 U.S.C. 5101) defined child maltreatment as a function of three components:

1. Act or failure to act produces risk of physical or emotional harm;
2. Victim of maltreatment is under 18 years of age;
3. Perpetrator of maltreatment is parent or caretaker of the child victim.

State laws generally define child *abuse* and *neglect* in broad terms to encourage reporting of all suspected cases (Doerner & Lab, 2015). Abuse is nonaccidental infliction of injury that impairs the physical or mental health of a child. Neglect is the withholding of essentials to sustain life, such as food, water, shelter, and medication. While some states recognize that parents hold religious beliefs that direct them to refrain from medical treatment, a court can intervene if a life-threatening situation or disability occurs.

The United States Department of Health and Human Services Children's Bureau has attempted to combine various definitions of child maltreatment into more specific categories (see Table 9.1) (Child Welfare Information Gateway, 2008).

Simply being a child puts an individual at risk for any of these forms of abuse. However, children who live in homes with drug and/or alcohol abuse, or domestic violence are at higher risk (National Child Abuse and Neglect Data System, 2015). Children who experience maltreatment can exhibit a variety of symptoms, including unexplained markings (e.g. bruises or welts), frequent absences from school, bad hygiene, and emotional and sexual inappropriateness. Abused children may also be delayed in development, experience nightmares, and attempt suicide (Child Welfare Information Gateway, 2013).

Table 9.1 Categories of Child Abuse

Abuse Category	Definition
Physical Abuse	Nonaccidental physical injury as a result of behaviors such as punching, kicking, shaking, throwing, or stabbing. Infliction of the injury must be by someone who was responsible for the child at the time. The injury is abuse even if it was not intended as such.
Emotional Abuse	Pattern of behavior that impairs a child's sense of worth or development. This can include threats, withholding love, and criticism. Due the nature of emotional abuse, it may be difficult to prove on its own, but it is almost always present with other forms of abuse.
Sexual Abuse	Activities by a caregiver, parent, or guardian that involve sexual touch, penetration, or exploitation, including production of child pornography.
Substance Abuse	This form of abuse can entail prenatal exposure to illegal drugs, manufacturing methamphetamine in presence of a child, selling or giving illegal substances to a child, and use of a controlled substance by the caregiver that impairs ability to care for a child.
Neglect	Failure of a parent or caregiver to provide basic physical, medical, educational, and emotional needs.
Abandonment	Abandonment occurs when the parent's whereabouts are unknown, child suffers harm after being left alone, or parent does not provide reasonable support for a given amount of time. It is often defined as neglect in many states.

Activity 9.3: Shaken Baby Syndrome

Shaken baby syndrome is a traumatic brain injury inflicted upon the child by being violently shaken. It can cause brain bruising, swelling, and bleeding that can lead to permanent brain damage, often resulting in cerebral palsy, intellectual disability, or even death. Prenatal and postnatal education on shaken baby syndrome is available to parents, as well as many other resources for stressful parenting management.

What resources are currently available in your area for parents? Is there evidence that these programs have effected a decrease in child abuse?

In fiscal year 2015, there were approximately 683,000 substantiated victims of child abuse and neglect, with over 4 million investigated reports (National Child Abuse and Neglect Data System, 2015). The large majority of the reports were for neglect (over 75%), but sadly over 1,600 children died as a result of abuse and neglect in 2015. The victimization rate was higher for children under the age of one (24.2 per 1,000 children in the population) and females (9.6 per 1,000 female children compared to 8.8 per 1,000 male children). The majority of substantiated reports of abuse and neglect were for white children (43.2%) (National Child Abuse and Neglect Data System, 2015).

In addition to immediate injuries, child abuse and neglect can have severe long-term effects (Daigle & Muftic, 2016). For instance, impairments to the brain can affect language, academic abilities, and cognitive abilities. Psychologically, abused and neglected children may develop anxiety or depression, posttraumatic stress disorder, and anger management issues. Children who are sexually abused may have problems with maintaining healthy relationships as adults, and suicidal thoughts are not abnormal. Lastly, abuse and neglect can increase involvement in delinquent and adult criminality (Jesperson, Lalumiere, & Seto, 2009; Widom, 2000).

Combating and preventing child abuse and neglect can be a difficult task, but states and the federal government have done quite a bit to address the issue in regard to laws and programming. As mentioned previously, a large percentage of child abuse cases involve children under the age of one, including baby abandonment and infanticide. There are parents, more often mothers, who are not prepared to have a child and may want to hide the birth of a newborn. Babies have been found in unhygienic public areas such as restrooms and Dumpsters. As a result of the increase in abandoned children, "safe haven" laws have been passed in every state to provide safe locations (e.g., hospitals, police stations, fire stations) where a parent can relinquish custody of a newborn without questions or legal repercussions (Child Welfare Information Gateway, 2010). However, mandatory reporting laws do require that employees of the state, such as law enforcement or social services, report all suspicions of child maltreatment no matter the age of the child (Daigle & Muftic, 2016).

Counseling options are available for parents who have perpetrated abuse and neglect, or fear that they may perform such acts. Parents Anonymous provides resources for parents needing support and positive parenting options for children of all types and special needs (Parents Anonymous, 2013, as cited in Doerner & Lab, 2015). Children's Advocacy Centers (CAC) incorporates multiple service agencies and criminal justice agencies to provide adept services for children who have been abused and neglected. These services can include counseling and treatment, as well as options to help the child maneuver through the court system with as little trauma as possible. The criminal justice system may also provide a guardian ad litem (GAL) to appear on behalf of a child in court (Daigle & Muftic, 2016).

Laws have been passed to increase punishment of violent offenders. After the rape and murder of seven-year-old Megan Kanka in 1993, President Bill Clinton signed Megan's Law in 1996 in order to allow for public notification of the presence of sex offenders in communities. Sex offenders are categorized by tier based on severity level, which predicates the type of notification that is used. For instance, states will inform the victim and law enforcement when offenders who are on the lowest tier are released. If an offender is in the highest risk category, communities can have press releases and flyers posted with the offender's history and current address. The Adam Walsh Child Protection and Safety Act, signed into law by President George W. Bush in 2006, created the National Sex Offender Registry (SORN) and introduced a series of rules and regulations for the SORN practices (Doerner & Lab, 2015).

Web Clips 9.4: Amber Alerts

In September 2016 the Federal Communications Commission approved additional functions of the Wireless Emergency Alerts system, which delivers critical alerts to cellular phone users. One of these is the national Amber Alert system. The Amber Alert website is at www.amberalert.gov/. What are other online options where you can utilize these reactive methods to retrieve lost children?

Summary

As can be seen from this chapter, many kinds of people can be victimized. While all victims should be handled with care with their individual needs considered, there are certain groups that need additional resources and considerations. The main question is: are we doing enough to protect these groups?

Discussion Questions

1. Is it possible to diminish the invisible racial divides in correctional facilities?
2. Victims of crime are often persons who cannot speak for themselves or cannot comprehend the extent of victimization. What safeguards are currently implemented to help these special groups?

Note

1   *Intellectual disability* is a contemporary term for mental retardation. Statutes applicable to the insanity defense often note mental retardation as standard for relief of legal responsibility, or mitigated responsibility, for criminal behavior. Both "intellectual disability" and "mental retardation" refer to IQ level, generally 70 points or under.

References

Appelbaum, P. S., Robbins, P. C., & Monahan, J. (2000). Violence and delusions: Data from the MacArthur Violence Risk Assessment Study. *American Journal of Psychiatry, 157,* 566–572.

Beck, A. & Harrison, P. (2003). *Prison and jail inmates at midyear 2003.* Washington, DC: Bureau of Justice Statistics.

Bureau of Justice Statistics. (2014). *Allegations of sexual victimization in prisons and jails rose from 2009 to 2011; substantiated incidents remained stable.* Retrieved from www.bjs.gov/content/pub/press/svraca0911pr.cfm

Center for Disease Control and Prevention (2015). *Key findings: Trends in the prevalence of Autism Spectrum Disorder, Cerebral Palsy, hearing loss, intellectual disability, and vision impairment, Metropolitan Atlanta, 1991–2010.* Retrieved from https://www.cdc.gov/ncbddd/developmentaldisabilities/features/dev-disability-trends.html

Child Welfare Information Gateway. (2008). *What are the major types of child abuse and neglect?* Washington, DC: U.S. Department of Health and Human Services, Children's Bureau. Retrieved from www.childwelfare.gov/pubs/factsheets/whatiscan.cfm

Child Welfare Information Gateway. (2013). *What are the major types of child abuse and neglect?* Washington, DC: U.S. Department of Health and Human Services, Children's Bureau. Retrieved from www.childwelfare.gov/pubs/factsheets/whatiscan.cfm

Covington, S., & Bloom, B. (2006). Gender responsive treatment services in correctional settings. In E. Leeder (Ed.), *Inside and out: Women, prison and therapy.* Philadelphia, Pennsylvania: Haworth Press.

Daigle, L., & Muftic, L. (2015). *Victimology.* Thousand Oaks, CA: Sage Publications.

Doerner, W., & Lab, S. (2015). *Victimology* (7th ed.). New York, NY: Routledge.

Family Caregiver Alliance. (2015). *Selected long-term care statistics.* Retrieved from www.caregiver.org/selected-long-term-care-statistics

Gido, R. L., & Dalley, L. (2009). *Women's mental health issues across the criminal justice system.* Upper Side River, NJ: Pearson Prentice Hall.

Haney, C. (2003). The psychological impact of incarceration: Implications for post-prison adjustment. In J. Travis & M. Waul (Eds.), *Prisoners once removed: The impact of incarceration and reentry on children, families, and communities* (pp. 33–66). Washington, DC: Urban Institute Press.

Harrell, E. (2015). *Crime against persons with disabilities, 2009–2013—Statistical tables* (NC 248676). Washington, DC: U.S. Department of Justice, Office of Justice Programs, Bureau of Justice Statistics.

Hassine, V. (2009). *Life without parole* (4th ed.). New York: Oxford University Press.

Hensley, C., Castle, T., & Tewksbury, R. (2003). Inmate-to-inmate sexual coercion in a prison for women. *Journal of Offender Rehabilitation, 37,* 77–87.

Hensley, C., Koscheski, M., & Tewksbury, R. (2005). Examining the characteristics of male sexual assault targets in a southern maximum-security prison. *Journal of Interpersonal Violence, 20,* 667–679.

Levin, A. (2005). People with mental illness more often crime victims. *Psychiatric News*. Retrieved from https://psychnews.psychiatryonline.org/doi/full/10.1176/pn.40.17.00400016

Maniglio, R. (2009). Severe mental illness and criminal victimization: A systematic review. *Acta Psychiatrica Scandinavica*, *119*, 180–191.

National Center for Elder Abuse. (2016). *Research*. Retrieved from https://ncea.acl.gov/whatwedo/research/statistics.html#ltc

National Child Abuse and Neglect Data System. (2015). *Child maltreatment*, *2015*. Retrieved from www.acf.hhs.gov/sites/default/files/cb/cm2015.pdf#page=66

Parekh, R. (2015). *What is a mental illness?* Retrieved from www.psychiatry.org/patients-families/what-is-mental-illness

Payne, B. (2011). *Crime and elder abuse: An integrated perspective* (3rd ed.). Springfield, IL: Charles C. Thomas Publisher, Ltd.

Petersilia, J. (2001). Crime victims with developmental disabilities: A review essay. *Criminal Justice & Behavior*, *28*(6), 655–694.

Robinson, L., de Benedictis, T., & Segal, J. (2011). *Elder abuse and neglect: Warning signs, risk factors, prevention, and help*. Retrieved from http://helpguide.org/mental/elder_abuse_physical_emotional_sexual_neglect.htm

Silver, E. (2002). Mental disorder and violent victimization: The mediating role of involvement in conflicted social relationships. *Criminology*, *40*, 191–212.

Teasdale, B. (2009). Mental disorder and violent victimization. *Criminal Justice & Behavior*, *36*(5), 513–535.

Wolff, N., Shi, J., & Siegal, J. (2009). Patterns of victimization among male and female inmates: Evidence of an enduring legacy. *Violence and Victims*, *24*(4), 469–484.

Chapter 10

Hate Crimes and Terrorism

Keywords

- Domestic Terrorism
- Hate Crimes
- International Terrorism
- PATRIOT Act
- Sentencing Enhancement

Ten days after Republican candidate Donald Trump won the presidential election, the Southern Poverty Law Center reported 867 accounts of hateful harassment or intimidation (Yan, Sgueglia, & Walker, 2016). President-elect Trump appeared on *60 Minutes* and asked individuals to stop posting xenophobic, anti-Islamic, and homophobic graffiti and abuse, and fortunately the amount of harassment has decreased (CBS News, 2016). However, there has been a definite resurgence of the commission of hate crimes in the past several years despite the public perception that we are a more tolerant society. In addition, terroristic acts (often as a result of bias or prejudice against a specific country or group) have grown over the past 20 years.

This chapter explores two forms of victimization: hate crimes and terrorism. Definitions of both are explored, as well as the various concepts and considerations associated with each. These forms of victimization can be hard to prove in that it is necessary to provide concrete evidence of the perpetrator's bias and prejudice.

Hate Crimes

Defining Hate Crimes

The Federal Bureau of Investigation has investigated hate acts since World War I, but assigned increased manpower to these events after the passing of the Civil Rights Act of 1964 (FBI, 2016a). Before the Civil Rights Act, the federal government took a hands-off approach to management of civil rights and viewed it as a local responsibility. However, when civil rights workers Michael Schwerner, Andrew Goodman, and James Chaney were abducted and murdered in Mississippi and it was determined the Ku Klux Klan and local law enforcement were involved, the federal government began taking a prominent role in investigating and combating hate crimes.

Feeling hate toward a person or group is not a crime, as it is a right protected by the Constitution. A hate crime is not a specific and unique crime, but instead is generally a "traditional" criminal offense like vandalism, arson, or murder. In order for it to be charged as a hate crime, there must be evidence that the crime was committed against an individual or property as a result of prejudice or bias based on "race, religion, disability, sexual orientation, ethnicity, gender or gender identity" (FBI, 2016a). It is important to note that it is irrelevant whether or not the victim of the crime actually possesses a specific characteristic, but it is imperative that the offender perceives that the victim exhibits a characteristic and acts on that perception. For example, if Susan vandalizes John's car with homophobic graffiti but John is a heterosexual, it could still be a hate crime, and as such, punishment is often more severe than it would be for a simple vandalism conviction. However, if she slashes his tires with no evidence indicating she acted out of prejudice or bias, she will be charged with vandalism.

Activity 10.1: Express Yourself

The First Amendment is one of the most constantly challenged and tested amendments. It is our constitutional right to speak our mind, even if it is not the majority opinion. Check out the website of the Ku Klux Klan, one of America's most infamous hate groups: www. kkk.com. Compare this website to two other websites that support a cause.

Hate Crime Legislation

On the federal level, the Civil Rights Act of 1964 (42 U.S.C. § 2000e) began the slow and steady movement to combat discrimination in the United States by outlawing unfair employment practices based on race, sex, nationality, or religion (Doerner & Lab, 2015). In 1968 an amendment to the Civil Rights Act extended the protection for equal access to housing (i.e., selling, renting, or financing any living abode). Related federal legislation was not passed again for another 25 years until the Hate Crime Statistics Act of 1990 (28 U.S.C. § 534), which required the United States Attorney General to compile information on bias-motivated crimes. The Federal Bureau of Investigation was already collecting crime statistics annually with the Uniform Crime Reporting Program, so it also became responsible for collecting data on hate crimes. As of this writing, the most recent and innovative addition by the federal government to address hate crimes is the Matthew Shepard and James Byrd Jr. Hate Crimes Prevention Act (18 U.S.C. § 249), passed in 2009, which extended protection against bias to those who are sexual minorities (i.e., gay, lesbian, bisexual, and transgender).

Case Study 10.1: Matthew Shepard and James Byrd Jr. Hate Crimes Prevention Act of 2009

Matthew Shepard, a young college student at the University of Wyoming, was robbed, beaten unconscious and left tied to a fence by two men who had offered to give him a ride home. He died a few days later in the hospital. The two men were later arrested and charged with murder, admitting they had assaulted Shepard after he made homosexual advances toward them. Both were given life sentences, in large part because Shepard's parents asked for mercy for the two men. Shepard's parents soon thereafter created the Matthew Shepard Foundation (www.matthewshepard.org) to provide resources and advocacy for LGBTQ persons.

James Byrd Jr. was an African-American man who was abducted by three white supremacists in Texas. He was chained by his ankles to the back of a pickup truck and dragged for three miles. He was conscious during the entire ordeal until his head and arm became severed from his body. Two of the men were sentenced to death, and the third is serving life in prison.

The brutal deaths of these two men in the same year (1998) spurred the passage of the first federal legislation extending protection for discriminatory acts against LGBTQ citizens since the 1969 Civil Rights Act, as well as providing additional resources for hate crime investigations and prevention. Signed into law by President Obama in October 2009, the act requires the FBI to track gender-related hate crimes. It gives federal law enforcement the ability to conduct hate crimes investigations not pursued by local law enforcement, as well as providing $5 million per year to state and local agencies for these investigations.

California was the first state to target hate crimes, in 1978, and other states began to do so in the 1980s. While state hate-crime laws may vary slightly, they all address the following issues:

- Discriminatory violence based on race, ethnicity, religion, sexual preference, disability, and age;
- Symbolic displays of hate, such as cross-burning or wearing hoods;
- Vandalism of places of worship or monuments;
- Training for law enforcement; and
- Data reporting.

(Doerner & Lab, 2015)

In addition, both federal and state hate crimes legislation provide *sentencing enhancement* for crimes committed based on one or more of the hate crimes requirements. Violence and actions based on discriminatory views are considered aggravating circumstances, allowing a judge to raise a penalty allowed under the sentencing laws. In the Supreme Court case of *Wisconsin v. Mitchell* (1993), where Mitchell (a black youth) and friends attacked a white youth simply because of his race and were given a sentencing enhancement, Mitchell appealed, stating the hate crime enhancement violated his First Amendment rights. The Supreme Court disagreed and upheld the decision, stating it was not Mitchell's prejudice but his actions that validated the use of the sentencing enhancement.

Not surprisingly, the Court has handled other cases arguing the First Amendment right to express hate. In *Virginia v. Black* (2003), one of the more famous cases that explained the "true threat doctrine" applied in other cases, the constitutionality of an anti-cross-burning statute was considered. The Court ruled that cross-burning activities implemented by the Ku Klux Klan were meant to send a message of intimidation to individuals not affiliated with the KKK, supported by a long history of KKK violence. Cross-burning insinuates a "true threat," which is a statement "where the speaker means to communicate a serious expressing of intent to commit an act of unlawful violence to a particular individual or group of individuals."

Responses by Stakeholders

Although legislation is in place, it is ultimately up to criminal justice stakeholders to determine how to respond to potential hate crimes. The first step in punishment for a hate crime is law enforcement response. According to the International Association of Chiefs of Police (2001), there are several key items that could indicate commission of a hate crime:

1. Perceptions of the victims and witnesses;
2. Perpetrator's behavior that indicates bias or prejudice;
3. Differences between the victim and perpetrator;
4. Similar incidents in the same area;
5. Incident occurred on a holiday or date of significance; and
6. Involvement of recognized hate group members.

However, even if these indicators are linked to the crime, the crime must actually get reported to law enforcement. This can be an issue depending on the victim. Some racial and religious groups do not trust law enforcement based on past experience. For example, there was a backlash against Muslims and Arab Americans in the United States after the September 11, 2001, terrorist attacks, and many minority citizens were perceived to be the enemy (Disha, Cavendish, & King, 2011). These perceptions may make it difficult for some citizens to trust that the police will treat reports fairly.

Prosecutors are also instrumental in determining the rate of punishment of hate crimes. Prosecutors use the same standards as law enforcement to determine if a hate crime has occurred. However, there is often a concern that the details of the crime are so complex that while trying to prove a hate crime occurred, jurors may get confused and acquit the offender altogether. Plea bargains are often accepted in exchange for at least some guaranteed punishment, but the plea bargain may decrease the severity of the punishment. Supreme Court decisions such as *Apprendi v. New Jersey* (2013) and *Alleyne v. U.S.* (2013) overturned lower court decisions that punished hate-crime offenders with sentencing enhancements based on issues of due process that the Court found were ignored.

Hate Groups

The Southern Poverty Law Center (SPLC) (2016a) developed a "Hate Map," a geographical map of the United States depicting all of the known hate groups and their locations (www.splcenter.org/hate-map). This list was compiled using publications, websites, and law enforcement reports. In 2015 the SPLC reported the presence of 892 separate hate groups in the United States. There is a concentration of hate group presence in the Northeast and Southeast regions of the United States, with a preponderance of white nationalists and similar groups.

In fact, there has been a surprising increase in the number of hate groups since 1999. Tentatively attributed to an increase in immigration numbers and disputes over deportation methods and issues, the number of hate groups rose from 457 in 1999 to 892 in 2015. The number of recognized hate groups peaked at 1,018 groups in 2011,with a quick spike around the 2009 inauguration of President Barack Obama.

The Ku Klux Klan (KKK) is one of the more infamous hate groups. Founded in 1866, it was the impetus of resistance in the white South to the Republican agenda for political equality for black Americans after the Civil War. Despite Congress' efforts to curb the KKK, Democratic victories in the states implemented a rule of white supremacy in the South. A reemergence of KKK activity in the 1960s during the Civil Rights movement involved acts of hate and violence— including murders, vandalism, and assaults—against minorities of all types. KKK membership has dwindled since that time, but KKK membership still numbers 5,000–10,000 members, and some can be seen participating in marches and demonstrations (History, 2016a).

Similar white supremacy groups are neo-Nazis in the United States. Neo-Nazi groups support Adolf Hitler and Nazi values, including a hatred for racial and sexual minorities and those who practice Jewish and (sometimes) Christian faith. While their propaganda is often targeted at European audiences, they are visible in the United States. White Nationalists and Christian Identity are also white supremacy groups with similar anti-minority values (Southern Poverty Law Center, 2016b; Southern Poverty Law Center, 2016c).

Frequency of Hate Crimes

Activity 10.2: Changing Our POV

United States Attorney General Loretta Lynch recently released a statement with information from 2015 statistics from the Federal Bureau of Investigation, noting that there was a 67% increase in hate crimes against Muslim Americans. There was also an increase of hate crimes against African-Americans, LGBT individuals, and Jewish citizens. However, it appears as if society as a whole (especially younger generations) is more supportive and accepting of differences.

What organizations, events, and university support are provided at your institution to promote acceptance and diversity? Do you believe your institution could do more?

Every year, the FBI requests arrest data from all local, state, and federal law enforcement agencies. It compiles these data into the Uniform Crime Report (UCR), which provides an annual summary to the public on the amount and types of crime known to law enforcement. The UCR separates criminal activity into two parts. Part I crimes are violent and property crimes, including aggravated assault, rape, murder, burglary, and arson. Part II comprises less serious crimes such as prostitution, drug offenses, vandalism, and fraud.

After the passage of the Hate Crime Statistics Act of 1990, the UCR also began providing information on hate crimes in the United States. In 2015 almost 15,000 law enforcement agencies reported 5,850 criminal incidents and 6,885 related offenses motivated by bias and prejudice against race, ethnicity, religion, sexual orientation, disability, and/or gender identity (FBI, 2016b). Of the single-bias incidents, there was a total of 7,121 victims, with 59.2% of the victims targeted due to race or ethnicity. In addition, 19.7% of the single-bias incidents were because of religion and 17.7% were due to sexual orientation. Of the hate crimes (n = 4,482) considered a crime against persons, 41.3% were classified as intimidation and 37.8% were simple assault. Approximately 2,300 hate crimes were against property, with 72.6% considered acts of destruction or vandalism (FBI, 2016b).

Information is also provided in the UCR on location of crimes and demographics of offenders. The majority of hate crimes in 2015 occurred near residences, indicating that offenders were trying to use intimidation based on the emotional ties of homes and families. Of the 5,493 known offenders, 48.4% were white and 24.3% were African-American (FBI, 2016b).

A method of collecting data possibly not known to law enforcement is the National Crime Victimization Survey (NCVS). More than 40,000 homes in the United States—a random sample—are polled every six months (seven times total). Pollsters request information on victimization experienced by people in the household. Only data on personal and household victimization are requested, not crimes against business.

In 2014, the NCVS released a report describing hate crime victimization from 2004 to 2012. Almost 294,000 violent and property hate crimes occurred in 2012 in households in the United States to persons 12 or older. Approximately half of the victims believed the crime to be a result of ethnicity bias, an increase from the past years. The amount of hate crimes motivated by religious bias rose from 10% in 2004 to 28% in 2012, while gender-bias hate crimes rose from 12% to 24% in the same time span. Hate crimes involving some form of violence rose from 78% in 2004 to 90% in 2012. Lastly, about 60% of hate crimes were not reported to police, a decline from the previous year (Wilson, 2014).

Web Clips 10.1: Hate Crimes and the Homeless

Many different types of people are protected under the Hate Crime Statistics Act of 1990, but our homeless population is often forgotten. Targeting a person simply because they are homeless makes it a hate crime. According to the National Coalition for the Homeless (2016), thrill seekers (often teenagers) are the primary offenders of hate crimes against homeless persons. Approximately 93% of these offenders were male and 17% of the attacks ended in death. Victims have included individuals of all sexes, ages, and races.

Find an example of a crime purposely committed against a homeless person. Do you believe the offender was punished appropriately? Was this crime charged as a hate crime? Why/why not?

Terrorism

Sadly, nowadays it is not unusual to see news reports about terrorism with increasing frequency. The feeling of safety and invincibility was shattered for millions of American citizens after the September 11, 2001, attacks. Since that time, terroristic acts have continued, not just in European and Middle Eastern countries, but also on American soil on a regular basis.

On April 15, 2013, two bombs exploded near the finish line of the Boston Marathon. Three spectators died and over 250 others were injured. Four days later, suspects and brothers Dzhokhar Tsarnaev (19) and Tamerlan Tsarnaev (26), were found in different locations by police. Tamerlan died in a shootout with officers, and Dzhokhar was arrested and taken into custody. Both Boston and America were stunned to learn that such a horrible act with fatal consequences could occur at what was supposed to be a happy and exciting time. This section will explore terrorism and how it can rage across the world.

Definition of Terrorism

It is not unusual to consider acts of terrorism as those that destroy large geographic areas and cause the deaths of hundreds of people. While that certainly does occur, terroristic acts can also occur on a smaller scale with few or no fatalities. The law 18 U.S.C. § 2331 provides the legal definition of terrorism in multiple different categories (FBI, 2016c):

International terrorism comprises activities with the following characteristics:

1. Violent acts or acts dangerous to human life that violate state or federal law;
2. Intent (i) to intimidate or coerce a civilian population; (ii) to influence the policy of a government by intimidation or coercion; or (iii) to affect the conduct of a government by mass destruction, assassination, or kidnapping;
3. Occur primarily outside the territorial jurisdiction of the U.S., or transcend national boundaries in terms of the means by which they are accomplished, the persons they appear intended to intimidate or coerce, or the locale in which their perpetrators operate or seek asylum.

Domestic terrorism comprises activities with the following characteristics:

1. Violent acts or acts dangerous to human life that violate state or federal law;
2. Intent (i) to intimidate or coerce a civilian population; (ii) to influence the policy of a government by intimidation or coercion; or (iii) to affect the conduct of a government by mass destruction, assassination, or kidnapping;
3. Occur primarily within the territorial jurisdiction of the U.S.

In addition, 18 U.S.C. § 2332b defines the *federal crime of terrorism* as:

1. Calculated to influence or affect the conduct of government by intimidation or coercion, or to retaliate against government conduct;
2. Violation of one of several listed statutes, including § 930(c) (relating to killing or attempted killing during an attack on a federal facility with a dangerous weapon); and § 1114 (relating to killing or attempted killing of officers and employees of the U.S.).

(FBI, 2016c)

Case Study 10.2: Oklahoma City Bombing

Called the worst case of domestic terrorism until the 9/11 attacks, the bombing of the Alfred P. Murrah Federal Building in Oklahoma City, Oklahoma, left 168 people dead (including children in the building's day care center). Over 600 people were injured and 300 buildings damaged or destroyed. Terry Nichols and Timothy McVeigh, both members of a radical right-wing survivalist group from Michigan, were arrested and convicted of the crime. Nichols was sentenced to life in prison and McVeigh was executed in 2001. He was the first federal prisoner executed since 1963 (History, 2016b).

Frequency of Terrorism

It is extremely difficult to report the total number of terrorist attacks occurring worldwide, simply because many acts are not reported and are in very remote areas of the world. The United States Department of State (2016) prepares a comprehensive annual report of known terroristic attacks. In 2015 there were 11,774 terroristic attacks worldwide, with over 28,000 individuals killed and 35,000 persons injured. Fatalities due to terrorist attacks peaked from April to July 2015, mainly due to attacks by the Islamic State of Iraq and the Levant (ISIL). Over 12,000 people were kidnapped or taken hostage, mainly in the countries of Syria, Afghanistan, Nigeria, and Iraq. However, the total number of terrorist attacks in 2015 represented a 13% decrease from 2014 (United States Department of State, 2016).

In 2015 terrorist attacks occurred in 92 countries, with 55% of the attacks occurring in Iraq, Afghanistan, Nigeria, India, and Pakistan (United States Department of State, 2016). The majority of terrorist attacks in these countries, as well as the other countries that experienced terrorism, were carried out by the following organizations: Taliban, ISIL, Boko Haram, Maoists, and Kurdistan Workers' Party. The most commonly used method of attack was bombing or an explosive device (52%), with armed assault in second place (23%). The majority of attacks involved private citizens or property as the target, with police and businesses as second- and third-,place targets, respectively (United States Department of State, 2016).

According to Plumer (2013), terrorist attacks in the United States have decreased in frequency since the 1970s but not in severity. Every American geographical region has been targeted multiple times by terrorist attacks. Most of these attacks are carried out by individuals, and bombings are generally the method of choice for attacks. However, while it may be impossible to stop all occurrences of terrorism, United States law enforcement agencies have become more successful in stopping attacks and North America experiences fewer terroristic events than the rest of the world (Plumer, 2013).

Web Clips 10.2

Read about the details of the 2015 Paris terror attacks at www.cnn.com/2015/12/08/europe/2015-paris-terror-attacks-fast-facts/. Using this website and other sources online, find out if there was any forewarning of the attacks. Is there anything private citizens can do to better protect themselves or be more aware of potential attacks?

Cyberterrorism

One of the newer forms of terrorism, still unrecognized by many, is cyberterrorism. Historically, *terrorism* refers to acts of physical violence such as bombings, kidnappings, and murder to make a political message. The term was coined by Barry Collin (1997). The Computer Fraud and Abuse Act (modified by the PATRIOT Act) defined cyberterrorism as the following:

Any conduct that causes (or, in the case of an attempted offense, would, if completed, have caused)—

(i)   Loss to one or more persons during any one-year period (and, for purposes of an investigation, prosecution, or other proceeding brought by the United States only, loss resulting from a related course of conduct affecting one or more other protected computers) aggregating at least $5,000 in value;

(ii)   The modification or impairment, or potential modification or impairment of the medial examination, diagnosis, treatment, or care of one or more individuals;

(iii) Physical injury to any person;

(iv)   A threat to public health or safety; or

(v)   Damage affecting computer system used by or for a government entity in furtherance or the administration of justice, national defense, or national security.

This definition is controversial, as an individual must have committed the act in question in order to be charged with cyberterrorism. The United States National Infrastructure Protection Center now defines cyberterrorism as a "criminal act perpetrated by the use of computers and telecommunications capabilities, resulting in violence, destruction and/or disruption of services to create fear by causing confusion and uncertainty within a given population to conform to a particular political, social or ideological agenda (Moore, 2011)."

The Internet benefits terrorist groups in that it is a cost-effective and easy method of recruiting new members, as well as a forum where supporters and potential members can learn about the group, join discussions, and participate in direct actions. Terrorist organizations have even used videos, comic-book-style propaganda, and games to provide incentives for children to join (Denning, 2010). During recruitment, terrorist organizations also educate interested individuals and raise funds. Online, potential recruits around the world can learn about the mission and purpose of the terrorist group in dozens of languages.

Combating Terrorism

Multiple agencies work together to combat and prevent terrorism. The National Joint Terrorism Task Force (NJTTF) leads more than 104 FBI Joint Terrorism Task Forces (JTTF) across the United States, creating a collaborative effort of local, state, and federal agencies. Established in the 1980s in New York and Chicago, the number of JTTFs almost doubled quickly after the 9/11 attacks. Now housed in the National Counterterrorism Center, the NJTTF works with the Department of Homeland Security, military branches, police departments, and the Federal Bureau of Prisons, as well as dozens of other agencies, to share and collect information on terrorism.

Possibly one of the United States' best-known methods of combating terrorism was the passage of the controversial PATRIOT Act of 2001. Essentially, the original PATRIOT Act and PATRIOT Act and Reauthorization Act of 2005 increased the surveillance abilities of law enforcement for terrorism investigations, updated laws to include technological terrorism crimes, and increased penalties for terroristic acts (United States Department of Justice, 2006). However, opponents of the act assert it is a violation of American citizens' right to privacy, allowing law enforcement to gather and monitor information that is unrelated to terrorist activities.

Web Clips 10.3: Edward Snowden: Terrorist?

Investigate online the events leading up to Edward Snowden's escape to Russia, where he is currently avoiding prosecution by the United States government. Do you believe Snowden's actions were an act of terrorism against the United States? Why or why not?

It is important to remember that there are victims of all crimes of terrorism and they must be treated fairly as well as compensated for any damages. In the United States, terroristic acts are federal crimes (Reno, Marcus, Leary, & Turman, 2000) and several pieces of legislation have been passed to address the needs of victims. The Hostage Relief Act of 1980 was passed after the Iran hostage crisis, providing victims, their spouses and dependents with benefits for medical expenses, taxes, and education costs. It did not, however, provide compensation for wages lost while held captive. In order to rectify this issue, President Ronald Reagan signed the Victims of Terrorism Compensation Act in 1986.

Victims of the 9/11 attacks specifically benefited from the Air Transportation Safety and System Stabilization Act (2001). This piece of legislation established a financial compensation fund for the victims and their immediate families. Financial awards based on lost projected future earnings varied per family. However, each family received $250,000 for each deceased person, plus $100,000 for a widowed spouse and each child (Levin, 2002). According to Dixon & Stern (2004), over $8.7 billion in benefits was awarded to victims of the 9/11 attacks.

Discussion Questions

1. Based on the focus on illegal immigration, do you foresee hate crimes becoming a prominent issue in criminal justice in the next few years? Why/why not?
2. Is it possible to combat hate speech without violating the First Amendment?
3. Which act of terrorism has had the most impact on law enforcement practices since 2007 and why?

References

CBS News (2016). *President-elect Trump speaks to a divide country*. Retrieved from www.cbsnews.com/news/60-minutes-donald-trump-family-melania-ivanka-lesley-stahl/

CNN Library. (2016). *2015 Paris terror attacks fast facts*. Retrieved from www.cnn.com/2015/12/08/europe/2015-paris-terror-attacks-fast-facts/

Denning, D. (2010). Terror's web: How the Internet is transforming terrorism. In Y. Jewkes and M. Yar, Eds. *Handbook on Internet Crime*. Willan Publishing.

Disha, I., Cavendish, J., King, R. (2011). Historical events and spaces of hate: Hate crimes against Arabs and Muslims in post 9/11 America. *Social Problems, 58*, 21–46.

Dixon, L. & Stern, R. (2004). Compensating the victims of 9/11. *Rand Corporation*. Retrieved from www.rand.org/pubs/research_briefs/RB9087.html

Doerner, W., & Lab, S. (2015). *Victimology* (7th ed.). New York, NY: Routledge.

FBI. (2016a). *Hate crimes*. Retrieved from www.fbi.gov/investigate/civil-rights/hate-crimes

FBI. (2016b). *Latest hate crime statistics released*. Retrieved from www.fbi.gov/news/stories/2015-hate-crime-statistics-released

FBI. (2016c). *Terrorism*. Retrieved from https://www.fbi.gov/investigate/terrorism

History. (2016a). *Ku Klux Klan*. Retrieved from www.history.com/topics/ku-klux-klan

History. (2016b). *Oklahoma City bombing*. Retrieved from www.history.com/topics/oklahoma-city-bombing

Levin, R. (2002). *September 11 victim compensation fund: A model for compensating terrorism victims?* Retrieved from www.kentlaw.edu/honorsscholars/2002students/Levin.html

Moore, R. (2011). *Cybercrime: Investigating high-technology computer crime (2nd ed)*. Burlington, MA: Anderson Publishing.

National Coalition for the Homeless. (2016). *Hate crimes and violence prevention*. Retrieved from http://nationalhomeless.org/campaigns/hate-crimes/

Plumer, B. (2013). Eight facts about terrorism in the United States. *Washington Post*. Retrieved from www.washingtonpost.com/news/wonk/wp/2013/04/16/eight-facts-about-terrorism-in-the-united-states/?utm_term=.3830690a0745

Reno, J., Marcus, D., Leary, M., & Turman, K. (2000). *Responding to terrorism victims: Oklahoma City and beyond*. Washington, DC: U.S. Department of Justice, Office of Justice Programs, Office for Victims of Crime.

Southern Poverty Law Center. (2016a). *Active hate groups in the United States in 2015*. Retrieved from www.splcenter.org/sites/default/files/splc-hatemap-2015.pdf

Southern Poverty Law Center. (2016b). *Neo-Nazi*. Retrieved from www.splcenter.org/fighting-hate/extremist-files/ideology/neo-nazi

Southern Poverty Law Center. (2016c). *White Nationalist*. Retrieved from www.splcenter.org/fighting-hate/extremist-files/ideology/white-nationalist

United States Department of Justice. (2006). *Fact sheet: USA PATRIOT Act Improvement and Reauthorization Act of 2005*. Retrieved from www.justice.gov/archive/opa/pr/2006/March/06_opa_113.html

United States Department of State. (2016). *Statistical information on terrorism in 2015*. Retrieved from www.state.gov/j/ct/rls/crt/2015/257526.htm

Wilson, M. (2014). *Hate crime victimization, 2004–2012—Statistical tables* (NCJ 244409). U.S. Department of Justice, Office of Justice Programs, Bureau of Justice Statistics.

Yan, H., Sgueglia, K., & Walker, K. (2016). *Make America White again: Hate speech and crimes post-election*. Retrieved from www.cnn.com/2016/11/10/us/post-election-hate-crimes-and-fears-trnd/

Index

Page numbers in *italic* indicate a figure, page numbers in **bold** indicate a table, and page numbers underscored indicate a numbered text box on the corresponding page.